Unity

Unity

Anglicanism's Impossible Dream?

Charlie Bell

scm press

© Charlie Bell 2024

Published in 2024 by SCM Press
Editorial office
3rd Floor, Invicta House,
110 Golden Lane,
London EC1Y 0TG, UK

www.scmpress.co.uk

SCM Press is an imprint of Hymns Ancient & Modern Ltd
(a registered charity)

Hymns Ancient & Modern® is a registered trademark of
Hymns Ancient & Modern Ltd
13A Hellesdon Park Road, Norwich,
Norfolk NR6 5DR, UK

British Library Cataloguing in Publication data
A catalogue record for this book is available
from the British Library

ISBN 978-0-334-06560-9

Typeset by Regent Typesetting
Printed and bound in Great Britain by
CPI Group (UK) Ltd

Contents

Acknowledgements   ix

Part 1 Where we find ourselves

1 Introduction   3
2 The Church of England: An introduction   16
3 Where the land lies: The Communion and
   contemporary polity   37
4 Anglican identity and unity   59

Part 2 Reflections on unity

5 *Ut unum sint*: A biblical reflection   79
6 Heresies and history: Creeds, councils and
   the patristic era   95
7 Dwelling together in unity: Ecumenism
   and relationship   110

Part 3 The search for Anglican unity

8 Rediscovering our common threads   131
9 Walking together and walking apart:
   Anglican unity in a time of crisis   151

Bibliography   168
Index of Biblical References   183
Index of Names and Subjects   185

To Bishop Christopher

Acknowledgements

The opportunity to travel and meet so many people from around the Anglican Communion, and just as importantly to hear their stories, has made this book possible. I am incredibly grateful to them, to those theologians and other Anglicans who still think ecclesiology matters, and – somewhat perversely – to those prelates whose blithe and often entirely unthinking use of the word 'unity' pushed my buttons enough to make me think more deeply about it. The errors are all mine – needless to say.

I am, of course, grateful to the clergy and laity of St John the Divine in Kennington, and most particularly to Fr Mark for an extraordinary and life-giving curacy. I am grateful, too, for the encouragement I have received from the congregation – particularly from our stellar churchwardens Jez and Venessa – and the fantastic pastoral team I have been privileged to minister alongside.

I am grateful, too, to my medical colleagues, to the Mistress and Fellows of Girton College, Cambridge, to Professor Woodward at Sarum, to the entire team at St Augustine's, and to Dean Malloy and all those at St John the Divine in New York City who appear to want to hear what I have to say!

As I have said previously, I am incredibly lucky to be in the Diocese of Southwark under authority of Bishop Christopher Chessun, to whom this book is dedicated. Bishop Christopher is a true servant of the church – pastoral not only to his clergy and people, but with a pastoral attitude towards the whole church. When Bishop Christopher speaks of unity, it is not a mere handwaving assertion, but a lived, hoped for, and prayed for reality. I hope this book might be at least a small token of gratitude to him for his support and fatherly care over the last few years.

My family continue – somehow – to tolerate my nonsense, and I am extremely grateful to them for that! And my Piotr not only encourages me in all things, but stimulates me to think more carefully, more deeply, about these things that we both care about. Piotr is a gift to the Church of England, and an unsurpassable gift to me. I cannot wait to marry him. Kocham Cię, babbington.

Charlie Bell
Feast of St Barnabas, Apostle
June 2024

PART I

Where we find ourselves

I

Introduction

The Church of England is in crisis. The Anglican Communion is in crisis.

So, at least, we are told. It seems that barely a month goes by without there being some prophecy of the end of either the Church of England or the Anglican Communion, at least in their current incarnations. Our ecclesial landscape – at least publicly – seems to be littered with endless conversations about splits, schisms, different groups being in or out of communion with one another, with nobody very content with the status quo and yet nobody really sure what to suggest as an alternative. We live in a church that seems to be determined to pursue endless splintering into ecclesial tribes, with ever more purist understandings of the 'true faith'. Words like 'orthodoxy' are weaponized, while the discipline of 'theology' is used to cover all kinds of sociological and political positioning.

The sheer volume of energy that appears to be wasted on this kind of infighting is, it would be fair to argue, energy that could – and surely should – be used in the core life, witness and work of the church. Of course, it's easy to declare sure blasé truisms in a vacuum of reality. There is no one single meaning of 'compromise', and neither do discussions of 'both sides' do justice to what is, to some degree hyperbolically and yet to some degree entirely reasonably, described as a fight for the heart of the Church of England and the wider Anglican heritage.

In the contemporary church, the presenting issue is that of sexuality, and to some degree gender. Different groups with different emphases, priorities, demographics and theologies seem to have coalesced on this topic as one that truly does have church-splitting potential. An avowed opposition to any attempts to 'agree to disagree' from those who oppose same-sex, same-gender relationships appears to position the church in an ever-increasing tension that many believe is unsustainable and cannot last. Talk of 'structural provision' for those who oppose the blessing of same-sex, same-gender relationships or marriage, or the licensing for ministry of those in 'active' same-sex relationships, is ultimately talk of visible, actual division – division that cuts across the heart of what it means to be Christian, the sharing in the body and blood of Christ at the altar.

Already there are Anglicans across the world who have declared themselves unwilling to receive communion along-side 'gay-partnered bishops and those who endorse same-sex unions'.[1] We will return to the implications, both theological and practical, of taking such a stand, but for now it is worth recognizing the sheer gravity of such an approach. Were the church – either the Church of England or the Anglican Communion – merely to be an institution, then the pick-and-choose option, in which only those who are thought to be the right kind of Anglicans are invited to the communion table, might make more sense. However, if we are to argue, that the Church of England or the Anglican Communion is part of the church catholic, and that there is some kind of metaphysical importance to the things that we do or don't do alongside one another, then we must surely recognize that our actions have consequences beyond the immediate.

While our disagreements might be likened to a family argument, nonetheless we need to be clear that the head of the family is Christ, and that our actions to exclude one another or refuse to commune with one another are actions that speak also of our church's relationship with and to Christ. That is not, necessarily, to say that refusing to commune with one another is wrong, or the least bad option, but it is to say that doing so cannot be done lightly, and most certainly cannot be done as a political bargaining tool. We must be sure, in other words, that in rejecting someone else as a guest at Christ's table, we are not assuming the judgement seat ourselves and in so doing laying up judgement upon our own heads.

It is easy to present the challenges facing the church in an overly simplistic way. It is certainly true that for many faithful

Christians in the pews, these wider issues of 'church politics' seem obscure at best and frequently rather tiresome. The fabled 'middle ground' of the church, who would rather just get on with loving God and neighbour, may indeed find the arguments tedious and the public scraps distasteful, and yet such people may find themselves directly or indirectly affected by whatever policy decisions are made by the church, whether that is because their son or daughter cannot get married in church, or because their faithful priest no longer feels able to minister in a church that will bless same-sex couples. While it is easy to portray the church's tensions in this area as an 'obsession with sex', the reality is that this particular issue is not going away, and nor are the wider questions about unity that it raises.

It is to that contested notion of unity that we turn in these pages. Unity is without doubt a key theological theme throughout Christian history and into the present, and, as we shall see, has been seen as the lodestar of episcopal polity and practice both within the Church of England and in the wider Anglican Communion. Yet, to date, the concept of unity remains at best imprecise and at worst a somewhat meaningless term (or rather a term with contested meaning) used apparently to trim the excesses of the fringes of the church and pursue a *via media* in church polity. The concept of *via media* may indeed have an important and helpful history in the development of Anglican theology and of the ecclesiology of the Church of England (in particular) but it objectively does not mean what it so frequently ends up referring to in contemporary debates, which is better described as 'unhappy compromise'.

Of course, even the idea of *via media* itself (and its use as a guiding light in current church disagreements) is open to fierce debate, but its application to the 'middle way' between Roman Catholicism and Puritanism is probably the most helpful way to engage with it and to recognize its complexity and contested progeny in the Anglican crises of the modern age.[2] Within the Church of England and the wider Anglican Communion, debates on the meaning, purpose, consequences and interpretation of the Reformation in England continue to rage, and in many ways these debates retain the general outline that they have done since the various historical moments of the sixteenth and seventeenth centuries that launched the peculiar form of Christianity now found under the umbrella of the Church of England (and Anglicanism).

Indeed, even the term Anglicanism is contested, and it is by no means clear that what is often referred to as Anglicanism in a global sense (that is, in reference to the Anglican Communion) is the same as what might be referred to as Anglicanism as a particular historical church polity within the Church of England.[3] It is not the purpose of this book to provide a comprehensive historical account of the development of the current Church of England or Anglican Communion, but it is important to recognize that the imprecise language so often used to discuss modern difficulties within the church can lead to fundamentally ahistorical assertions, and, in the same way, a lack of basic understanding of the history of the development of the church (and Communion) as it is now can lead to similarly unjustifiable propositions. At the centre of the Church of England, and its spread globally through the imperial project, are contradictions, contests and at times incoherence, and yet any discussion of unity in the contemporary church needs to address the church as it is and was, rather than a sanitized version or a narrative of the church that speaks with a single voice. It is easier, of course, to ignore reality and find uniformity where there is none, but this will not aid us in addressing the matter at hand, namely what unity might look like in our context, and whether it might be anything more than an impossible dream.

It is because unity and uniformity are not the same that a renewed focus on what is meant by unity is so important if we are to address the institutional challenges not only of this generation but of those to come. In the contemporary world, it is tempting to focus on structures and hierarchies, and to view the church in a way that is analogous to a secular institution, rather than see it as ultimately something mystical and hence primarily metaphysical. It is not our primary purpose here to critique the creeping secularization of leadership found in the Church of England in particular, nor the increasing centralization of the Anglican Communion, although both of these things do appear to be a result, at least in part, of a withdrawal from the metaphysical and a retreat into the managerial.

Of course, it would be naive to suggest that there is not something of the secular institution to these current ecclesial bodies, and indeed it would be impossible for them to exist were there not due attention paid to how their underlying theological vision might be played out in the public square. However, the contention of this book is that unless and until the theological vision is properly engaged with, then attempts to somehow create unity as a primarily sociological or political entity will simply continue our current instability, at best creating a mirage and more likely losing sight of unity as a theological virtue and replacing it with a coping strategy that wrestles the primacy from God and places it in powerful human hands.

One of the key challenges that the modern church faces is that the imprecision and lack of theological depth underlying talk of 'unity' has become commonplace. As we shall see in these pages, there is much made of the importance – even centrality – of unity to the future of the church, and yet what is being referred to is all too frequently intangible and undefinable. The risk here is that theological terms are not somehow value neutral; the use of the word 'unity' in the context of the church suggests a theological meaning, and yet if this meaning is neither theological nor agreed, then the secular concept of uniformity (or whatever else might be posing as a polity of unity) becomes baptized, and hence takes on an importance and a sacredness that it does not deserve. As a result, talk of unity becomes a useful tool both to manage the church's 'warring parties' and as the ultimate silencing tool of those in authority to use against any who disagree.

An example would be in the debates on sexuality in the light of the *Living in Love and Faith* project. For those in the current Church of England who have been arguing for either doctrinal change or pastoral accommodation for couples of the same sex, 'unity' as a tool has been frequently employed in order to retain the status quo and prevent any meaningful change. Whether this is an appeal to the 'unity' of the Church of England, or 'unity' in the wider Communion, there is then an inevitable privileging of stasis, turning unity into a tool of conservatism rather than a theological virtue in its own right. As we shall see, there are reasonable arguments to be made about the catholicity of the church, and the need for consensus and 'travelling together' on disputed matters of ethical living or Christian morality. Yet far too often the real issues at stake are not separated out, and hence conversations about lack of consensus, *adiaphora*, or legitimate theological diversity and spaciousness are silenced in the name of 'unity'. In many ways, 'unity' then acts as a trump card or an appeal of last resort, and entirely appropriate conversations (let alone decisions) are deemed too dangerous lest 'unity' is threatened.

Yet by its nature 'unity' is not something that can be manufactured, nor is it something that can be pretended into existence. Refusing to engage with matters of theological controversy or difficulty does not make such matters go away; instead, silencing these debates in the name of unity does damage to the church's ability to grow and develop its theological understanding. In a sense, making unity something that is aimed for – something to achieve – rather than recognizing it as part of the essence of the church means that we as creatures overstep our rightful place and run the risk of focusing on human politics rather than on the endless search for truth. Doing so, we fail to pay due attention to the work of the Holy Spirit.

Indeed, no discussion of unity would be complete without proper attention being paid to the Holy Spirit. Here we find a tension so often revealed in the Christian narrative: the love of God being both unchanging and yet ever new. That love, propelled through the world in the Holy Spirit, not only leads us into all truth (John 16) but also calls us to unity in the bond of peace (Ephesians 4). Such a tension is challenging and, as we shall see, these challenges have pressed themselves in on the church from the early days of the Christian faith. Yet while true unity and the work of the Spirit are not in opposition – indeed, they are one and the same – it is entirely possible that political constructions of 'unity' may themselves lead us to prioritize agreement, consensus and uniformity over a theological spaciousness and contingency in which openness to the Holy Spirit's movement (or, indeed, otherwise) is enabled. A simple example of this might be the arguments over the rightness or wrongness of slavery and the emphases that different churches gave to the political and the theological, the unifying and the vivifying. While there is a place for careful conservatism and consensus in the catholic nature of the church, this surely cannot be at the cost of ignoring or silencing the prophetic. It is in holding this creative tension that unity reveals itself.

The determination to create (an illusion of) rather than allow the revealing of unity speaks, perhaps, to the current loss of, and in many places total lack of, confidence in the church by its leadership, both as an institution and – tragically – as Christ's own bride. As churches' financial situations, congregational numbers and influence wane in the western world, there is a temptation to find the magic bullet that will enable churches to stem decline and grow. Attempts to do this are themselves somewhat theologically suspect. Of course it is entirely reasonable for churches to try to get their houses in order and ensure they are communicating and engaging missionally with the world as effectively as possible, but the idea that their 'success' (itself a loaded term) is in their own hands, or that there is a simplistic way of refilling the pews (through particular expressions of worship or doctrine) does appear to be a misreading of the very nature of the church and its total reliance on the goodness and generosity of God. Yet equally fascinating is the turn towards uniformity as a tool for growth; the idea that young people, in particular, are looking for churches that have a uniformity of message, which is clear and unbending. Research in this area is mixed and suffers from methodological and interpretative challenges (for example, while churches of a particular theological bent may have a large number of young people at one point in time, interpreters frequently fall into the causation-correlation fallacy, and similarly ignore the millions of young people who do not darken the doors of any church whatsoever).

Of course, a key problem with enforcing 'unity' is that the credibility of the church's message and its ability to engage with wider society is significantly impaired. Those watching the church's debates on sex and sexuality, for example, are unlikely to be convinced by the – until recently – absurd public image that the members of the Church of England's House of Bishops all agreed on almost everything, a position defended in the name of 'unity'. When 44 bishops finally openly stated that they did not, in fact, agree with the current prohibition on the blessing of same-sex relationships or clergy entering into same-sex marriages,[4] these bishops were not somehow damaging 'unity', as was claimed by a number of commentators at the time, but instead were revealing the current theological spaciousness and in so doing providing an honest appraisal of the diversity of views of those holding leadership positions under the banner of the Church of England.

Such honesty is surely to be lauded, even if the diversity it reveals may prove challenging in institutional terms. Yet these bishops, and LGBTQIA Christians more widely, were accused of destroying the unity of the church.[5] To return to our earlier point, mistaking conservatism and stasis for unity – and in this case, suggesting that even advocating for change from the status quo is an insult to the unity of the Body of Christ – ultimately means that nothing can, should or ever will change in the way the church exists, acts or engages. This is demonstrably absurd and is a clear indication of the politicization of what should be a theological concept. Unfortunately, to date, this misreading of the meaning of unity has become so commonplace that its unthinking repetition forms the backbone of episcopal reports, synodical discussions and international theological engagement, doing damage not only to our credibility as a church but to our ability to conceive ourselves appropriately in theological terms.

It is from this starting place that debates on the receiving of communion alongside one another and our willingness to declare ourselves 'out of communion' with fellow Christians finds its genesis. That so many different Christian denominations refuse to come to the Lord's table together remains one of the greatest scandals in the witness of the church universal. Yet for this process of othering and rejection to find its way into the internal life of a denomination is nothing short of shameful. Indeed, it is extremely hard to defend any form of denominational cohesion when such a policy is adopted, and similarly extremely difficult to see how those who refuse to receive communion from one another might be reasonably described as being part of the same 'church'.

A counterpoint to this would be that the refusal to receive communion alongside fellow Christians is not in itself anything new, but rather just a visible manifestation of an already extant lack of unity in the Body. This may well be true, but at that stage it is hard to see what thread remains that unites members of a denomination in such circumstances. In other words, how might that situation be described in ways other than the simple moniker 'schism'? The link between genuine unity and communion is strong, and thus we return to the muddied waters of 'unity' as an institutional descriptor and as a theological imperative. In the context of the current Church of England, the refusal of some members to receive communion alongside others, and yet a determination to 'preserve unity', suggests that what is really being talked about is not unity at all but institutional survival. Such conversations are not in themselves problematic; what is problematic is the elision of discussions of a theological concept with conversations about institutional self-understanding.

In other words, being part of the Church of England, or being 'Anglican', is as much an institutional statement of belonging as it is a theological one, and yet those two different facets have become interlinked to such a degree that conversations are ineffective and dishonest. By surrendering the theological and metaphysical, and focusing entirely on the institutional, we ultimately do damage to who we believe ourselves to be as Christians. In many ways, we put 'being Church of England' or 'being Anglican' ahead of 'being in the church'. Hence discussions of 'unity' in Anglicanism so frequently end up sounding as though institutional survival (or institutional 'unity') is of a higher priority than, for example, the theological unity of all Christians. This does huge potential damage to the ecumenical project and means that our reference points for discussions about unity become structures, historical events or institutional instruments, rather than a recognition that unity itself transcends the denominational. While it may find expression in particular visible ways within particular ecclesial communities, that is not its final destination.

This is not to suggest that these structural elements do not matter, or that they do not present particular challenges to visible unity. An example might be the response to the ordination of women (most particularly to the episcopate) in the Church of England, opposition to which is not uniform in its theology, and yet it directly impacts on the 'ability' of some within the church to receive communion from others given the implications of disagreement on matters of church order. Whether the current polity is successful or sustainable is moot;[6] it remains challenging to argue that there has not been some level of genuine break in unity as a result of this disagreement. While this situation has once again led to accusations by some of those holding to the conservative view that those proceeding to the ordination of women are 'to blame' for the break in unity, the situation is much more accurately described as being one in which two (or more) views held with theological integrity are simply incompatible with the mutual reception of communion (from at least one direction).

There is not the space here to go into the complexity of this particular question, and there remain some problematic, unfinished and contested theological questions around the theology of 'taint' and the episcopal office.[7] However, what is clear is that matters of church order are not merely institutional but themselves can have an impact on the theological self-understanding and manifestation of a church's life, and this is brought into clearest relief when addressing the question of holy communion. It is certainly interesting when considering the relative importance given to 'unity' and questions of theological or church order 'purity' in such circumstances. For those who come to a minority view on a particular theological issue, the opportunity arises as to whether to give primacy to a concession to visible unity (for example, to receive communion from a female priest or alongside a gay person) or to the integrity of a personally held theological conviction.

These questions become increasingly complex, not least

given the relationship between what might be called local unity (within the Church of England, for example) and unity per se (that is, within the wider church catholic). Here, individuals may consider their commitment to wider unity more important or compelling than their commitment to denominational unity. Hence, to return to questions around the ordination of female clergy, some of those opposed (from the traditionalist Anglo-Catholic wing of the Church of England) are so because of their belief that the Church of England should not (and indeed cannot) move on a question of such fundamental importance without that movement being a joint discernment across the church catholic.[8] There is no neat line between such an argument and the refusal to then accept a denominational decision; indeed, it is arguable that even were one to hold this view, the commitment to a local expression of catholic life that has gone through a joint (albeit limited) discernment on this topic requires those with doubts to commit with obedience to the decision, yet pray for wider discernment and alignment (in whatever direction).

What becomes evident when addressing these and other questions of unity is that there is no clear, neat dividing line between the institutional and the theological, and yet imprecision about language in any such discussions can lead conversations in unhelpful and ultimately unfruitful directions. Institutional manifestations of unity (or disunity) are inevitable when the church is an institution in both a human and a mystical sense, yet while it is tempting to start with institutional questions and focus on the manifestations themselves, it is absolutely key that the theological takes precedence. This is particularly difficult in a church run by what is effectively a political decision-making body like General Synod; yet it is the responsibility of all those – and most particularly bishops – who speak of unity, to do so in a way where the primacy is given to the theological, which can then be worked out in the context of the institutional.

To date, this has been increasingly, and dangerously, missing, with the church behaving primarily either like a political entity (with all the associated horse-trading) or as an object of stasis (where willingness to hold together is predicated on an obscuring of diversity and a strong-arming, through misuse of theological language, by those who resist change) – occasionally both at the same time. If the church is to regain its sense of its mystical self, if unity is to become something revealed rather than something used, and if the Church of England and the wider Anglican Communion are to be genuine good faith actors in internal and external engagements, then there is a deep need to revisit, refine and re-engage with what it is we mean when we talk about unity. It is to that task that we turn in these pages.

Notes

1 Pat Ashworth, 'Lambeth 2022: Global South Bishops press for re-affirmation of Resolution 1.10', *Church Times*, 29 July 2022, https://www.churchtimes.co.uk/articles/2022/5-august/news/world/lambeth-2022-global-south-bishops-press-for-re-affirmation-of-resolution-110 (accessed 2.1.24).

2 Don S. Armentrout and Robert Boak Slocum, eds, 'Via Media', in *An Episcopal Dictionary of the Church: A User Friendly Reference for Episcopalians* (New York: Church Publishing Inc, 2000), https://www.episcopalchurch.org/glossary/via-media/ (accessed 2.1.24).

3 Jeremy Morris's *A People's Church: A History of the Church of England* (London: Profile Books, 2022) is an excellent introduction to the complexity of this debate. Readers may also wish to consult Mark Chapman, *Anglican Theology* (London: T&T Clark, 2012).

4 Gloucester Diocese, 'A statement from 44 bishops on LLF', https://gloucester.anglican.org/2023/a-statement-from-44-bishops-on-llf/ (accessed 4.1.24).

5 Catherine Pepinster, 'Evangelicals Fear LGBT Blessings Proposal Would Split the Church of England', *Christianity Today*, https://www.christianitytoday.com/news/2023/february/church-of-england-synod-lgbt-blessings-marriage-evangelical.html (accessed 20.1.24).

6 Church of England, 'The Five Guiding Principles', https://www.churchofengland.org/sites/default/files/2017-10/the_five_guiding_principles.pdf (accessed 20.1.24).

7 In particular, the precise meaning of 'sacramental assurance' and the stated need by those who oppose the ordination of women to be ordained by male bishops who have never ordained women. See The Society, 'A Catholic Life in the Church of England', https://www.sswsh.com/uploads/A_Catholic_Life_for_web.pdf (accessed 12.1.24).

8 Interestingly, what defines 'the church catholic' is itself often a political or institutional decision, and far too frequently simply refers to 'the Roman Catholic Church outside England'. This is not indefensible as an idea, but should be more clearly stated by those who hold to it. Frequently, imprecise language is used that suggests that no movement should occur without 'the church catholic', which appears to ignore vast swathes of other denominations engaged in the ecumenical enterprise who have moved on this question, and often on questions of sexuality. We shall engage with this more in later chapters.

The Church of England:
An introduction

As we have discussed in Chapter 1, unity is not uniformity, and nor is it all about institutions. However, if we are to have a fruitful conversation about unity in the particular context of Anglicanism, then we need to address the realities of the institutional context in which attempts to manifest 'unity' are made. These realities are hugely complex and contested, and hence it is impossible to do justice to the multitude of ways in which communion is or is not experienced by members both of the Church of England and of the wider Anglican Communion. However, despite their disputed received meanings and utility, there are a number of commonalities of life and structural realities that form at least the narrative, if not the reality, of the essence of the form of Christianity that is found within Anglicanism.

The Church of England

While its contemporary role in the Anglican Communion is widely contested, and even rejected,[1] the See of Canterbury and the Church of England by association is historically found at the centre of the form of Christianity now colloquially referred to as Anglicanism (although, as we noted in Chapter 1, this is not quite the right term in a historical sense). The Archbishop of Canterbury, by virtue of being the metropolitan archbishop of the Southern Province in England and the Primate of All England, is the most senior bishop in the Church of England and thus its spiritual head. Given the Established nature of the Church of England, the Supreme Governor of the Church of England is the monarch, meaning that the leadership (in its various meanings) of the church is not entirely simple, yet in the contemporary church the Archbishop of Canterbury is afforded effective autonomy in spiritual leadership, albeit alongside other members of the House of Bishops and in collaboration with the General Synod of the Church of England. There are, of course, exceptions, but for our purposes this is a reasonable starting point.

The Church of England is comprised of two provinces, with the smaller Province of York presided over by its metropolitan, the Archbishop of York. While these two provinces are theoretically separate, nonetheless much of the business of the church is done with both provinces brought together as 'The Church of England'. Seven administrative bodies make up the National Church Institutions, including the two archbishops, the Archbishops' Council, the National Society, Church Commissioners, Central Services and the Pensions Board.[2] These National Church Institutions were formally instituted in 1998 as part of the National Institutions Measure, with the express intention of enabling 'them better to serve the work and mission of the Church'.[3] Of note, while there have been breaks in the historical episcopal leadership structures of the Church of England, these central institutions nonetheless serve the entire church and as yet there have not been any serious attempts to separate out 'central' services on theological grounds.

There are 42 dioceses in the Church of England, each with a diocesan bishop and an array of other bishops who assist the diocesan. In different dioceses this might include area bishops (with geographical jurisdiction), bishops suffragan and assistant bishops (retired or working outside of a primarily episcopal role, such as a principal of a theological college). The Common Worship order for the Ordination and Consecration of a Bishop describes the role of bishops as follows:

Bishops are ordained to be shepherds of Christ's flock and guardians of the faith of the apostles, proclaiming the gospel of God's kingdom and leading his people in mission. Obedient to the call of Christ and in the power of the Holy Spirit, they are to gather God's people and celebrate with them the sacraments of the new covenant. Thus formed into a single communion of faith and love, the Church in each place and time is united with the Church in every place and time.[4]

It further states:

> Bishops are called to serve and care for the flock of Christ. Mindful of the Good Shepherd, who laid down his life for his sheep, they are to love and pray for those committed to their charge, knowing their people and being known by them. As principal ministers of word and sacrament, stewards of the mysteries of God, they are to preside at the Lord's table and to lead the offering of prayer and praise. They are to feed God's pilgrim people, and so build up the Body of Christ.
>
> They are to baptize and confirm, nurturing God's people in the life of the Spirit and leading them in the way of holiness. They are to discern and foster the gifts of the Spirit in all who follow Christ, commissioning them to minister in his name. They are to preside over the ordination of deacons and priests, and join together in the ordination of bishops.
>
> As chief pastors, it is their duty to share with their fellow presbyters the oversight of the Church, speaking in the name of God and expounding the gospel of salvation. With the Shepherd's love, they are to be merciful, but with firmness; to minister discipline, but with compassion. They are to have a special care for the poor, the outcast and those who are in need. They are to seek out those who are lost and lead them home with rejoicing, declaring the absolution and forgiveness of sins to those who turn to Christ.
>
> Following the example of the prophets and the teaching of the apostles, they are to proclaim the gospel boldly, confront injustice and work for righteousness and peace in all the world.

In the creation of what are effectively tiers of bishops (diocesans and others), we meet the understandable tension between the institutional and the theological: while there is a theoretical equality of bishops by virtue of their ordination, nonetheless there are particular roles given to each in the life of the institutional church. Given the way that the Church of England makes decisions, as we discuss below, this does ultimately mean that some bishops inhabit a fundamentally different role from others, for example in the setting of 'national policy' and in the way that discipline is meted out in dioceses. It is unfortunate that there has been so little attention paid to the tensions implicit in an episcopal ordering that includes suffragans,[5] and it is likely that further work on the implications of episcopal collegiality would benefit the church in ways beyond the practical crisis management that appears to loom over the contemporary Church of England.

The current practical structural arrangements for bishops mean that such collegiality is nominally found in the form of the College of Bishops.[6] The College of Bishops includes all serving bishops in the Church of England, and while it is a place where conversation, debate and solidarity might be expressed, it is not a formal decision-making body. This body is the House of Bishops, itself a formal part of the General Synod of the Church of England, and includes all diocesan bishops, the Bishop of Dover (functioning as diocesan Bishop of Canterbury), the Bishop to the Armed Forces, and nine elected suffragan bishops. Six female suffragan bishops and three provincial episcopal visitors (of which more below) are also invited to speak but not vote at the House.

Given these arrangements, and the synodal relationship that is found at the heart of Church of England polity (of which more below), it is clear that bishops (and most particularly diocesans and those elected from suffragan roles) hold a responsibility not only to the local diocese but to the national church. While it is understandable that the House is formulated the way it is, given its role in General Synod, nonetheless this does mean that there is a fundamental disconnect between the expression of collegiality as a theological good and collegial decision-making as a practical reality. To coin a phrase, all bishops are equal but some bishops are more equal than others. The implications of this for 'unity' are significant, not least when clear decisions of the College of Bishops are disregarded by the House of Bishops.[7]

The bishop's role in the Church of England is multifarious. Diocesan bishops are not only the chief pastor of their diocese (with the ability in theory, if not in practice, to set large parts of diocesan policy independently of the national church bodies), but also have a collegial role in the life of the church corporately. Twenty-six bishops of the Church of England also sit in the House of Lords,[8] including both archbishops, the Bishops of London, Durham and Winchester, and 21 others who sit by seniority.[9] In recent years, there has been a tendency for more areas of public life to be allocated a 'lead bishop' or spokesperson, which enables the Church of England to speak publicly with one voice on a variety of issues where there is general agreement (although this particular role is not without its difficulties, and moves to formalize what seems to be a more cabinet form of 'church government' appear to have stalled[10]). At present, the Church of England remains committed to a geographical form of episcopacy (in the main) and were this to be changed it would be a fundamental challenge to the ecclesiology of the institution.

It is this geographical nature of the Church of England that is one of its key, distinctive elements, and one that has been threatened in recent years by talk of 'differentiation' as a result of disagreement on matters of church order or ethics. The Church of England talks of being 'a Christian presence in every community',[11] which has historically referred to parish churches covering almost the entire length and breadth of England. In recent years, this too has been under strain, as campaigns such as 'Save the Parish' and Alison Milbank, a member of its steering committee, have argued convincingly,[12] and as dioceses such as Truro and Leicester have increasingly and intentionally aimed to loosen the link between the parish and local ministry. These decisions appear to have been driven by two different impetuses, one financial and the other theological.

As the numbers and finances in dioceses of the Church of England continue to decline, it is inevitably the case that decisions will need to be made on the appropriate use of finances, central, diocesan and local. Yet it is not at all clear that financial difficulties necessarily lead to such a significant shift in the

Church of England's ecclesiology as that found in some future planning. There has been a woeful lack of focus on this ecclesiology and its underlying theology in discussions on the future of the Church of England, and the lack of transparency and the often entirely avoidable elision of different driving forces in discussions on this topic have been deeply unhelpful. The focus on 'diocesan strategies' often leaves rather a lot to be desired in theological hard work. Hence new ideas and projects can take on a seemingly unstoppable form that pays little regard to the historical expressions of Christianity in the form of the Church of England.

It is important, of course, not to focus solely on the historical formulations and expressions of the Church of England, but to ignore them is surely a grave error, particularly if we are looking to discuss unity. Unity cannot merely refer to the here and now: unity must require us to look for the thread of historical continuity and tradition found within any Christian expression. While those opposing women's ordination or same-sex blessings may make reference to this historical continuity, there has been far too little attention paid to the ahistorical implications of their own demands for structural separation. A key example might be the separation of the geographical from the expression of episcopal oversight in parishes that refuse the ordination of women; here, a commitment to one understanding of catholic order (the male-only priesthood) leads to a rejection of another (the geographical diocese). This is not to say that this is the right structural outcome, but it is to bring attention to the complexity of these discussions and decisions that is so often missed. Unity and catholicity do not come in a single shape or size.

The contemporary Church of England does appear somewhat reticent to include a theology of the church in its conversations about structural changes, whether that is in response to financial difficulty or theological diversity. The drive towards 'fresh expressions of (the) church' is a good example of this, not least since the publication of *Mission-Shaped Church*,[13] which has had a significant impact on the Church of England's self-understanding in recent years. It is fascinating that there is such a focus on growth per se rather than growth being seen as a result of a focus on, for example, the bringing in of the Kingdom of God, or effective, engaging and credible mission and evangelism, which has historically been best provided at the level of the parish. In dismantling or defunding parish ministry, there has instead been a focus on untested yet 'shiny' schemes that sit without the historical expression of the Church of England, and where even the need for ordained ministry is shunned (again, an example of fundamentally un-Anglican theological visions and financial circumstances leading to muddied waters and unsatisfactory outcomes).[14]

The growth of what appear to be groups calling for and implementing fundamentally un-Anglican forms of church order within the Church of England is quite astonishing. For example, the Gregory Centre for Church Multiplication was, until recently, operationally part of the Diocese of London,[15] and is led by the Bishop of Islington, whose role is intentionally non-geographical, even if he is a member of the London College of Bishops. The sheer confusion about the relationship between these initiatives and the Church of England is bewildering, and yet money and time continue to be invested in these 'new ways of being (the) church' without any apparent qualms about the challenge to our ecclesiology (in fact, quite often the opposite).[16] The mention of clergy as 'limiting factors',[17] and of 'passengers', is not an aberration: it is central to much thinking on the future of the Church of England.[18]

These moves to reorder the way that the Church of England is formulated matter because this alteration in the expression of the church in its structures ultimately says something about the church's own self-understanding and our ecclesiology as Anglicans. This may seem somewhat peripheral to our discussion of unity, yet it is abundantly clear that our unity *as Anglicans* (separate from our unity *as Christians*, of which more in later chapters) does require us to understand and – to a large degree – agree on what 'being Anglican' means in terms of our engagement with wider society. This is particularly important for us as an Established church: part of our identity in England is that very Establishment and its geographical and parochial implications. There are, of course, debates about the appropriateness or otherwise of continued Establishment, but even were this to be challenged and even lost in the future, nonetheless it forms part of our heritage and hence must form at least some part of our identity.

Indeed, when looking for the thread that runs through our common identity, the geographical nature of the Church of England is surely a stronger candidate than reference to common doctrine or even practice. Since its formation, and to differing degrees, the Church of England has embodied a variety of different forms of worship (not least since the decline of the common use of the Book of Common Prayer), vesture, self-understanding and theologies, but has – through the three-fold ministry and the geographical nature of parishes and their associated dioceses – ultimately been a church of place. It is quite notable how organizations and groups that appear most willing to jettison this place-based ecclesiology are also those that reject theological diversity on matters of sexuality. It appears that this is, at least in part, built on a false premise of what the Church of England's ecclesiology is – or, indeed, a failure to recognize that this ecclesiology is front and centre of Anglican identity.

The link with place is perhaps best seen when considering the 'cure of souls', and the professed role of the Church of England as being the church for everyone in the parish, whatever their religion or connection to the parish church itself. Until recently, this has manifested itself in the availability of the Church of England's solemnization of marriage to all those who live in the parish (or have the requisite connection). While remarriage after divorce has complicated this relationship, the point-blank refusal of the Church of England to marry couples of the same sex has meant that for the first time in its history, the local parish is no longer available to everyone in the parish in the same way as it was previously. This has led, too, to protracted and unconvincing debates about the difference between Holy Matrimony and marriage,[19] but it is interesting in the decade since same-sex marriage was introduced by the state quite how little attention has been paid to this ecclesiological issue. Focus has instead been entirely on the doctrinal meaning (or, more correctly, on the politics of developing doctrine), so that the significant changes to ecclesiology have been an unacknowledged casualty of what is presented as doctrinal purity. Whether this is truly an Anglican way of proceeding is moot.

A not dissimilar issue arises when considering the availability of funerals or baptisms. The Church of England's website states that 'a Church of England *funeral is available to everyone, giving support before, during and after the service*, for as long as it's needed',[20] and similarly baptism is open to all, whether individuals (or parents) are regular churchgoers or not.[21] However, in recent years stirrings of debate have begun on whether infant baptisms should be permitted, whether preparation for baptism should be a formal requirement, or whether funerals should be restricted to members of the congregation only. Far too infrequently has the 'church of place' self-identity of the Church of England been seen to hold much sway. Once again, narrow definitions of 'doctrine' trump a recognition that a conception of a 'church of place' is itself doctrinal in nature, and little attention is paid to those who advocate for the 'church of place' as a theological virtue.

In this and in other discussions about our ecclesiology that weigh directly in on our debates about the nature of the 'church' in which we seek for unity, there is a focus on policy-making devoid of theological depth; all too frequently they happen in the context of crisis management (whether through threats of schism or financial catastrophe, or both). A culture of fear holds back serious engagement with the church's theological underpinnings, and the Church of England has found itself engaged in 'crisis' after 'crisis' in the past 30 years, many of which have impacted directly on our ecclesiology. In current discussions about 'structural provision' for a 'time of uncertainty',[22] it is notable that any reference to the inherited forms of geographical church order appears to vanish into thin air.

We must not, of course, be beguiled by talk of a 'church of place' so that we create a false history (or indeed present) of uniformity across the parishes of the Church of England, nor of a mythical 'anything goes' in belief and practice. It has long been the case that different 'parties' (whether liberal, evangelical, catholic, or something besides) have existed within the Church of England, although it is not true that there have never been boundaries to what is held within the church. We might think, for example, of the Great Ejection following the Act of Uniformity of 1662 in England: in this case, the 1662 Book of Common Prayer became the tool that defined the bounds of the Church of England.[23]

There has always been a creative tension between different theological (and doctrinal) streams, and the development of the Book of Common Prayer, and perhaps even more so *Common Worship* (2000), has enabled these different streams to worship with common liturgy, albeit with different emphases and even different understandings of the purpose and nature of worship. A particular example might be the multiplicity of beliefs and understandings held about the Eucharist,[24] which is manifest in the diversity of Eucharistic Prayers found in *Common Worship*.[25] Yet while Section B of the Canons of the Church of England is clear about which forms of worship may or may not be used,[26] in recent years it is increasingly unsurprising when these rules are stretched at best, and ignored at worst, in Church of England worship. This has led to an almost complete break-down in uniformity of worship in any meaningful sense. And given the sheer variety of materials already available for use in the multiple *Common Worship* volumes, even the use of authorized liturgy would mean the possibility of very little overlap between worshipping communities.

Here again, then, we meet a tension between diversity and uniformity, and it is a particular tension given the role that liturgy has played in developing Church of England identity. There is not the space to do justice to the early years of pressure to revise the 1662 Book of Common Prayer, but the failure of Parliament to pass the revised 1928 Book of Common Prayer (which had been approved by both the Church of England Convocations and Church Assembly in the previous year) did prove a turning point in any attempt to have a single, authorized book of common liturgy (although, of course, the Book of Common Prayer remains authoritative in liturgy and, to some degree which is itself debated, doctrine). This becomes all the more important in a church that holds to an understanding of *lex orandi, lex credendi*, where the 'performance of the church's practices – in its prayer life and liturgy – is inherently connected to its beliefs'.[27] In the contemporary Church of England, a lack of common prayer and common liturgy is surely, at least in part, connected with the revealed lack of unity. Whether it is cause or effect, or a mixture of the two, remains up for debate.

It is for this reason that the contemporary Church of England has already lost something of its historical character. While the parties within the church are not new, historically the liturgy of a Church of England parish would be recognizable and similar to that in another – perhaps with its own idiosyncrasies and particular emphases, but nonetheless making use of the same words and the same patterning of those words. Since the Book of Common Prayer's withdrawal from many parishes, this is no longer the case, meaning that not only might the preaching and teaching be different from one parish to another (itself a development since the Books of Homilies, appointed for use by Article 35 of the 39 Articles, of which more below), but so too the form of worship. The consequence of this is that attending a 'Church of England' service on a Sunday morning is now effectively a meaningless term.

It is not only the Book of Common Prayer that was held in common in the Church of England: it forms part of the formularies. Gerald Bray describes these as

> designed by Archbishop Thomas Cranmer (1489–1556) to give the English Church a solid grounding in the three fundamental areas of its life – *doctrine, devotion* and *discipline*. The Articles provided its doctrinal framework, the Prayer Book settled the pattern of its devotional life and the Ordinal outlined what was expected of the clergy, whose role was the key to the church's discipline.[28]

These formularies remain central to Church of England identity, through the Declaration of Assent, which, according to Canon C15, is 'made by deacons, priests and bishops of the Church of England when they are ordained and on each occasion when they take up a new appointment'.[29] The Preface to the Declaration states:

> The Church of England is part of the One, Holy, Catholic and Apostolic Church, worshipping the one true God, Father, Son and Holy Spirit. It professes the faith uniquely revealed in the Holy Scriptures and set forth in the catholic creeds, which faith the Church is called upon to proclaim afresh in each generation. Led by the Holy Spirit, it has borne witness to Christian truth in its historic formularies, the Thirty-nine Articles of Religion, *The Book of Common Prayer* and the Ordering of Bishops, Priests and Deacons. In the declaration you are about to make, will you affirm your loyalty to this inheritance of faith as your inspiration and guidance under God in bringing the grace and truth of Christ to this generation and making Him known to those in your care?[30]

The Declaration itself then states:

> I, *A B*, do so affirm, and accordingly declare my belief in the faith which is revealed in the Holy Scriptures and set forth in the catholic creeds and to which the historic formularies of the Church of England bear witness; and in public prayer and administration of the sacraments, I will use only the forms of service which are authorized or allowed by Canon.

We see here that while the assenter speaks of the formularies bearing witness, this is not precisely the same as stating that they embody the faith and doctrine of the Church of England as it is now – which they objectively and demonstrably do not.[31] Similarly, the 'Ordering of Bishops, Priests and Deacons' referred to is not that used in the vast majority of ordinations in the contemporary church. It is not possible merely to disregard the formularies, Ordinal and Book of Common Prayer, given their fundamental place in the development of the Church of England, yet it is also implausible to make use of them as an unchangeable and once-for-all expression of the faith of the Church of England. To date, there has been a limited amount of work done in bridging this gap, not least because of the perceived difficulty in coming to a common mind across the wings of the Church of England.

This is perhaps best exemplified in how different 'parties' within the church might see the Church of England in relation to other churches. For some, it is in continuity with the pre-Reformation church, and is therefore the contemporary expression of English Catholicism. For others, it is primarily a church of the Reformation, and Protestant in character.[32] For others, it is a *via media* of the Reformation, in which closer associations with Roman Catholicism were maintained than in other churches of the period. This self-conception has implications for unity, not least in whether the Church of England is seen primarily as a denomination or primarily as a wing of the church catholic (albeit a disputed one). It is clear that at the Reformation a break was made in the English church; it is the meaning and nature of that break which remains contested today.

This brings us back to the importance of the threefold order in the Church of England. While some other churches of the Reformation did away with this, it remains central to the ordering of the Church of England. This has had practical implications, not least proposals to enable intercommunion with the Methodist Church (which in its English form does not hold to the threefold order).[33] As we have seen, this threefold order is intrinsically linked to geography, and attempts by other 'Anglican' churches to 'plant' bishops in England is fundamentally at odds with a basic understanding of Church of England ecclesiology.[34]

It remains true that there is disagreement about the exact nature of priestly (or presbyteral) ministry within the Church of England, yet at present there remain some particular sacramental actions that are reserved to priests, most universally the celebration of the Eucharist. Others have lamented the creeping ascent of leadership language over the language of sacramental ministry in the church's understanding of priestly ministry, yet while there has been a preponderance of new ministries in recent years (among them the confusing title 'worship pastor', which would previously have been called 'Director of Music'), these have been predominantly lay and there has been no serious attempt within the Church of England to separate sacramental ministry from priestly ordination. The close relationship we have discussed between *koinonia* and unity suggests that this sacramentality – and our ability to discern a common if varied view of it – is key to our pursuit of unity.

Not only is the threefold order important for our sacramental understanding, but it is also expressed in the way that decisions – at least in part – are made in the church. The General Synod (and the associated Diocesan and Deanery Synods) replaced the Church Assembly in 1970, and 'considers and approves legislation affecting the whole of the Church of England, formulates new forms of worship, debates matters of national and international importance, and approves the annual budget for the work of the Church at national level'.[35] It has a tricameral structure – Houses for Bishops, Clergy and Laity – and is elected in a somewhat arcane way (particularly in the House of Laity), which means that it is infrequently 'representative' in any true sense of the Church of England in its entirety. The phrase 'synodically governed and episcopally led' is frequently used to describe the way the Church of England's structures work, but it has been heavily criticized, not least because bishops lead in synod and govern in their dioceses, and the role of General Synod is primarily legislative rather than executive.

The challenge of a synodical church is that the precise location of authority is not always clear, or, if it is clear, then it is not always clear-cut. While a two-thirds majority of the General Synod is required when voting on major matters of doctrine,[36] teaching authority (and associated discipline) resides with the bishops by virtue of their episcopal office. The result is that the bishops corporately can veto anything that might otherwise pass through the General Synod, but need the consent of the Houses of Clergy and Laity to make changes to Canon or liturgy. Recognizing the 'elusive' 'outworking of this polity', the National Church Governance Report and Recommendations described it as follows:

The notion of 'the Bishop-in-Synod' much more accurately describes Anglican polity, recognizing that where bishops lead the Church into making decisions about its life, policy and ministry, they do so in consultation, both with their episcopal colleagues in the deliberations of the House and College of Bishops, and in and with the wider body of clergy and laity represented in the General Synod, respecting the calling, wisdom and experience of the whole people of God.[37]

This then brings us full circle to a discussion of bishops once again. It is worth considering why – in wider church debates about structural provision and unity – we so frequently return to such a discussion. Of course, this is in part because of our threefold order, but it is also because many bishops refer to themselves as being the 'focus of unity', exemplified by reference to the Archbishop of Canterbury as 'a unique focus of unity'.[38] It is not at all clear what is meant by this statement – and this perhaps lies at the very root of our investigations here. Such a statement has had a number of implications for our common life, and these frequently tend towards a church in which bishops appear to fear saying anything or making any definitive statement in order that this 'unity' not be put at risk.[39] In the Church of England this has become a point of policy: a unified voice from the House of Bishops has been put forward on almost every decision on matters of sexuality until this fragile consensus began to break in 2023.[40] While it is to be welcomed that the contours of honest debate are now intentionally seeping out from episcopal gatherings,[41] it has been a long time coming, and the recourse to 'unity' appears to remain the standard *modus* at the heart of the Church of England's central apparatus.

An example of this might be the current Archbishop of Canterbury's bizarre decision to abstain in the final vote on same-sex blessings in the General Synod in November 2023, and his public statement that he would not use the prayers because of 'my pastoral care and responsibility of being a focus of unity for the whole communion', despite being 'extremely joyfully celebratory of these new resources'.[42] The Archbishop's press release explaining his abstention on the final vote stated:

Archbishops of Canterbury must always work for the maximum possible unity in the Church, however impossible that may seem and however deep our differences. For that reason, I abstained on yesterday's vote because my pastoral responsibility extends to everyone in the Church of England and global Anglican Communion.[43]

It is not at all clear how his decision to abstain from the vote, or not use the prayers, is a tool of unity. Indeed, in this circumstance, it appears to be more a tool of dishonesty, and does not appear in a good light when read alongside his speech to the Anglican Consultative Council in Ghana where he intimated that General Synod members were uninterested in the impact of decisions on other parts of the Communion, and his contention that 'Archbishops do not chair the General Synod and do not organize its business or debates'. It is simply not credible to suggest that the Archbishop can be a 'focus of unity' by saying one thing in one place and another in another, but this appears to be a symptom of the wider malaise on the topic of unity and of English bishops' unwillingness to ask precisely what the phrase 'focus of unity' might mean.

While the phrase 'focus of unity' has grown in its public presence and in ecumenical theological conversation,[44] it is not found in the ordination liturgies of either *Common Worship* or the Book of Common Prayer, nor in the associated Canons. Fascinatingly, the word 'unity' does not appear at all in the Book of Common Prayer's Consecration liturgy, and *Common Worship* merely has the archbishop asking episcopal ordinands, 'Will you promote peace and reconciliation in the Church and in the world; and will you strive for the visible unity of Christ's Church?', with the new bishop welcomed 'as a shepherd of Christ's flock' who is commended to 'build up the Church in unity and love, that the world may believe' (and, indeed, priests are called to 'discern and foster the gifts of all God's people, that the whole Church may be built up in unity and faith').[45] Other Anglican churches do contain clearer reference to unity (for example, The Episcopal Church's reference to the guarding of 'faith, unity and discipline'[46]).

This is not to say that this phrase does not have utility, or indeed that bishops are not to be a 'focus of' or 'focus for' unity, but it is to say that if such a moniker is to be used, then a clear definition of what this means in practical terms needs to be developed, one that is grounded in Anglican identity and polity (albeit in conversation with ecumenical partners). Simplistic reference to such a phrase, with the absurd practical outcomes outlined above, ultimately leads to a situation where being a 'focus of unity' means doing and saying absolutely nothing whatsoever and hence creating an episcopacy of the lowest common denominator. Of course there is a need for bishops to be circumspect in how they act and appropriately generous in how they provide space for their clergy and people, but that is a long way from the idea that bishops should follow the 'seen and not heard' mentality of Victorian children!

There is more to be said about the way that the processes for selecting bishops might impact on a genuine striving after unity, and similarly questions remain about how recent developments in Provincial Episcopal Visitors have impacted the way the Church of England conceives of sacramental episcopal ministry. For now, however, we can see that there are a number of threads that run through the structures that make up what has become the contemporary Church of England, among them geography, parochial ministry at the heart of diocesan structures, Establishment, the threefold order, sacramentality and the importance of the bishop – albeit contested in practical outworking. These different facets are central to the Church of England, and yet to differing degrees are more or less part of the essence of other Anglican communities. Whether these can provide part of the basis for a Communion-wide definition and demonstration of unity is the question we now seek to address.

Notes

1 Kirk Petersen, 'GAFCON Rejects Archbishop Justin Welby's Leadership', The Living Church, 21 April 2023, https://livingchurch.org/2023/04/21/gafcon-rejects-archbishop-justin-welbys-leadership/ (accessed 15.1.24).

2 Church of England, 'National Church Institutions', https://www.churchofengland.org/sites/default/files/2024-01/nci-structure-chart-january-2024.jpg (accessed 12.1.24).

3 Hansard, 'National Institutions Measure', https://hansard.parliament.uk/Commons/1998-06-18/debates/ad2c352e-b388-4b59-9e75-5a10e414f489/NationalInstitutionsMeasure (accessed 23.2.24).

4 Church of England, 'Common Worship Ordination Services', https://www.churchofengland.org/prayer-and-worship/worship-texts-and-resources/common-worship/ministry/common-worship-ordination-0 (accessed 20.1.24).

5 An exception to this, albeit not recent, is here: House of Bishops, 'Suffragan Bishops', 2004, https://www.churchofengland.org/sites/default/files/2023-01/gs-misc-733-suffragan-bishops.pdf (accessed 10.1.24).

6 Church of England, 'House of Bishops', https://www.churchofengland.org/about/general-synod/structure/house-bishops (accessed 9.1.24).

7 Francis Martin, 'Bishops' divisions over same-sex marriage exposed', Church Times, 26 October 2023, https://www.churchtimes.co.uk/articles/2023/27-october/news/uk/bishops-divisions-over-same-sex-marriage-exposed (accessed 20.1.24).

8 Samuel White, 'House of Lords: Lords Spiritual', House of Lords Library Briefing, 4 September 2017, https://researchbriefings.files.parliament.uk/documents/LLN-2017-0056/LLN-2017-0056.pdf (accessed 161.24).

9 In recent years there has been accelerated seniority given to women diocesans since the 2014 vote to allow women to become bishops in the Church of England. The Bishop of Sodor and Man has a legislative role in their own jurisdiction of the Isle of Man.

10 Kaya Burgess, 'Behold the Bishop of Brexit as church models itself on politics', The Times, 7 February 2022, https://www.thetimes.co.uk/article/bishop-of-brexit-church-models-itself-politics-vd8mv2fgg (accessed 20.1.24).

11 Church of England, 'No ordinary ministry', https://www.churchofengland.org/life-events/vocations/no-ordinary-ministry (accessed 24.1.24).

12 Alison Milbank, The Once and Future Parish (London: SCM Press, 2023).

13 Graham Cray, ed., Mission-Shaped Church (London: Church House Publishing, 2012).

14 Alison Milbank's letter to the Church Times, 26 May 2023, makes

clear that the original proposal did not require the priest to hold Cure of Souls, https://www.churchtimes.co.uk/articles/2023/26-may/comment/letters-to-the-editor/letters-to-the-editor (accessed 10.1.24).

15 Diocese of London, 'New Charitable Status for the Gregory Centre for Church Multiplication (CCX)', 6 April 2023, https://www.london.anglican.org/articles/new-charitable-status-for-the-gregory-centre-for-church-multiplication-ccx/ (accessed 16.1.24).

16 Madeleine Davies, 'Clarification: Not 10,000 but 20,000 new lay-led churches; not a strategy but a vision', *Church Times*, 9 July 2021, https://www.churchtimes.co.uk/articles/2021/16-july/news/uk/clarification-not-10-000-but-20-000-not-a-strategy-but-a-vision (accessed 16.1.24).

17 'Leader comment: "key limiting factors"', *Church Times*, 9 July 2021, https://www.churchtimes.co.uk/articles/2021/9-july/comment/leader-comment/leader-comment-key-limiting-factors (accessed 16.1.24).

18 Catherine Pepinster, 'CofE's "transformation" with 10,000 lay-led communities angers clergy fearing the end of the parish', Religion Media Centre, 9 July 2021, https://religionmediacentre.org.uk/news/cofes-transformation-with-10000-lay-led-communities-angers-clergy-fearing-the-end-of-the-parish/ (accessed 16.1.24).

19 'The Church of England's Doctrine of Marriage', https://southwell.anglican.org/wp-content/uploads/2023/01/The-Church-of-Englands-Doctrine-of-Marriage-paper.pdf (accessed 2.1.24).

20 Church of England, 'Funerals', https://www.churchofengland.org/life-events/funerals (accessed 10.1.24).

21 Church of England, 'Parents' guide to christenings', https://www.churchofengland.org/life-events/christenings/parents-guide-christenings (accessed 11.1.24).

22 Church of England, 'GS2328 *Living in Love and Faith*: Setting out the progress made and work still to do', February 2023, https://www.churchofengland.org/sites/default/files/2023-10/gs-2328-llf-nov-2023.pdf (accessed 10.1.24).

23 It is once again notable that so many of those who currently speak of 'unity' in matters of doctrine appear so willing to ignore 'unity' in the use of authorized liturgy.

24 Charles Bell, 'The Eucharistic Feast: Participation, representation and sacramental integrity in the time of social distancing', Anglicanism.org, https://anglicanism.org/the-eucharistic-feast-participation-representation-and-sacramental-integrity-in-the-time-of-social-distancing (accessed 10.1.24).

25 Church of England, 'Holy Communion Service', https://www.churchofengland.org/prayer-and-worship/worship-texts-and-resources/common-worship/holy-communion-service (accessed 10.1.24).

26 Church of England, 'Canons of the Church of England: Section B', https://www.churchofengland.org/about/leadership-and-governance/legal-services/canons-church-england/section-b (accessed 10.1.24).

27 Ashley Cocksworth, 'David F. Ford', in Stephen Burns, Bryan Cones and James Tengatenga, eds, *Twentieth Century Anglican Theologians* (London: Wiley, 2021), p. 198.

28 Gerald Bray, *The Faith We Confess: An Exposition of the Thirty-Nine Articles* (London: The Latimer Trust, 2009), p. 1.

29 Church of England, 'The Declaration of Assent', https://www.churchofengland.org/prayer-and-worship/worship-texts-and-resources/common-worship/ministry/declaration-assent (accessed 10.1.24).

30 Church of England, 'The Declaration of Assent'.

31 One might think here of Article 37's reference to the death penalty, of 33, in its reference to 'excommunicate persons', or 35, of the Homilies.

32 We might think here of the Coronation Oath, in which the King declares his willingness to maintain 'the Protestant Reformed Religion established by law'. Available in the official Order of Service: https://www.royal.uk/sites/default/files/documents/2023-05/The%20Coronation%20Order%20of%20Service.pdf (accessed 11.1.24).

33 Madeleine Davies, 'Anglican Catholic Future raises concerns about Methodist proposals', *Church Times*, 4 July 2019, https://www.churchtimes.co.uk/articles/2019/5-july/news/uk/anglican-catholic-future-raises-concerns-about-methodist-proposals (accessed 10.1.24).

34 For example, Bishop Andy Lines, 'Missionary Bishop to Europe' of the Anglican Network in Europe.

35 Church of England, 'General Synod', https://www.churchofengland.org/about/general-synod (accessed 5.1.24). The relationship between Synods and Parliament is long and complex, but it is possible to see synodality working through these various bodies in different ways and with different levels of effectiveness throughout the church's long history.

36 Tim Wyatt, 'Factsheet: The Church of England's General Synod', *Religion Media Centre*, 13 February 2020, https://religionmediacentre.org.uk/factsheets/synod-factsheet/ (accessed 10.1.24). Interested readers may consult the Standing Orders of the General Synod, specifically Standing Order 36 (4), available here: https://www.churchofengland.org/sites/default/files/2024-03/standing-order-updated-february-2024.pdf) (accessed 15.5.24).

37 Church of England, 'GS2307: National Church Governance Report and Recommendations from the National Church Governance Project Board', June 2023, https://www.churchofengland.org/sites/default/files/2023-06/gs-2307-national-governance-review-synod-july-2023-final_0.pdf (accessed 10.1.24).

38 Church of England, 'The Anglican Communion', https://www.churchofengland.org/about/building-relationships/anglican-communion (accessed 11.1.24).

39 Charles Bell, *Queer Holiness* (London: Darton, Longman and Todd, 2022), ch. 12

40 Interestingly, it was broken initially by those who have made the most overt appeals to 'unity' as a reason for not blessing same-sex couples.

41 Church of England, 'House of Bishops meeting: 29 November', 29 November 2023, https://www.churchofengland.org/media/press-re leases/house-bishops-meeting-29-november (accessed 10.1.24).

42 Oliver Slow and Andre Rhoden-Paul, 'Archbishop will not give new prayer blessing for gay couples', BBC News Online, 20 January 2023, https://www.bbc.co.uk/news/uk-64342940 (accessed 10.1.24).

43 Archbishop of Canterbury, 'Living in Love and Faith: Statement by the Archbishop of Canterbury', 16 November 2023, https://www. archbishopofcanterbury.org/news/news-and-statements/living-love-and-faith-statement-archbishop-canterbury (accessed 10.1.24).

44 For example, World Council of Churches, 'Baptism, Eucharist and Ministry: Faith and Order Paper No. 111', 1982, https://www.anglican communion.org/media/102580/lima_document.pdf (accessed 11.1.24).

45 Church of England, 'Common Worship Ordination Services', https://www.churchofengland.org/prayer-and-worship/worship-texts-and-resources/common-worship/ministry/common-worship-ordination-o (accessed 20.1.24).

46 The Episcopal Church, 'The Ordination of a Bishop', https://www. bcponline.org/EpiscopalServices/ordination_of_a_bishop.html (accessed 20.1.24).

3

Where the land lies:
The Communion and
contemporary polity

It may appear surprising that, until now, we have made little mention of those things classically associated with Anglicanism, such as Hooker's (fabled) three-legged stool. There are several reasons for this. First, the history of the Church of England remains contested, and while various interpretations of the breadth and variety of practices and beliefs continue to be debated, there remains considerable disagreement that is unlikely to aid in the development of a path for unity. Second, and related to this, while the *via media* approach of Anglicanism may prove a helpful concept to some degree, it can easily become a political approach, and therefore prove unacceptable to those who come to disagree with how it might be applied in the present day.

Third, there appears to be some benefit to addressing the Church of England as it *is* now and as it *has been* structurally, rather than engaging in ultimately fruitless debates about doctrinal purity or acceptability of contemporary ideas to those who wrote or promulgated its formularies. There is a great risk that we become fossilized in documents and find the finer points of our doctrines unchangeable because they were formulated during the Reformation, and in so doing become unwilling and unable to return to Scripture as our prime authority, or be open to the call of the Holy Spirit. By engaging with how we have been experienced, how we relate, how we self-identify, how we have manifested 'being Anglican', we have the opportunity to ask questions about how this influences and engages our identity in the contemporary church, and thus ensure that we do justice to an ecclesiology that has been worked out as much practically as it has been doctrinally.

Finally, it is important for us to recognize that the situation within England is fundamentally different to that in the rest of the Communion. While we refer to the Anglican Communion, it is patently absurd for us to suggest that this 'Anglicanism' (in its identarian use rather than party use) is expressed in one and the same way everywhere, because the contemporary context in which Anglicans live out their faith is so different across the globe, and because of the historical development of these communities.[1] Talk of 'unity' in the Communion must surely start with an understanding of what it really means to be 'Anglican' in a Communion that lacks the context of the English church and that is the result – in the main – of British imperial ambition in a bygone age. This is not to denigrate or show disrespect to Anglicans outside England, but it is simply to state the fact that some of those things – particularly the geographical nature of the church, its relationship to Establishment and its governance – are fundamentally different outside England.

This is true even within those parts of the United Kingdom outside England. The Church in Wales, for example, was disestablished (and disendowed) as a result of the Welsh Church Act 1914, leading to a different form of church, albeit one that retained much similarity with its Established cousin. Here was seen a more extreme version of identity development compared to that in England, as the Church in Wales existed in a context in which the majority of the population were Nonconformists and hence where an Established church appeared at best an anomaly and at worst anathema. During the preceding centuries in England, a similar formation of identity 'in opposition' to other forms of Christianity (and, eventually, other or no religions) developed, meaning that being Church of England no longer directly aligned with being a Christian in England. While it appears somewhat strange to consider this in modern Britain, this move towards being one 'denomination' among many surely formed part of the growing pains of contemporary English Anglican identity.[2]

While it is understandable from a historical perspective that the Church of England remains Established despite being the organ of a minority religion, it is entirely possible that this status will be more seriously challenged in the coming years. Whether or not the Church of England remains Established, it surely has much to learn from other expressions of Anglicanism in discovering its identity in an ever-changing, multi-religious and multicultural world. In many ways, remaining Established is a greater challenge for the Church of England's identity – seeking to be the Christian presence in every community while there may be competing Christian presences and while there may also be an antipathy or even direct opposition to the Church of England playing this role (particularly, for example, in its political activity in the House of Lords).

That is to ask, both from an English perspective and from a wider Communion perspective, whether – given the continued arguments about the meaning of *via media* and the acceptable breadth of doctrinal understandings, and the mixed and contested range of voices in defining the acceptable and unacceptable in Anglicanism – there is something that can be called distinctly Anglican, beyond its birth in the English Established context. If there is, then what might that be, and where might it be found (in liturgy, in structures, in ecclesiology, and so on)? Is what we have relied on – and in particular the Instruments of Unity we will discuss below – fit for purpose in a postcolonial landscape? Can they be bettered, or replaced? Will that be enough, and if not, what can shore up the situation? If we cannot answer those questions, then we surely face much more than a crisis of unity: we face a crisis of fundamental identity.

There remains the risk that in Anglicanism our appeal to 'unity' really means everyone thinking, or believing, the same thing, which, as we have seen, is ahistorical in the extreme and does little credit to the legitimate diversity that has been found within Anglicanism.[3] Hyperbolic references to particular biblical interpretations as being 'un-Anglican' is easy shorthand,[4] but fails to do anything like justice to the varied and intelligent engagement with Scripture that Anglicans of all times and places have undertaken. There are legitimate arguments to be made about Anglican interpretative method and the role of Scripture (although even these are contested), but far too often debates fall into discussions of *beliefs* being 'un-Anglican' (or simply 'unorthodox' or 'revisionist'). This is simply not a valid way of engaging in identity formation if we are to do so with even cursory respect to those things that might rightly be called Anglican.

Of course, for some the idea of Anglicanism as a distinct identity *at all* is deeply suspect. Among these might be those who see the Church of England as a continuation of the church *in* England at the Reformation, or those who see it as primarily a Reformed national church whose missionary (and imperial) endeavours have led to an overseas body of affiliated Christians who feel a sense of 'family attachment' to the Church of England and its historical formularies. This view is in the minority, at least in the way that the current Anglican Communion appears to self-identify and in the formation of the Instruments of Communion, which do suggest that it is in some particular way an entity (if not a denomination). It is perhaps interesting to reflect on how the Church of England might have developed an identity were the wider Communion not to have formed, and yet the existence of vast numbers of global Anglicans and their clear affinity to – if also frustration with – the Archbishop of Canterbury and the English church requires us to take seriously the reality that the Communion does, in some way at least, exist, and if we are to say that there is no such thing as Anglican identity or Anglicanism as a denomination, that is simply not within our gift.

We may wish simply to retreat from the wider Communion, but much of the current talk of schism and 'impaired communion' comes from the fact that the imperial history of the Anglican Communion has not been addressed. More scandalously, there appears to be very little willingness to address it in the contemporary church. The Anglican Communion is effectively a child of empire, not only in its structures, but in its assumptions, its ways of working, its Europe-centredness, and its continued operations. While many formerly imperial organizations and institutions have at least begun to do the work of decolonization and applied postcolonial analysis to their current manifestations, the Church of England and the wider Anglican Communion far too often appear to be content with living in a world in which the hard work of engaging with imperial history is unnecessary or inconvenient.

It is perhaps for this reason that so much money is spent by rich western groups, including both genuine but also entryist self-identified 'Anglican'-esque groups, seeking to further their particular ideological or theological agendas in poorer parts of the Anglican Communion. The Anglican Communion becomes, in such situations, merely a proxy political playground for rich conservatives, meaning that theological decision-making is mired in financial dishonesty and lacks the integrity it so desperately requires. 'Unity' is a frequent flier in such conversations, and the 'but the Communion' argument has been used to significant effect when moves have been made in progressive directions in the Church of England. That is not to say that there are not deeply held beliefs, some of which are conservative, in different parts of the Anglican Communion, but it is to say that the use of the Communion as a tool is deeply damaging, and it is hard to square this with a Christian ethic of money.

One difficult and yet essential part of any conversation on the Anglican Communion has to be that of culture and context. While the use of 'Global South' has been lazily used by both progressives and conservatives alike, it is nonetheless self-evidently the case that in large parts of the Anglican Communion in global-majority areas, the dominant cultural narrative is (from a western perspective) more conservative on matters of gender and sexuality, two issues that have proved extremely divisive in recent years. Here we find theology and culture coming into conflict, or indeed finding synergy with one another, and creating a heady mix that it has proved challenging to separate out.

It is beyond the scope of this book to fully outline the history of anti-LGBTQIA beliefs, views and behaviours in those parts of the world where queer people still face active oppression and violence, yet it is demonstrably the case that in places where the British Empire held control, such positioning was part and parcel of the imperial expansion, whatever the original cultural norms of the colonized people.[5] This is of particular importance when considering the genesis of the Anglican Communion: in 2022, 34 out of 54 Commonwealth countries continued to criminalize same-sex relations.[6] In many of these places, the Church of England was hand in glove with government in the promotion of these repressive laws, and hence it is understandable that culture and theology find some alignment. It is similarly understandable that as the Church of England has moved in its understanding in this area (if only in peripheral matters) there is resentment by leaders across the Communion that having been told to do one thing, they are now being told to do another. Whether this is a fair representation of what is happening is somewhat immaterial to the way in which it is received.[7]

Since the publication of *Fiducia Supplicans* by the Roman Catholic Church, this relationship between culture and particular expressions of Christian sexual ethics has become clearer still.[8] This declaration, which recommended very limited pastoral provision for those in same-sex relationships, was received with a mixture of disbelief and anger in many parts of the world, and particularly in parts of the African Roman Catholic Church.[9] Here, direct reference was made to culture, with Fridolin Cardinal Ambongo, the President of the Symposium of Episcopal Conferences of Africa and Madagascar, stating, 'We, the African Bishops, do not consider it appropriate for Africa to bless homosexual unions or same-sex couples because, in our context, this would cause confusion and would be in direct contradiction to the cultural ethos of African communities.' This is a clearer articulation of what has been implicit or explicit in statements from African Anglican Primates,[10] although such pronouncements often blur the lines between culture and theology.[11]

This is a deeply problematic state of affairs, made more difficult because of the spectre of colonialism and the deep concern that bishops of white, western provinces have about being perceived to lecture their Global South brother and sister bishops. Yet it remains racist, albeit in a more subtle way, to refuse to treat bishops from the Global South with enough respect to challenge their views and challenge them to do the work of separating culture from theology. Not to do so fails the Global South and the Global North, and the Communion as a whole, as it fails to engage with the reality of cultural factors and prevents a complex and yet much required conversation about culture and norms.[12] To fail to have this conversation out of a sense of postcolonial guilt, while retaining the symbols and institutions of colonialism within the Anglican Communion, is little short of absurd.[13]

Similar conversations must surely take place over the role of women within the Anglican Church. At the most recent Lambeth Conference (2022), there were 97 women bishops,[14] yet the vast majority of them were white and from the Global North. Indeed, in Communion discussions, there remains an almost total absence of female ordained leadership. There is a multiplicity of views on women's ordination across the Communion, yet there remains an unwillingness to asks questions of the relationship between this and culture. While many conservative leaders have berated the Church of England and other western churches for 'capitulating to culture', any conversation on cultural and contextual integration of Anglicanism will need to have a far wider remit than the Global North alone.

Yet surely similarly unacceptable is the argument sometimes heard in more progressive circles that those coming from Communion churches with conservative views should simply be ignored or refused a seat at the table. We shall consider the potential risks of a 'unity at all costs' strategy towards the end of this book, but for now it is important for us to recognize that any serious engagement with the Communion by those in the Global North, and in particular those in the Church of England, requires us to face the colonial legacy head on, and in so doing recognize the continued power imbalance at the heart of our institutions and structures. To do so, though, would necessitate the genuine surrendering of power, and it may be that the Church of England is not yet in the position of being willing to do so.

We will return to our need to seek to understand our history and undertake a proper postcolonial analysis,[15] and put this into practice, towards the end of this chapter, but for now let us turn to the Communion as it is currently constituted. The Anglican Communion describes itself as 'one of the world's largest Christian communities',[16] with 'members in more than 165 countries around the globe'.[17] There are 41 provinces and five extra-provincial areas, which are described as being 'in communion – or a reciprocal relationship – with the See of Canterbury and recognize the Archbishop of Canterbury as the Communion's spiritual head'. However, there is 'no central authority', and the provinces are 'autonomous ... free to make their own decisions in their own ways ... guided by recommendations from the four Instruments: the Archbishop of Canterbury, the Lambeth Conference, the Primates' Meeting and the Anglican Consultative Council'.

The Communion's website makes reference to the first 'Anglican' worship taking place outside Britain in Canada in 1578, and recognizes the importance of the mission agencies in developing this mission. Interestingly, reference is also made to the ordination of the first bishop of The Episcopal Church (in the USA) by a Scottish bishop, 'a move seen by some as the beginnings of an Anglican Communion with autonomous member Churches'. In the earliest days of the Communion, many of these churches were run either from England or by Englishmen ordained as bishops in the mission territories, but over time this has changed so that leadership (and governance) is now based in the territories themselves, leading to the development of increasingly autonomous and independent churches.

Not only does the Anglican Communion exist as an ecclesial grouping, but it also has representation at a political level (for example at the United Nations), and hence behaves as a single body.[18] This is perhaps the clearest example of the complexity of the Communion; it is both a single body but also a collection of autonomous (or, perhaps better, interdependent) churches for which there is no single point of overarching authority or binding decision-making ability. At its most fruitful, it is a remarkable opportunity to bring together a huge variety of Christians from hugely different contexts in a bond of friendship, and yet as we have seen in recent years this bond can be severely tested, even to breaking point (of which more below).

As described, the Anglican Communion has four 'Instruments' of communion, and it is these that are served by the Anglican Communion Office and that are represented by the Office at major international bodies.[19] As we have described previously, the Archbishop of Canterbury is one of these Instruments, and according to the Anglican Communion Office 'is the Focus for Unity for the other three Instruments of Communion ... and therefore a unique focus for Anglican unity'.[20] He is described as the 'leader' of the Anglican as *primus inter pares* of the Primates, although this is certainly a disputed label and ultimately unhelpful in trying to describe Anglican polity.

In recent years, this 'leadership' role of the Archbishop has become increasingly fraught, not least given the rather unconvincing appeals to 'unity' that we saw in the last chapter. As Archbishop of Canterbury, the office-holder is both Primate of All England and 'leader' of the Anglican Communion, and it is questionable that it will be practical or possible to continue with this combined role into the future if the Communion continues to experience the divides that it does, and if the Church of England is not to sink into mere stasis in the name of 'unity'. Yet it is surely also the case that continuing to have leadership that is inevitably situated in the Church of England is also simply unsustainable in the light of any serious reflection on the colonial history of such a role. To date, the vast majority of the holders of this role have been English (with notable and honourable exceptions), they have all been male, and white (in modern times). This is simply incompatible with a Communion that is intentionally global in its make-up and that takes seriously the ramifications of the imperial project, enslavement of Black people by white people, the role of the Church of England in the architecture of the slave trade, and so on.

Given the key role of the Archbishop in the 'unity' of the Communion, this is an urgent matter, and yet one that has been given little to no airtime in recent years. In 2022, proposals were brought to the General Synod of the Church of England to change the way that the Archbishop of Canterbury was chosen, which would specifically increase the Anglican Communion representation in the appointments panel (called the Crown

Nominations Commission).[21] Yet carefully hidden within these proposals was the fact that the English would nonetheless have a majority in the final decision-making, and similarly there remained significant confusion about how these Communion 'representatives' would be chosen.[22] By undertaking this form of tinkering, rather than engaging in appropriate and deep reflection on the role and nature of Anglican leadership, the opposite of the intended outcome (of reducing the colonial nature of the appointment) appears to have been cemented. The comments of the Archbishop of Canterbury are telling and representative of much discussion on this topic within the English church:

> From the richest to the poorest nations, the Anglican Communion spans a hugely diverse tapestry of societies, cultures and human experience.
>
> Anglicans worldwide have a profound and historic relationship with the See of Canterbury, and the Archbishop of Canterbury has the great privilege of serving as a focus of unity for Anglican churches across the globe.
>
> It is only right that this international family of churches is given a voice in the process of selecting the 'first among equals' of the bishops of our global communion.
>
> That is why I am pleased that General Synod has voted to increase the representation of Anglicans from around the Communion in the process of choosing future Archbishops of Canterbury.
>
> This small but important step will ensure that the Crown Nominations Commission for the See of Canterbury has balanced and diverse representation from the entire Anglican Communion.
>
> I also want to thank the Diocese of Canterbury for giving up three seats on the Canterbury CNC to enable this change.
>
> I pray that this significant step will bind us more closely together as disciples of Jesus Christ, called to share his good news with a world in need.[23]

Here there appears to be little (if any) recognition that the issue is not with the appointment of the Archbishop of Canterbury per se, but rather the fact that it is the Archbishop of Canterbury who, by right as an English Archbishop, heads the Anglican Communion. It remains astonishing that this simple fact has not been engaged with at the level of the General Synod or the wider Anglican Communion, and yet such a conversation is surely necessary if the historical imbalances and felt injustices of the Communion structures are to be rectified. That there is a 'profound and historic relationship' with Canterbury is not in doubt, but it is hugely disappointing that there appears to be no willingness to challenge whether this profound and historic relationship is the right 'focus of unity' for the modern Communion.

This becomes even more important when we consider the fact that 'being in communion with' (or the rather more vague 'reciprocal relationship' with) the See of Canterbury is a prerequisite for being Anglican. Breakaway self-identified 'Anglican' groups such as the Anglican Church in North America challenge this, apparently suggesting that it is possible to be authentically Anglican outside the structures of communion.[24] Such an argument is unconvincing not least in the vagueness of its content: it is not clear at all what 'Anglicanism' is according to such a church's definition. It is fascinating that so many churches wish to retain the identity of Anglican, yet without any clear definition; this does appear to amount to little more than a name and an assertion of requirements that are either exceedingly general or lacking in historical precedent. We shall return to further examples of these below.

We will engage more deeply with questions of 'being in communion' as we progress our argument, but for now it is enough to recognize that the requirement to be in communion with an English see is itself problematic and yet is historically a reasonable definition of Anglican identity (and perhaps an early example of Anglican identity as 'being in opposition' to other denominations). As we have seen, the other Instruments of Communion similarly find their reference point in this see: the Lambeth Conference (which Canterbury calls), the Anglican Consultative Council (over which Canterbury presides), and the Primates' Meeting (which Canterbury chairs).

The Anglican Consultative Council (ACC) was created in 1968 through a Resolution of the Lambeth Conference,[25] and is primarily in the business of relationship building, information sharing, policy development, ecumenical work and mission.[26] The Anglican Communion Office describes it as 'the most representative body of gathered Anglicans among the Instruments of Communion',[27] which is a curious phrase, and appears to refer to the presence of both lay and ordained Christians who come as 'representatives' from the different provinces (albeit without clearly defined representative roles or responsibilities). While the ACC is somewhat incidental to the lives of most Anglicans worldwide, it is likely that the ACC will be the forum where future developments on the structure of the Anglican Communion will be discussed. It remains to be seen whether the ACC will have the membership and courage to do so in a way that does justice to the topic in a truly postcolonial way.

The Primates' Meeting and the Lambeth Conference have both proved to be hotspots of division and threatened (even attempted) schism in recent years, not least because they are both places where episcopal disagreement is at its most visible and intense. The first Lambeth Conference in 1867 was called by the Archbishop of Canterbury Charles Thomas Longley, in part in response to concerns about Bishop John Colenso, missionary Bishop of Natal. Bishop Colenso had been removed from office by Bishop Robert Gray over concerns about his 'liberal' biblical interpretation, including his views on the acceptability of polygamy in South Africa,[28] but this had been overruled by the Privy Council in London.[29] Division was present at that first Conference, with the non-attendance of the then Archbishop of York, and the refusal of permission to use Westminster Abbey for particular highlights.[30] Since then, there have been a number of controversial topics discussed at Lambeth Conferences, including in recent years debates on the permissibility of same-sex relationships (despite Longley's declaration that 'questions of doctrine' were not to be discussed at such conferences).[31]

Up until and including the Conference of 1998, Resolutions were passed at Lambeth Conferences. These Resolutions, together with any other decisions made at the conference, have no legal effect or standing whatsoever, although they were intended to shape debate at the level of the national churches. It was in this context that the Lambeth Resolution I:10 in 1998 was passed, which made headline reference to the forbidding of blessings for same-sex couples and the refusal of Holy Orders for those in such unions, and which continues to significantly influence Communion polity and debates to this day.[32] Since 2008, there have been no Resolutions, and at the 2022 Lambeth Conference (delayed in part by the global pandemic and in part by the ongoing boycott of some bishops because of the attendance of LGBTQIA bishops (though not their spouses who were explicitly not invited))[33] there were a series of 'Calls', which themselves did not pass entirely without controversy.[34]

In many ways it remains fascinating that the Resolutions (and later Calls) retain so much importance in the mind of many Anglicans, not least given the hottest topic – that of doctrine relating to same-sex relationships – has not been debated in any meaningful sense since 1998. In the wake of the Lambeth Conference of 2022, there has been an explicit push to encourage lay and ordained people from across the Communion to engage with the content of the Calls, with varying degrees of success,[35] which appears to be a recognition that the Lambeth Conference remains somewhat aloof from and ultimately limited in its impact on ordinary Anglicans. That said, there was recognition during the last Lambeth Conference of the potentially damaging impact, particularly on LGBTQIA people in churches who affirmed their relationships and ministry, of hearing an 'Anglican' perspective that appeared to be in direct contradiction to the polity of their own churches.[36] This tension remains unresolved, and yet is perhaps inevitable in the context of a Communion of such widely divergent cultural and theological understandings.

There remain two further Lambeth Conference related issues to address in the context of Anglican identity and the search for unity, which we shall do in the next chapter, but for now it is worth asking the question: what is the point of the Lambeth Conference? It remains unclear as to its purpose, given it is neither legislative nor executive, and the refusal of some bishops to attend to share fellowship with those with whom they disagree. It is, perhaps, an exercise in relationship building, and a place for discussion, but at present it is hard to identify its particular role in being an 'Instrument of Communion'. Given the vast expense (covered in no small part by a church, The Episcopal Church, that is so vehemently opposed by many of the attendees because of its views on same-sex relationships, and that covers not only the travel and accommodation for bishops, but for their (opposite sex) spouses as well), it is surely important to first identify the purpose of such a huge gathering before continuing it into the future as an Instrument. It may be that an intentional focus on episcopal relationship would be helpful to a focus on 'unity', but the current haziness of purpose does not help in this regard.

The final Instrument of Communion is the Primates' Meeting, which was established in 1978 by Archbishop Donald Coggan 'as an opportunity for "leisurely thought, prayer and deep consultation"'.[37] The Anglican Communion describes Primates as having 'no authority as a body', and 'their own national churches determine how their ministry is carried out in their own context'. Once again, however, the Primates' Meeting has been a place where political disagreement has been brought to the fore, particularly over matters of sexuality.[38] While the Primates have made pronouncements on punishments for churches,[39] such as The Episcopal Church (USA), for their 'divergence' from Communion polity (itself a very contested notion),[40] it is not at all clear what actual authority, in a real sense, is invested in this particular Instrument.[41]

Two further groups are important contributors to the current landscape of the Anglican Communion. The first of these is the Global South Fellowship of Anglicans (GSFA), which was formally set up during the Lambeth Conference of 2022, and describes itself as a 'koinonia' of 11 provinces who have signed up to their covenantal structure (from 25 who joined initially).[42] Of note, not all of these provinces are in communion with the See of Canterbury and some have been newly founded (in an arguably schismatic way) to 'supersede' already extant provinces, which is hard to defend as being within the bounds of historical Anglicanism. Their purpose and history is not entirely clear from their website, although they do state that the current organization is a formalization of the Global South Conferences that have met since 1994. The GSFA has members who are both in schism with and in communion (albeit in some cases impaired) with Canterbury, and has committed itself to 'taking decisive steps towards resetting the Anglican Communion' and questioned the Archbishop of Canterbury's 'fitness to lead' the Communion.[43]

While GSFA has focused primarily on opposing 'liberalization' on matters of sexuality, following the 'deep darkness of rebellion to the truth of God's word' supposedly entered into by provinces that are not 'orthodox' and are presenting 'false teaching', there does appear to be a recognition of the need for a focus on 'strong identity' for Anglicans.[44] Interestingly, the GSFA describes its covenantal structure as 'a locus of structural unity for the orthodox of the whole Communion', suggesting that the 'Anglican Orthodox Leaders' would meet annually 'to continue this link to one another, to be refreshed by Spirit-filled fellowship, to take counsel together on Communion matters, and to collaborate on mission and ministry'. In many ways, this appears to be a re-envisaging of the Communion, yet at present on a scale that is implausible and with an identity that primarily relies on opposition to homosexuality.

The second group that has had an impact on discussions of unity in the Anglican Communion has been GAFCON, the 'Global Anglican Future Conference'. It describes itself as 'a global family of authentic Anglicans standing together to retain and restore the Bible to the heart of the Anglican Communion'.[45] They were set up in 2008, 'when moral compromise, doctrinal error and the collapse of biblical witness in parts of the Anglican communion had reached such a level that the leaders of the majority of the world's Anglicans felt it was necessary to take a united stand for truth' (a reference, presumably, to homosexuality, given the formation of GAFCON in opposition to the ordination of Bishop Gene Robinson).[46] GAFCON has met a number of times since then and claims to be a 'global movement within the Communion which represents the majority of all Anglicans'.[47]

There are a number of links between GSFA and GAFCON, including members of the leadership of both organizations, although GSFA appears to be more willing to work within the structures of the Communion, while GAFCON contains more Primates who have declared themselves out of communion with Canterbury. This was demonstrated in the Kigali Commitment at GAFCON IV, which reported:

> The leadership of both groups affirmed and celebrated their complementary roles in the Anglican Communion. Gafcon is a movement focused on evangelism and mission, church planting and providing support and a home for faithful Anglicans who are pressured by or alienated from revisionist dioceses and provinces. GSFA, on the other hand, is focused on establishing doctrinally based structures within the Communion.[48]

Given this, it appears that there is more hope within GSFA that the original Instruments of Communion might be reformed, whereas in GAFCON there is a clearer willingness to re-envisage the meaning of Anglicanism (although there is clearly overlap between the membership and aims). To this end, the Kigali Commitment rejected the idea of 'good disagreement' that had been proposed by the Instruments of Communion, stating that 'we cannot "walk together" in good disagreement with those who have deliberately chosen to walk away from the "faith once for all delivered to the saints"'.[49] They described the 'leadership role' of the Archbishop of Canterbury as 'entirely indefensible' and called for repentance, stating:

> We long for this repentance but until they repent, our communion with them remains broken.
>
> We consider that those who refuse to repent have abdicated their right to leadership within the Anglican Communion, and we commit ourselves to working with orthodox Primates and other leaders to reset the Communion on its biblical foundations.

WHERE THE LAND LIES

While it remains the aim of the Anglican Communion to rebuild and 'walk together', it is hard to see how this might happen in the current circumstances given the absolute refusal of GAFCON, and its associated provinces, to do so. GAFCON continues to 'recognize new orthodox jurisdictions' and 'Gafcon-aligned networks', a direct challenge to the authority of the Anglican Communion. The Kigali Commitment spelt this out:

> We acknowledge their agreement that 'communion' between churches and Christians must be based on doctrine (Jerusalem Declaration #13; GSFA Covenant 2.1.6). Anglican identity is defined by this and not by recognition from the See of Canterbury.
>
> We welcome the GSFA's Ash Wednesday Statement of 20 February 2023, calling for a resetting and reordering of the Communion. We applaud the invitation of the GSFA Primates to collaborate with Gafcon and other orthodox Anglican groupings to work out the shape and nature of our common life together and how we are to maintain the priority of proclaiming the gospel and making disciples of all nations.
>
> Resetting the Communion is an urgent matter. It needs an adequate and robust foundation that addresses the legal and constitutional complexities in various Provinces. The goal is that orthodox Anglicans worldwide will have a clear identity, a global 'spiritual home' of which they can be proud, and a strong leadership structure that gives them stability and direction as Global Anglicans. We therefore commit to pray that God will guide this process of resetting, and that Gafcon and GSFA will keep in step with the Spirit.

Such a 'resetting' is particularly interesting given the definition of Anglicanism on which it is predicated, that 'Anglican identity' is defined by an 'agreement that "communion" between churches and Christians must be based on doctrine'. This is ahistorical as an Anglican understanding, yet if the language of the Commitment is taken at face value (that they represent 85 per cent of global Anglicans), then it is important not to dismiss this out of hand and recognize that this is now a competing claim for the marker of Anglican identity. Of course, the claim that GAFCON 'represents' a proportion of the Communion is open to significant challenge, and similarly a reliance on numbers does not appear to be a Christian virtue or part of an authentic Anglican patrimony. Nonetheless this kind of positioning is important when considering exactly what 'unity' is now thought to rely on in the context of Anglicanism, and how the current conclusions have been reached.

Alongside this, the fact that there is such an explicit rejection of the need to be in communion with Canterbury, and the celebration of new provinces based on doctrine and in direct contradiction of the historically important geographical parish, diocese and provincial structure, does suggest that fundamentally divergent understandings of Anglicanism have now developed, which are in competition with one another. This poses a challenge to any understanding of 'unity', not least given the apparent need for any such understanding to command widespread acceptance. It may be, of course, that any conception will need, at the minimum, a long period of discussion, engagement and reception, and at worst we may be beyond the point where a shared understanding can command the loyalty of the Communion. We may be in a position whereby impaired communion is inevitable for a prolonged period.

Whichever of these turns out to be the case, we must now ask: is there something that makes an ecclesial community and communion distinctly Anglican? Does it matter that such a thing, or group of things, exists? Does Anglican identity still find a purpose and calling within the church catholic? If so, how might we go about finding that identity, and thus our renewed locus of unity? Several attempts have been made to do just that, and we look to those before fleshing out what such unity might look like given our current English and wider Communion context.

Notes

1 Mark Chapman and Jeremy Morris's books outlined in the Introduction are helpful in this regard.

2 Mark Chapman, *Anglican Theology* (London: T&T Clark, 2012), p. 159.

3 We might think here, again, of the intentional nature of producing a common liturgy that can embody a number of different particular beliefs on matters such as justification, Eucharist, and so on.

4 Sam Allberry, 'Why Homosexuality is an Issue of First Importance', *The Village Church*, 9 April 2015, https://www.thevillagechurch. net/resources/articles/why-homosexuality-is-an-issue-of-first-import ance (accessed 10.1.24).

5 An excellent summary is found in Enze Han and Joseph O'Mahoney, *British Colonialism and the Criminalization of Homosexuality: Queens, Crime and Empire* (London: Routledge, 2018).

6 Civicus, 'LGBTQI+ Rights in the Commonwealth: Time for Change', Civicus Lens, 21 June 2022, https://lens.civicus.org/lgbtqi-rights-in-the-commonwealth-time-for-change/ (accessed 2.1.24).

7 Indeed, in some contexts homosexuality continues to be described, against all the evidence, as being 'forced' on countries by 'foreign actors'. See Harriet Sherwood, 'Justin Welby criticizes Ugandan church's backing for anti-gay law', *The Guardian*, 9 June 2023, https://www.theguardian. com/world/2023/jun/09/justin-welby-criticises-ugandan-church-back ing-for-anti-gay-law (accessed 20.1.24).

8 Dicastery for the Doctrine of the Faith, 'Declaration: *Fiducia Supplicans*, On the Pastoral Meaning of Blessings', 18 December 2023, https://www.vatican.va/roman_curia/congregations/cfaith/documents/ rc_ddf_doc_20231218_fiducia-supplicans_en.html (accessed 10.1.24).

9 ACI Africa, 'No Blessing for "same-sex couples" in Africa, Catholic Bishops Declare, Vatican Agrees', ACI Africa 11 January 2024, https://www.aciafrica.org/news/9998/no-blessing-for-same-sex-couples-in-africa-catholic-bishops-declare-vatican-agrees (accessed 11.1.24).

10 Andrew Brown, 'The latest hate speech from the Church of Nigeria', *The Guardian*, 13 March 2009, https://www.theguardian.com/ commentisfree/andrewbrown/2009/mar/13/religion-anglicanism-akinola-nigeria (accessed 12.1.24).

11 Kirk Petersen, 'Bishops in Ghana Endorse Anti-Gay Bill', The Living Church, 20 October 2021, https://livingchurch.org/2021/10/20/ bishops-in-ghana-endorse-anti-gay-bill/ (accessed 10.1.24).

12 Thabo Msibi, 'The Lies We Have Been Told: On (Homo) Sexuality in Africa', *Africa Today* 58(1), 2011, pp. 55–77.

13 We might think here of how long it took senior bishops in the Church of England, including the Archbishop of Canterbury as 'focus of

unity' in the Anglican Communion, to make any kind of public remark on the active episcopal sponsoring of homophobic laws in Uganda and Ghana.

14 Diocese of London, 'Bishop of London joins 650 bishops from 165 countries at Lambeth Conference', https://bishopoflondon.org/news/bishop-of-london-joins-650-bishops-from-165-countries-at-lambeth-conference/ (accessed 10.1.24).

15 An excellent example is found in Kwok Pui-lan, *The Anglican Tradition from a Postcolonial Perspective* (New York: Seabury Books, 2023).

16 Anglican Communion, 'What is the Anglican Communion?', https://www.anglicancommunion.org/structures/what-is-the-anglican-communion.aspx (accessed 10.1.24).

17 It is not entirely clear what is meant by 'member' in this context; similarly, what is meant by bishops 'representing' a particular number of Anglicans in their context. The latter of these is certainly not grounded in anything like a meaningful Anglican ecclesiology.

18 Anglican Communion, 'Presence at the United Nations', https://www.anglicancommunion.org/mission/at-the-un.aspx (accessed 11.1.24).

19 Anglican Communion, 'Anglican Communion Office', https://www.anglicancommunion.org/structures/anglican-communion-office.aspx (accessed 11.1.24).

20 Anglican Communion, 'Archbishop of Canterbury', https://www.anglicancommunion.org/structures/instruments-of-communion/archbishop-of-canterbury.aspx (accessed 10.1.24).

21 Church of England, 'GS2253: Consultation on Proposed Changes to the Membership of the Crown Nominations Commission for the See of Canterbury', February 2022, https://www.churchofengland.org/sites/default/files/2022-01/gs-2253-consultation-on-proposed-changes-to-the-canterbury-cnc.pdf (accessed 10.1.24).

22 Sarah Meyrick, 'Five global regions to have reps on CNC for Archbishop Welby's successor', *Church Times*, 22 November 2023, https://www.churchtimes.co.uk/articles/2023/24-november/news/world/five-global-regions-to-have-reps-on-crown-nominations-commission-for-archbishop-welby-s-successor (accessed 16.1.24).

23 International Anglican–Roman Catholic Commission for Unity and Mission, 'Global Anglican Communion given greater voice in choosing future Archbishops of Canterbury', 12 July 2022, https://iarccum.org/2022/global-anglican-communion-given-greater-voice-in-choosing-future-archbishops-of-canterbury/ (accessed 20.1.24).

24 Anglican Church in North America, 'What is Anglicanism?', https://anglicanchurch.net/anglicanism/ (accessed 10.1.24).

25 Anglican Communion, 'The Lambeth Conference: Resolutions Archive from 1968', https://www.anglicancommunion.org/media/127743/1968.pdf (accessed 10.1.24).

26 Anglican Consultative Council, 'Articles of Association', https://www.anglicancommunion.org/media/39479/the-constitution-of-the-anglican-consultative-council.pdf (accessed 20.1.24).

27 Anglican Communion, 'Anglican Consultative Council', https://www.anglicancommunion.org/structures/instruments-of-communion/acc.aspx (accessed 11.1.24).

28 Mark Chapman, *Anglicanism: A Very Short Introduction* (Oxford: Oxford University Press, 2006), p. 111.

29 The Lambeth Palace Library Blog, 'The first Lambeth Conference', https://monumentoffame.org/2020/07/03/the-first-lambeth-conference/ (accessed 10.1.24).

30 Randall T. Davidson, *The Five Lambeth Conferences* (London: SPCK, 1920), p. 12.

31 Encyclopaedia Britannica, 'Lambeth Conference', https://www.britannica.com/topic/Lambeth-Conference (accessed 11.1.24).

32 Anglican Communion, 'Section I.10 – Human Sexuality', https://www.anglicancommunion.org/resources/document-library/lambeth-conference/1998/section-i-called-to-full-humanity/section-i10-human-sexuality (accessed 20.1.24). It is interesting to note the content of some of the amendments.

33 Mary Frances Schjonberg, 'Same-sex spouses not invited to next year's Lambeth Conference of bishops', Episcopal News Service, 18 February 2019, https://www.episcopalnewsservice.org/2019/02/18/same-sex-spouses-not-invited-to-next-years-lambeth-conference-of-bishops/ (accessed 20.1.24).

34 David Paulsen, 'Archbishop of Canterbury's remarks on human dignity lift up traditional and progressive marriage beliefs', Episcopal News Service, 2 August 2022, https://www.episcopalnewsservice.org/2022/08/02/at-lambeth-conservative-bishops-work-the-sidelines-to-reaffirm-majority-opposition-to-same-sex-marriage/ (accessed 10.1.24).

35 Lambeth Conference, 'The Lambeth Calls', https://www.lambethconference.org/phase-3/the-lambeth-calls/ (accessed 11.1.24).

36 Pat Ashworth, 'Draft Lambeth Conference "call" threatens to reignite 1998 row over homosexuality', *Church Times*, 22 July 2022, https://www.churchtimes.co.uk/articles/2022/29-july/news/world/draft-lambeth-conference-call-threatens-to-reignite-1998-row-over-homosexuality, and Episcopal News Service, 'Bishops who support full LGBTQ+ inclusion release statement from Lambeth Conference', Episcopal News Service, 3 August 2022, https://www.episcopalnewsservice.org/2022/08/03/bishops-who-support-full-lgbtq-inclusion-release-statement-from-lambeth-conference/ (accessed 10.1.24).

37 Anglican Communion, 'Primates' Meeting', https://www.anglicancommunion.org/structures/instruments-of-communion/primates-meeting.aspx (accessed 11.1.24).

38 Antony Bushfield, 'Tense primate meeting on LGBT Christians

gets underway', Premier Christian News, 11 January 2016, https://premierchristian.news/en/news/article/tense-primate-meeting-on-lgbt-christians-gets-underway (accessed 10.1.24).

39 Communiqué from the Primates' Meeting 2016, Anglican Communion New Service, 15 January 2016, https://www.anglicannews.org/features/2016/01/communique-from-the-primates-meeting-2016.aspx (accessed 10.1.24).

40 Primary Christian News, 'US Episcopal Church defiant on primates meeting: "Nothing will change"', Premier Christian News, 17 January 2016, https://premierchristian.news/en/news/article/us-episcopal-church-defiant-on-primates-meeting-nothing-will-change (accessed 15.1.24).

41 It is described as a 'powerful and morally forceful guideline' in the Archbishop's speech, which is a curious and ambiguous turn of phrase. Justin Welby's Presidential Address to the General Synod, *Episcopal News Service*, 15 February 2016, https://www.episcopalnewsservice.org/2016/02/15/archbishop-justin-welby-unpacks-primates-communique/ (accessed 10.1.24).

42 Global South Fellowship of Anglican Churches, 'Who we are', https://www.thegsfa.org/about-us (accessed 19.1.24).

43 Justin Badi Arama, 'Global South archbishops question Welby's "fitness to lead" the Anglican Communion following synod vote on gay blessings', Anglican Ink, 9 February 2023, https://anglican.ink/2023/02/09/global-south-archbishops-question-welbys-fitness-to-lead-the-anglican-communion-following-synod-vote-on-gay-blessings/ (accessed 10.1.24).

44 Global South Fellowship of Anglican Churches, 'GSFA brings hope and builds orthodox unity in the Anglican Communion', https://www.thegsfa.org/news/gsfa-brings-hope-and-builds-orthodox-unity-in-the-anglican-communion (accessed 10.1.24).

45 GAFCON, 'About GAFCON', https://www.gafcon.org/about (accessed 10.1.24).

46 GAFCON, 'History', https://www.gafcon.org/about/history (accessed 11.1.24).

47 GAFCON, 'Global Movement', https://www.gafcon.org/about/global-movement (accessed 10.1.24).

48 GAFCON, 'GAFCON IV – The Kigali Commitment', 21 April 2023, https://www.gafcon.org/news/gafcon-iv-the-kigali-commitment (accessed 11.1.24).

49 GAFCON, 'GAFCON IV – The Kigali Commitment'.

4

Anglican identity and unity

As we discussed in the previous chapter, the first Lambeth Conference of 1867 was not a huge success, and yet it paved the way for many more such conferences. As preparations were in train for the third such conference, the bishops of the Protestant Episcopal Church in the United States met in Chicago, in 1886, for their own General Convention and, more from ecumenical impulse than from an aim to address issues of Anglican identity, they adopted the ideas of Episcopal priest William Reed Huntington in his book *The Church Idea: An Essay Towards Unity* (1870) in the form of the Chicago Quadrilateral. The aim of this quadrilateral was to push towards reunification of the churches, which the Episcopalian bishops believed was possible through adopting 'principles of unity exemplified by the undivided Catholic Church during the first days of its existence'.[1]

The Lambeth Conference of 1888 debated the Quadrilateral,[2] and passed Resolution 11, which modified the wording to create an agreed definition that would be used in the pursuit of unity:

> That, in the opinion of this Conference, the following Articles supply a basis on which approach may be by God's blessing made towards Home Reunion:
>
> 1 The Holy Scriptures of the Old and New Testaments, as 'containing all things necessary to salvation', and as being the rule and ultimate standard of faith.
>
> 2 The Apostles' Creed, as the Baptismal Symbol; and the Nicene Creed, as the sufficient statement of the Christian faith.
>
> 3 The two Sacraments ordained by Christ Himself – Baptism and the Supper of the Lord – ministered with unfailing use

of Christ's words of Institution, and of the elements ordained by Him.

4 The Historic Episcopate, locally adapted in the methods of
its administration to the varying needs of the nations and
peoples called of God into the Unity of His Church.[3]

With our prior caveat that Resolutions of the Lambeth Conference are not binding, nonetheless this particular formulation
continues to hold widespread support within the Anglican
Communion, and in recent times has been seen as a pointer
towards Anglican identity as much as it has to the ecumenical
venture.

The failure of the Quadrilateral to further ecumenical dialogue is perhaps best exemplified in two ways, which relate
to the fourth of the statements, on the Historical Episcopate.
While Anglicans and Roman Catholics may indeed be willing
to agree on this particular formulation in principle, nonetheless
since the unfortunate Apostolic letter *Apostolicae Curae*, issued
by Pope Leo XIII in 1896, it remains Roman Catholic polity
that Anglican orders are 'absolutely null and utterly void'.[4]
While there have been attempts since this period to reconsider
the matter,[5] this declaration means that while the Historical
Episcopate may indeed supply a basis for reunification, the
Roman Catholic position is that the Anglican Church has no
part in this particular order.

While this has been a stumbling block for ecumenical purposes, it is nonetheless an interesting reflection on the importance
of the threefold ministry for Anglican identity. This has proved
problematic in attempts at reunification with the Methodist
Church (as we described in previous chapters), given their
lack of episcopal orders in some branches, including England.
Yet despite these two ecumenical issues, this does somewhat
cement the episcopate as an important part of Anglicanism, and
perhaps adds justification to the focus on the importance of the
episcopate for visible unity within the Communion. To date
there have been limited attempts to subvert this order, which
have primarily related to issues of sacramental ministry and
presiding at the Eucharist by those not ordained as priests,[6]

but this position has gained very little wider support outside Sydney, Australia.

Interestingly, when faced with the tension between church order (that is, who might be ordained) and sacramental order (who might administer the sacraments), the Diocese of Hong Kong came down in favour of sacramental order and irregularly ordained a woman to be a priest before such a possibility had been agreed with the wider church. On 25 January 1944, Florence Li Tim-Oi was the first woman to be ordained in the Anglican Communion, to enable the Eucharist to be celebrated in Macau, which could not be accessed by visiting clergy because of the Second World War.[7] This act of necessity was met with hostility after the war had ended, but in itself identified the key importance of priestly ordination for sacramental ministry and hence the centrality of the threefold order to Anglican identity when addressed in a practical sense.

The Lambeth Quadrilateral itself builds on the historical formularies of the Church of England, and does so in a way that is both generous to the inheritance and appropriate to the circumstances in which it was itself formulated. The first Article reflects Article 6 of the 39 Articles, and the third reflects Article 25. Criticisms have been made that this third Article does not make mention of the further five sacraments frequently associated with the church catholic (confirmation, penance, orders, matrimony and extreme unction), but given the wide and long-standing variety of beliefs within both the Church of England and the wider Communion on the status of these further sacraments, it does appear reasonable for the two dominical sacraments to be the prime identifiers of Anglican identity (most particularly from an ecumenical perspective).

What is particularly interesting is the limited reference to specific doctrines made in the Quadrilateral.[8] The second Article merely makes mention of the creeds of the church, which themselves form the backbone for the agreed doctrine of the vast majority of Christian denominations. While this does appear to be a generous agenda for ecumenical dialogue, it does not perhaps do justice to the particularity of Anglican doctrine, which may be as much in its method (which may itself be disputed, as we shall see below) as in its content. In a sense, the Lambeth Quadrilateral does give us a 'minimum understanding' of what it means to be Anglican, but whether it really gives enough to describe an identity as *distinctly* Anglican is not clear. Of course, that is not its initial purpose – and in many ways its more 'bare bones' approach is entirely appropriate for the ecumenical enterprise. The question we might ask, however, is whether the Lambeth Quadrilateral can provide a basis for internal unity as well.

An attempt to provide a clearer understanding of the doctrinal integrity required for internal unity came with the publication of the Windsor Report (2004) and the associated Anglican Communion Covenant in 2006. Coming as it did out of a period of crisis, it is perhaps a salutary reminder that such periods do not necessarily provide the most comprehensive and level-headed canvases on which to draw such fundamental conclusions about the nature of Anglican doctrinal identity. In response to The Episcopal Church's (USA) ordination of Gene Robinson (a publicly gay man in a same-sex relationship) as a bishop in 2003, and the authorization of a rite for the blessing of same-sex unions in the Diocese of New Westminster, Canada, the Primates of the Anglican Communion met and released a lengthy statement, lamenting that the decision

> will tear the fabric of our Communion at its deepest level, and may lead to further division on this and further issues as provinces have to decide in consequence whether they can remain in communion with provinces that choose not to break communion with the Episcopal Church.[9]

This is an early and fascinating example of where the directionality of blame is so firmly established as lying on the side of those who have developed their doctrinal understanding in good conscience and in line with the Anglican theological method. We shall return to this later, but it is notable that 'unity' is seen here as something from which a group have demurred or walked away, rather than as something that sits above decisions that are made and which is a fundamental part of Anglican identity. 'Unity', as defined here, appears to be a defence of the status quo majority position, and there is the implicit suggestion that movement from a defined position (defined, indeed, by whom?) is an active process of assault on that 'unity'. This appears to run the risk of conceptualizing 'unity' as a means to an end rather than as a metaphysical reality. In other words, it mistakes visible unity for unity itself, suggesting that the essence of unity is present only when humanly expressed and recognized. This seems to do damage to the understanding of unity as a theological imperative and as a gift of the Holy Spirit, as we discussed in Chapter 1.

The 2003 statement from the Primates also spoke of 'the Anglican inheritance of faith and order', and a 'firm desire to remain part of a Communion, where what we hold in common is much greater than that which divides us'. In particular they 're-affirm[ed] [their] common understanding of the centrality and authority of Scripture in determining the basis of [their] faith', acknowledging a 'legitimate diversity of interpretation' which 'does not mean that some of us take the authority of Scripture more lightly than others'. In so doing, they appeared not to be questioning the centrality of Scripture to the American churches (in contrast to the more recent accusations that we saw in the last chapter), but instead were concerned about the 'mutual respect' that needed to be shown by provinces in addressing the way that the 'possible effects' of interpretation of Scripture by one province might be received in or impact upon another.

It is hard to take issue with this particular call for mutuality, but once again it is fascinating that the Primates did not appear to recognize that this mutuality is a two-way process. This appears to be an appeal to numbers (as we saw in the last chapter, and given that Resolutions are ultimately a process of a majority non-binding vote, this seems to be routinely the case when reference is made to Lambeth I:10). What is really being called for is restraint by provinces with a minority view, rather than a genuine mutuality whereby the 'possible effects of' the interpretation of *any* province's interpretation of Scripture on any others should be considered. There is little here, for example, or in later pronouncements, about the impact of the openly homophobic nature of episcopal statements in some 'Global South' provinces on those provinces that have taken an affirming position on sexuality.

This is further illustrated by the reference to the decisions of The Episcopal Church (USA) and the Anglican Church of Canada being a risk to the 'mission and witness' of the Anglican Communion 'in a world already confused in areas of sexuality, morality and theology, and polarized Christian opinion', suggesting that there is a univocal 'mission and witness' within the Anglican Communion. The Primates state that they speak 'as a body', which is unclear in its meaning (given the nature of the Primates' Meeting), and while they recognize that 'it is not for us to pass judgement on the constitutional process of another province', and 'recognize the sensitive balance between provincial autonomy and the expression of critical opinion by others on the internal actions of a province', 'nevertheless, many Primates have pointed to the grave difficulties' that they state arose as a result of the election of Bishop Robinson's 'lifestyle'.[10] In addition, the Primates spoke specifically of the jeopardizing of 'sacramental fellowship' because the 'recent actions in New Westminster and in the Episcopal Church (USA) do not express the mind of our Communion as a whole'.

Two questions might quite rightly be asked at this juncture. First, given the diversity of doctrinal understandings across the Communion (including, as we have noted, on justification and on the Eucharist) and issues of church order (for example, the ordination of women), why is it that this particular issue is one that has led to division that seems impossible to resolve?[11] Second, and relatedly, to what extent is the Primates' reasoning representative and reflective of genuine markers of Anglican identity, and to what extent is it primarily political posturing in response to a single issue?

While the Primates' statement appears to be clear in its condemnation and in its assessment of the damage done to the Communion as an entity (if such a thing exists), the statement also began the process that led to the Windsor Report and the ecclesiology that underpinned the ultimately unsuccessful Anglican Covenant. Here we find a declared understanding of mutuality that requires those with a minority position (however 'Anglican') to make no move in some matters of doctrine[12] until the majority agree, that further cements the idea that there is a 'Communion' position on matters of doctrine, and that appears to privilege certain doctrinal issues over others as relates to unity. The Primates do not explain why homosexuality is the issue of doctrine that fits this bill, nor do they explain why doctrine per se (beyond the Quadrilateral) has become a pillar of Anglican identity.[13] This is a shift in Anglican ecclesiology: it points towards a centralizing Communion structure with a unified 'mission and witness', in which doctrine is agreed by majority decision, and in which particular doctrines (specifically in this case pastoral and disciplinary approaches to homosexuality) define the bounds of 'sacramental fellowship'.

This appears to be a fundamental break with historic Anglican self-understanding, and yet its apparently uncritical reception by many, including the current leadership of the Anglican Communion, has led to our current difficulties when defining internal notions of 'unity'. It is interesting to question whether this particular centralizing tendency would have been furthered were homosexuality not to be the issue of the day. Similarly, it is worth recognizing that while the 2003 Primates meeting has indeed reset the Communion's polity in favour of majority thinking, it has not addressed the fundamental issues of colonialism and colonial structures. Homosexuality as an issue has overtaken any serious consideration of the appropriateness (or otherwise) of the current Communion's make-up, and changes to the Communion's self-understanding have been crisis-led and issue-focused rather than intentional and analytical.

To return to the Windsor Report: this was set up in the light of the concerns of the Primates, and was chaired by Archbishop Robin Eames, who was at that time Primate of All Ireland.[14] Its purpose was not to opine on the rightness or wrongness of homosexuality, but rather to make recommendations on the future structures of the Anglican Communion in the light of these disagreements. It did so by suggesting a way, the Anglican Covenant, in which the 'mutuality' (or 'mutual interdependence and responsibility in the Body of Christ', as the Report quotes the third 'Anglican Congress' of 1963) is to some degree legislated for and differences constrained.

The Windsor Report makes reference to the 'Ten Principles of Partnership', which consist of local initiative, mutuality, responsible stewardship, interdependence, cross-fertilization, integrity, transparency, solidarity, meeting together, and acting ecumenically.[15] While these are useful pointers in understanding the way the Communion acts, they are contestable notions and, in a similar way to the Quadrilateral, do not get to the heart of what it is that is specifically 'Anglican' about the Communion.[16] It also appears (paragraphs 22–30) to take as read, following the example of the Primates, the authority of the Lambeth Conference in setting the bounds of acceptable doctrinal development within the Communion (itself highly contestable and indeed contested even within the report, for example in paragraph 42), and addresses homosexuality as primarily a doctrinal rather than a pastoral issue. It did recognize the disputed nature of the question at hand (principally whether it was a thing indifferent or not), and also the problems with trust, understandings of subsidiarity, and procedure.

Key outcomes from the Windsor Report, alongside the Anglican Covenant, were a call for a period of repentance (primarily from The Episcopal Church (USA) and the Anglican Church of Canada) and reconciliation, a moratorium on the consecration of gay people to the episcopate, a moratorium on public rites of same-sex blessing, and a call to avoid, except in 'situations where there has been an extreme breach of trust, and as a last resort', the intrusion of episcopal ministry into another's diocese or province. In terms of the Covenant, the Windsor Report produced a draft and suggested that this

> would make explicit and forceful the loyalty and bonds of affection which govern the relationships between the churches of the Communion. The Covenant could deal with: the acknowledgement of common identity; the relationships of communion; the commitments of communion; the exercise of autonomy in communion; and the management of communion affairs (including disputes).[17]

The Covenant was finalized by the Covenant Design Group.[18] The final document did not contain any new markers of Anglican identity, basing itself primarily on the Lambeth Quadrilateral and the Instruments of Communion. Concerns were raised, nonetheless, that the Covenant defined the Anglican faith too narrowly, was overly centralizing, and was ultimately designed to cement the status quo and exclude churches whose doctrine (specifically on homosexuality) had developed.[19] In England, despite episcopal support, the Covenant was defeated, and there were a number of similar defeats across the Communion, although some provinces did approve it.[20] Predictably, some progressive provinces felt that the Covenant was too restrictive, and some conservative provinces felt that it did not go far enough.

One of the key issues with the Covenant was the fourth section, 'Our Covenanted Life Together'. Here, it was proposed that the Standing Committee of the Anglican Communion was to be given the authority to 'monitor the functioning' of the Covenant, 'make a declaration that an action or decision is or would be "incompatible with the Covenant"', and 'recommend to any Instrument of Communion relational consequences which may specify a provisional limitation of participation in, or suspension from, that Institution'. There is a not-so-subtle shift here in the workings of the Instruments of Communion, away from being foci of unity with no central authority, to becoming authoritative in determining the bounds of what is and is not acceptably Anglican. This would have created an entirely new entity in place of the current Communion – essentially an entity that would exist in and of itself, rather than as an expression of unity among its members. This would, in many ways, have been a definitive step in the direction of denominationalism, yet towards a denomination that would remain structurally colonial. It is unlikely such a move would have even been considered were opposition to homosexuality not the impetus.

In rejecting the Covenant, there was an implicit recognition that not only were centralizing tendencies to be avoided but also that a focus on doctrine as a unifying identity was not something that commanded widespread support. This acts as a rebuke to the direction charted in the 2003 Primates' statement, and at the Lambeth Conference of 2022 the Archbishop of Canterbury's intervention on the Call on Human Dignity made clear that some lessons had been learnt:

> I am very conscious that the Archbishop of Canterbury is to be a focus of unity and is an Instrument of Communion. That is a priority. Truth and unity must be held together, but Church history also says that this sometimes takes a very long time to reach a point where different teaching is rejected or received. I neither have, nor do I seek, the authority to discipline or exclude a church of the Anglican Communion. I will not do so. I may comment in public on occasions, but that is all. We are a Communion of Churches, not a single church.[21]

In the same speech he recognized that 'there is no attempt to change people's minds', and that 'careful theological reflection and a process of reception' had been exercised in churches who had moved on the issue of same-sex relationships. 'They have not arrived lightly at their ideas that traditional teaching needs to change ... they are not careless about scripture ... they do not reject Christ.' While it is startling that such a statement was required, nonetheless it shows a commitment by the current Archbishop, Justin Welby,[22] to try to move away from the binarism of the current debate and the assumption, embodied in much Communion dialogue since 2003, that the 'gay issue' would and should be the doctrinal issue that defined Anglicanism. If this position is held to, and widely received, then there is hope that the Communion might refocus on genuine markers of Anglicanism rather than get caught up in endless debates on sexuality. To date, however, this remains a hope and not a reality.

Let us return to those things that might be better indicators of Anglican identity, and hence the grounds for unity. Prominent among these, as we have seen, is the threefold order and in particular the episcopate. Anglican understanding has consistently given homage to the idea of apostolic succession,[23] as a marker of the catholicity of the Church of England (and wider Communion).[24] Building on the Church Fathers, Archbishop Michael Ramsey suggests that this term has several meanings: 'the succession of Bishop to Bishop in office' securing 'a continuity of Christian teaching and tradition'; the succession of the Apostles 'in the sense that they performed those *functions*, of preaching and ruling and ordaining, which the Apostles had performed'; and 'to signify that grace is handed down from the Apostles through each generation of Bishops by the laying on of hands'.

This definition is helpful, in that it does not rely merely on the laying on of hands in an unbroken line (not least given historical realities). However, while apostolic succession itself may (in its various forms) be held to be a key marker of Anglicanism (if not an entirely distinctive one), it is important to recognize that both the exercise of this episcopal ministry (and its relationship to particular expressions of synodality) and the election or appointment of those to this role differs markedly from province to province. While in the English church, bishops are appointed, in the vast majority of the Communion there is a process of election.

Indeed, in England, given the Established nature of the church, bishops are officially appointed by the Crown (with the spiritualities of the see granted by the archbishop and the temporalities by the monarch).[25] Diocesan bishops[26] are appointed through the Crown Nominations Commission (CNC), an outdated and secretive process that was historically intended to provide advice for the Prime Minister, whereas suffragan bishops are appointed by the diocesan bishop in concurrence with the archbishop.[27] While the CNC contains members nominated by and from the General Synod and by and from the diocese, together with the archbishops, there is a very limited level of pan-church consent given for the appointed candidate.[28]

This is in marked contrast to other provinces, for example in The Episcopal Church (USA). Here, bishops (both diocesan and suffragan) are elected by Diocesan Convention, but this election must be consented to by both a majority of diocesan standing committees and from a majority of bishops exercising jurisdiction in The Episcopal Church.[29] Such a mechanism gives practical expression to the idea that bishops are elected to serve the whole church, and similarly enables a practical expression of collegiality.[30] It is interesting that this is the direction in which many Anglican expressions have moved once no longer bound by Establishment, and may point to a distinctly Anglican model, in which there is ordained episcopal leadership which is granted by consent of clergy and laity, and in collegiality with other bishops.

It is also of note that the Instruments of Communion (except the ACC) are also episcopal and collegial in nature, yet the ACC – together with the varieties of convocations and synods in each province – suggest that effective Anglican episcopacy is not expressed by the bishop alone but by bishops in college and by bishops with consent. This is the case across the Communion, and is a key reminder of the importance given to lay and ordained in the development of Anglican identity and polity. This is found in the formulation of Anglican canon law,[31] which is derived and promulgated separately in national churches rather than centrally, yet which contains a similar emphasis on the make-up of the church. Archbishop Rowan Williams describes it as follows:

> Canon Law begins from that basic affirmation of equity which is the fact of membership in the Body of Christ – a status deeper and stronger than any civil contract or philosophical argument. And it seeks clarity about who may do what and who is answerable to whom, because every Christian has to know how to work out their responsibility to God within the context of the various relationships and obligations they are involved in.[32]

However, a lack of Establishment in the vast majority of the Communion has removed the absolute necessity of being 'a church for the entire people' rather than for the congregation/s, which does run the risk of Anglicanism behaving more like a denomination (and hence increasing its focus on doctrinal matters) in the wider Communion than in England. In England itself, an increasing focus on doctrine as a marker of Anglicanism has similarly led to greater emphasis being placed on this denominational character. As a particularly 'English' facet of Anglican identity, it is perhaps challenging to determine how this might be effectively embodied in situations where Anglicanism *is* one among many different churches, although it may be that a commitment to open occasional offices or similar could aid in that purpose. It does seem that this comprehensiveness in action and service, if not in theology and doctrine, is a potential gift of Anglicanism's history that has not been effectively exploited to date.

Throughout our exploration so far, we have intentionally shied away from an association of Anglicanism with particular interpretations of the *via media*, or particular doctrinal understandings, or even of doctrinal and interpretative methodology. This is not because Anglicanism has not been associated with them – it has, quite often rather forcefully, by those who take entirely opposing perspectives, both historically and in the contemporary church – but rather because a dogmatic assertion of Anglicanism's being one thing or the other, as either method or doctrine, in this regard is simply historically inaccurate.[33] Because this process of 'identity formation' through selective use of history is nothing new, even our history is littered with it (often history formed in the heat of conflict), making the task even more complicated!

Thus, while it may indeed be reasonable to say that particular theological methods or self-identifications are *within* the stream of Anglicanism (for example, the three-legged stool of Scripture, tradition and reason, wrongly associated with Hooker, or the fabled *via media*) it is not really true to say that these are the *only* true examples of Anglican theological method (by which we mean Anglican as a 'denomination' rather than as a seam of thought, as we described in Chapter 1). In other words, the primacy of Scripture, and the use of reason and tradition, most certainly do find themselves within the broad stream of Anglicanism, and thus are not 'un-Anglican', but it is not clear that this is enough to define Anglicanism – or, indeed, whether if we were to do so, we would be doing justice to the wideness of the stream. Anglicanism's lack of 'key texts' adds to the complexity of such a task, meaning that there is an inevitable set of 'competing versions as to what counts as authentic historical Anglicanism'.[34]

In Jeremy Morris's review of Stephen Sykes's work – an Anglican theologian who wrote *Unashamed Anglicanism*[35] and who did believe there was something distinctive about Anglican theology and doctrinal understandings 'not only in their formularies, but also in their public worship, canon law, and indeed in the practices and operative norms by which they conducted their business' – he notes how Sykes 'showed how intricately related theology, polity, liturgy, devotion and practice really were' in Anglicanism, and in so doing 'complicated questions of identity'.[36] Similarly, Mark Chapman describes Anglican theology as emerging 'from a combination of text, institution, context and practice, both ecclesiastical and secular and drawn from a number of key periods', which must surely include our own.[37] He concludes, 'sometimes the boundaries between historical myth, ecclesiastical ideology and theology are remarkably thin'. As we seek to understand an Anglican identity that might aid us in developing a locus for unity, this is a helpful reminder of the complexity and the politics that are inextricably linked to this project.

In these few chapters, we have sketched out some of the present and past 'ways of being' that might help us find something of the somewhat elusive 'Anglican identity'. Among the keys to Anglican polity is church order, and yet the way that authority is held and exercised in an Established church does not easily translate to an authority held in an 'interdependent family of churches' such as the Anglican Communion. The Instruments of Communion, while imperfect and in need of reform, go some way in showing how authority might be collegially and collectively held, but the failure of the Anglican Covenant has illustrated the sheer level of difficulty there is in resolving disputes in the family. While the Formularies of the Church of England are helpful in charting how we have got to where we are, in themselves they do not present a clear answer to the questions of unity our current disagreements raise. Similarly, while Scripture is Anglicanism's greatest authority, matters of interpretation are not so easily resolved. Indeed, in each of the Lambeth Quadrilateral's articles – creed, Scripture, sacraments, and the episcopate – we see more clearly how Anglicanism can engage outwardly than inwardly.

There is, perhaps, something most distinctly Anglican about the tradition's ability to engage so openly with other traditions while firmly situating itself within historic understandings of what it is to be an ecclesial body, its identity beyond being merely 'church' being found in its outward rather than its inward focus, and indeed about the 'ungrudging awareness of [the] incompleteness' of Anglican ecclesiology in that context.[38] While there has been an inevitable slide into denomination-alism, there nonetheless remains something of an attempt to be at least open to those who need *church*, when they need church, embedded within the DNA of Anglican churches. Lacking 'absolute and exclusive claims', it is a church that is grounded in and – when at its best – stirs up the very best in the society in which it finds itself. For a church that has become churches, from one context to many, this is a significant challenge, and yet perhaps it is in the *doing* this that we really understand what Anglicanism might mean as a global stream of Christianity.

Yet that global stream, as we spoke of it at the start of this book, is in crisis – or at least, that is what we are led to believe – and that crisis is a crisis of unity. Before we return to Anglican identity and look for where that unity might be found despite all the diversity, let us look to some traditional sources of theology for Anglicans beyond our own history – Scripture, the Fathers, our ecumenical ventures and encounters – and ask: what might this unity mean theologically? Does it matter, and if so, why? And just as importantly, how do we understand unity as more than simply holding things together and hoping they won't break? It is in asking those questions that we might begin to understand how to hope for unity in our own context, and beyond.

Notes

1 Don S. Armentrout and Robert Boak Slocum, eds, 'Chicago-Lambeth Quadrilateral', in *An Episcopal Dictionary of the Church, A User Friendly Reference for Episcopalians* (New York: Church Publishing Inc., 2000), https://www.episcopalchurch.org/glossary/via-media/ (accessed 2.1.24).

2 Robert Slocum, 'The Chicago-Lambeth Quadrilateral: Development in an Anglican Approach to Christian Unity', *Journal of Ecumenical Studies* 33(4), Fall 1996.

3 The Anglican Church of Canada, 'The Lambeth Quadrilateral', https://www.anglican.ca/about/beliefs/lambeth-quadrilateral/ (accessed 10.1.24).

4 Pope Leo XIII, '*Apostolicae Curae* (Apostolic letter on Anglican Ordinations)', 13 September 1896, https://iarccum.org/doc/?d=622 (accessed 10.1.24).

5 Malines Conversations, 'Sorores in Spes', 15 December 2021, https://www.malinesconversations.org/sorores-in-spe/ (accessed 10.1.24).

6 Brian Douglas, *The Anglican Eucharist in Australia* (Leiden: Brill, 2022), pp. 284–97.

7 Women's Ordination Worldwide, 'Florence Li Tim-Oi', 25 January 2020, http://womensordinationcampaign.org/blog-working-for-womens-equality-and-ordination-in-the-catholic-church/2020/1/25/rev-florence-li-tim-oi-first-woman-ordained-in-anglican-communion (accessed 20.1.24).

8 Not least the absence of any mention of sex or marriage, either as a sacrament or a doctrine, given the huge impact that this particular doctrine has had on the divisions within the Anglican Communion since (including same-sex marriage, but also contraception and divorce).

9 Primates Meeting of the Anglican Communion, 'A Statement by the Primates of the Anglican Communion meeting in Lambeth Palace', https://www.fulcrum-anglican.org.uk/wp-content/uploads/2016/01/primates2003lambeth.pdf (accessed 20.1.24).

10 Statements from the Primates Meetings are, unfortunately, littered with this kind of unfortunate language, which is a clear result of cultural rather than theological outworking.

11 Readers may wish to consult Christopher Craig Brittain and Andrew Mackinnon, *The Anglican Communion at a Crossroads* (Philadelphia, PA: Penn State University Press, 2018) and William L. Sachs, *Homosexuality and the Crisis of Anglicanism* (Cambridge: Cambridge University Press, 2009).

12 Legitimate questions might also be asked as to whether what was being undertaken by The Episcopal Church (USA) and the Anglican Church in Canada was truly a change in doctrine, or whether it was

more akin to pastoral accommodation and changes in church discipline and order. This nuance did not appear to worry the Primates.

13 The Windsor Report makes reference to Resolution III.2, 'The unity of the Anglican Communion', from the 1998 Lambeth Conference, which relates to the ordination of women, and states that 'although some of the means by which communion is expressed may be strained or broken, there is a need for courtesy, tolerance, mutual respect, and prayer for one another, and we confirm that our desire to know or be with one another, remains binding on us as Christians', similarly recognizing that 'those who dissent from, as well as those who assent to, the ordination of women to the priesthood and episcopate are both loyal Anglicans'. It appears to be rather a shame that this kind of polity (and indeed language) has not been made available in matters of sexuality.

14 The Lambeth Commission on Communion, 'The Windsor Report', 2004, https://www.anglicancommunion.org/media/68225/windsor2004full.pdf (accessed 20.1.24).

15 Mission Issues and Strategy Advisory Group II, 'Towards Dynamic Mission: renewing the Church for Mission', 1993, https://www.anglicancommunion.org/media/108031/MISAG-II-Towards-Dynamic-Mission-1992.pdf (accessed 10.1.24).

16 In many ways, they are closer to providing a definition of what is 'communion' about the Communion rather than what is Anglican. This is also the case more generally in the Windsor Report itself.

17 The Lambeth Commission on Communion, 'The Windsor Report', 2004, paragraph 118.

18 Anglican Communion, 'The Anglican Communion Covenant', https://www.anglicancommunion.org/media/99905/The_Anglican_Covenant.pdf (accessed 10.1.24).

19 Diarmaid MacCulloch, 'The Anglican church can start afresh', *The Guardian*, 25 March 2012, https://www.theguardian.com/commentisfree/2012/mar/25/anglican-covenant-bishops-division (accessed 20.1.24).

20 Matthew Davies, 'England: Anglican Covenant defeated in majority of dioceses', Episcopal News Service, 26 March 2012, https://www.episcopalnewsservice.org/2012/03/26/england-anglican-covenant-defeated-in-majority-of-dioceses/ (accessed 20.1.24).

21 Archbishop of Canterbury, 'Lambeth Call on Human Dignity: Read Archbishop Justin's remarks', https://www.archbishopofcanterbury.org/speaking-writing/speeches/lambeth-call-human-dignity-read-archbishop-justins-remarks (accessed 10.1.24).

22 In a way more successful than that outlined in previous chapters.

23 Robert David Redmile, *The Apostolic Succession and the Catholic Episcopate in the Christian Episcopal Church of Canada* (Maitland, FL: Xulon, 2006), p. 10.

24 Michael Ramsey, *The Gospel and the Catholic Church* (Peabody, MA: Hendrickson, 2009), pp. 69–70.

25 David Pocklington, 'Bishops: From announcement to installation', *Law & Religion UK*, 20 April 2016, https://lawandreligionuk.com/2016/04/20/bishops-from-announcement-to-installation/ (accessed 5.1.24). Church of England, 'Leadership and governance', https://www.church ofengland.org/about/leadership-and-governance (accessed 10.1.24).

26 Excluding the Bishop of Gibraltar in Europe, whose appointment is somewhat different.

27 House of Bishops, 'The Nomination Process for Suffragan Bishops', 2016, https://www.churchofengland.org/sites/default/files/2017-11/nom ination-process-for-suffragan-bishops.pdf (accessed 20.1.24).

28 Church of England, 'Crown Nominations Commission', https://www.churchofengland.org/about/leadership-and-governance/crown-nominations-commission (accessed 20.1.24).

29 Armentrout and Slocum, 'Bishops', in *An Episcopal Dictionary of the Church*, https://www.episcopalchurch.org/glossary/via-media/ (accessed 2.1.24).

30 The downside being, of course, the risk that a College of a particular bent will only ever allow the election of a bishop of a similar persuasion.

31 The Primates recognized in 2003 that there were 'shared principles of canon law ... [which] may be understood to constitute a fifth instrument of unity in the Communion'. To date, this role as a 'fifth instrument of unity' has not been further explored, but work continues on developing these joint principles. See Ecclesiastical Law Commission, 'The Principles of Canon Law Common to the Churches of the Anglican Communion', 2nd edn, 2022, https://www.anglicancommunion.org/media/483121/UFO_Principles-of-Canon-Law_Second-Edition_2022.pdf (accessed 10.1.24). It is not entirely clear how this 'fifth instrument' might be envisaged as working – at first sight it is more a commonality and less an instrument.

32 Anglican Communion, 'Canon Law', https://www.anglicancom munion.org/structures/canon-law.aspx (accessed 10.1.24).

33 Mark Chapman's *Anglican Theology* (London: T&T Clark, 2012) is an interesting rollick through the history, which shows quite how non-sensical such a position is. He cautions against 'trawling through the past in the hope of finding an elusive Anglican identity', which we have attempted to avoid in these pages!

34 Chapman, *Anglican Theology*, p. 3.

35 Stephen Sykes, *Unashamed Anglicanism* (London: Darton, Longman and Todd, 1995).

36 Jeremy Morris, 'Unashamed Integrity: Stephen Sykes and the "crisis" of Anglican Ecclesiology and Identity', *Ecclesiology* 15(1), pp. 62–80.

37 Chapman, *Anglican Theology*, p. 154.

38 Further explored in Paul Avis, *The Anglican Understanding of the Church: An Introduction* (London: SPCK, 2013).

PART 2

Reflections on unity

5

Ut unum sint: A biblical reflection

So far, we have been introduced to both the Church of England and the Anglican Communion as they are currently formulated. Of course, neither the Church of England nor the Anglican Communion are uncontested organisms, and there will be plenty within each who will challenge the vision provided here. We have focused on these two ecclesial institutions because it is fundamental to recognize that 'unity' is not a purely abstract term and cannot be spoken about in such a way without ultimately doing a disservice to the ecclesial venture. Yet in these next chapters, we take a step back from the institution and ask what Scripture and tradition might have to tell us about the meaning of unity and its application in our context.

In our next chapter, we will consider the witness of the patristic and conciliar eras, but first let us consider the witness of Scripture itself. Of course, any engagement with Scripture leads to questions of interpretation and emphasis, and we will meet some of these here. Lacking a Magisterium or some other central, authoritative interpretative method or institution, one of the great gifts of the Reformed churches – that Scripture is for the people, and the ultimate authority in matters of faith – can nonetheless sound rather easier to apply in theory than in practice. As we have seen, Anglicanism is no stranger to this kind of controversy. Addressing questions of unity in Scripture leads us to potentially uncomfortable questions, a key example for our purposes might be the reconciliation of John 17.21 ('that they may all be one') and salvation by faith not works, with talk of sheep and goats, or Paul's writing to the Corinthians regarding sexual immorality (Corinthians 5.11: 'Do not even eat with such a one').

We will tease out more of the inevitable tensions as we pass through this chapter, but for now it can generally be stated that, despite the nuances and the contested weight given to the behaviour of believers, the cause for such behaviours, and the way these might relate to both visible and invisible unity, not only is unity a key part of the scriptural narrative as relates to God's people and God's church (and indeed, in some readings, all creation), but unity is explicitly not something created by humankind and adopted by God. In other words, as Prayer G of the *Common Worship* Eucharistic Prayers of the Church of England puts it,[1] we ask God to 'reveal [the church's] unity, guard her faith, and preserve her in peace'. Here again we meet the key tension between unity, faith and peace, yet here too we recognize that while visible disunity is a wound in the church and can impact negatively on mission, evangelism and credibility, and even threaten the ability of the church as an institution to survive, nonetheless visible unity is something revealed by God that reflects something of a deeper, metaphysical unity that belongs to God. When we declare ourselves 'out of communion' or bewail others having destroyed the unity of the church, it is helpful to be reminded that we may only be privy to, and able to describe, the part of the iceberg above the waterline.

Our first task when approaching Scripture on matters of unity is to ask in what context and for what purpose Scripture is written and is speaking, both then and now. Recent debates about the relationship of unity to discipline[2] are not alien to Scripture – we might think first of Paul's Epistles, and the way in which a break in discipline in a particular church community is linked with a break in unity. Yet we must be careful that we do not ignore the author's context or seek to oversimplify. In Paul's case, he is writing to nascent churches whose identity remains central to their 'success'; yet it is also true that Paul's focus on behaviour change in the Christian *as* Christian is far from incidental to his developing theology.[3] To take individual commands from Paul as the 'last word' on unity is therefore not only poor hermeneutics but dangerous theology, and we must remember that while the presenting issue might be unity, there are many other parts of both Old and New Testament that Anglicans cannot agree on. Among these, and highly relevant to the interpretations of Paul and unity, is the Eucharist, and we will return to this as we look to chart a way forward for the future of the Anglican Church.

Our key question is whether there is a narrative that can be drawn from Scripture – across its various genres and both Testaments – to help us in our discussion of the contested understanding of unity in the church of today. It is certainly true that reams have, will and should be written about this particular question, and therefore in this chapter we merely seek to draw out these themes and bring ourselves to a more coherent understanding of unity, which, as the biblical record suggests, is more than mere uniformity and yet does not entirely remain either abstract or ephemeral. The Bible's relentless 'earthwards' focus of theology means that we cannot talk of unity in the Kingdom of God being something away from the here and now, even if its fulfilment is indeed something eschatological and not something temporal. If we are to talk about unity as a theological concept – which we should – then we also need to somehow embed it, however imperfectly, in our institutional church too, as the biblical writers so clearly outline. Yet, like them, we must not lose sight of the ultimate essence of unity and recognize that our institutional manifestations may be messy, contextual and challenging.

While we primarily focus here on the New Testament, as it specifically relates unity to the church, there are nonetheless a number of examples of the importance of unity in the Old Testament, often relating to matters of the unity of the nation under God and the avoidance of faithlessness to God through disunity (e.g. 2 Chronicles 30.12; Malachi 2.10). Psalm 133 is possibly one of the most spontaneously joyful and beautiful descriptions of the blessings of unity that we find in the Old Testament:

How very good and pleasant it is
  when kindred live together in unity!
It is like the precious oil on the head,
  running down upon the beard,

on the beard of Aaron,
    running down over the collar of his robes.
It is like the dew of Hermon,
    which falls on the mountains of Zion.
For there the LORD ordained his blessing,
    life for evermore.

Jesus' apparent reference to this psalm in the Farewell Discourse of John 17 is notable. He speaks both of unity (as we have seen) and also 'life for evermore', noting, 'And this is eternal life, that they may know you, the only true God, and Jesus Christ whom you have sent' (John 17.3). Jesus' reference to unity in the Farewell Discourse follows this pattern throughout and is distinctly Trinitarian in formulation. Jesus asks the Father to 'protect [the disciples] in your name that you have given me, so that they may be one, as we are one' (John 17.11), and talks of giving the disciples 'the glory that you have given me ... so that they may be one, as we are one, I in them and you in me, that they may become completely one' (John 17.22–23).

In the first instance, therefore, we see unity as being a reality at the heart of the Trinity, and we might see this unity being particularly characterized by the work of the Third Person, the Holy Spirit, who 'abides with' the disciples, and 'will be in' them (John 14.17). The unity of the church is primarily orientated towards God; the disciples are called not only to oneness with one another, but oneness with Christ, something that will come to completeness through the work of the Holy Spirit as Christ becomes 'in them' just as the Father is 'in' Christ. It is from this unity with (and in) God that unity between Christians might flow.

The unity that Christ speaks of appears to be related to the truth that Jesus speaks of in John 16.12–15. The glorification that will be given to the disciples, and the glorification of Christ to the disciples, will be 'because [the Spirit] will take what is mine and declare it to you'. This Spirit will 'guide you into all the truth', a truth that – with unity – will slowly become more manifest as the church grows ever more into the likeness of Christ. There is a danger here, of course, in equating truth with doctrinal purity, and similarly in denying the role of the Holy Spirit in the ever-greater manifestation of the glory and truth of God, both of which allow the disciples to be ever more 'one' in him. Being open to work of the Spirit while recognizing the importance of revealed truth in the concept of unity is another tension in our understanding of the word.[4]

There are a number of other themes in Jesus' words on oneness that are striking. One of these is the missional importance of unity:

> 'I ask not only on behalf of these but also on behalf of those who believe in me through their word, that they may all be one. As you, Father, are in me and I am in you, may they also be [one] in us, so that the world may believe that you have sent me.' (John 17.20–21)

The importance of church unity for mission (as, for example, in the Primates' statement of 2003) is a contemporary concern, yet it is not entirely clear that what is being referred to in Jesus' words here is a confected unity *for the purpose of better missional outcomes*. Instead, what Jesus speaks of here is the oneness of the disciples springing from their oneness in and with Christ being a way of demonstrating and revealing Christ to those who come to believe. This is further described where Jesus prays that the disciples may 'become completely one, so that the world may know that you have sent me and have loved them even as you have loved me' (John 17.23). Similarly, Jesus asks that the disciples be 'with me where I am, to see my glory' (17.24). The entire passage of the high priestly prayer suggests that the directionality remains primarily to and from Christ, and not among the disciples themselves, and makes clear that the unity that is being spoken about is a reflection and not a confection. This is not a unity by numbers, in which the minority fall behind the majority; it is a unity by Trinitarian overflow, requiring the disciples to first find their oneness in the life of the Trinity.

This conception becomes clearer when reading these passages on unity in the light of the 'true vine' dialogue in John 15. The disciples cannot 'bear fruit' unless they abide in Jesus as he abides in them (15.4), with the Father as the vine grower (15.1). Christ is the vine, the disciples are the branches (15.5), suggesting a deep connectedness and intimacy to the unity of Christ and church. This intimacy is further strengthened by Jesus' use of 'love' as the lifeblood that flows through the Trinity and into the oneness of Christ with the disciples. 'As the Father has loved me, so I have loved you; abide in my love ... I have said these things to you so that my joy may be in you and that your joy may be complete' (15.9–11). We meet here a vision of unity that is not enforced or based on a set of rules, but is instead fuelled by and manifested through love and joy (cf. Galatians 5.22).

This link of unity with love becomes clearer in the following verses. 'This is my commandment, that you love one another as I have loved you'; 'I am giving you these commands so that you may love one another' (15.12, 17). By making love such an explicit element of the disciples' horizontal relationship with one another, and making this contingent on his love for them, Jesus here makes clear that the sign of manifest unity is the reflection of his love for his church in the way that the disciples love and serve one another. 'By this everyone will know that you are my disciples, if you have love for one another' (John 13.35).[5]

Before leaving the Farewell Discourse, it is important to reflect briefly on the context in which these words of Jesus are being spoken. At the start of John 13, Jesus has washed his disciples' feet, much to the chagrin of Simon Peter, the same Simon Peter who, despite protestations of loyalty, will shortly betray Jesus. Yet while Jesus speaks of Simon Peter's betrayal (13.36–38), nonetheless it is on this 'rock' that Christ then builds his church (Matthew 16.18), the visible sign of the unity of his disciples. Unity is anything but complete or perfect or simple, and yet in these final moments of the life of Christ, he prays that it might become ever more manifest in the church through love, seen in the joy and companionship (in its sense of fellowship with the breaking of bread) of the disciples, built up by the Spirit of truth, whose truth is in testifying to Jesus, the way, the truth and the life, and whose truth can be found in the unity of the disciples with Christ and with one another.

The Gospel of John has a substantial portion of Jesus' speech given over to unity. While this isn't the case in the other Gospels, there are incidents of Jesus' teaching and actions that are pertinent to (primarily temporal) unity. We might think here of Matthew 18.15–17 where Jesus speaks of reproving others who sin (interestingly following a parable in which Jesus makes clear that it is the will of the Father that none of 'these little ones should be lost' (18.14)), Matthew 15 in which Jesus reproves the Pharisees and scribes, or Mark 7 where there is a similar incident and then the famous encounter with the Syrophoenician woman. The religious landscape of Jesus' time was not one – unsurprisingly – in which there was absolute doctrinal agreement, and because of this it is to be expected that he would speak clearly and forthrightly about the Kingdom of God.

Yet it is clear that in the founding of the church – and in the early Acts stories that recount the early days of the nascent church – there is a commitment to a visible unity that speaks to something of the nature of God and is fundamental to the essence of the church itself, rightly ordered. Jesus' teaching on reproving a brother and sister is not incompatible with this wider vision, not least given his teaching on forgiveness (in the context of sin), and the importance of finding the lost sheep. In our contemporary church, the rush to 'differentiate'[6] belies a belief that some doctrinal matters supersede the command to embody love in unity despite our differences. It is somewhat hard to see how this can be justified in the light of Jesus' own command to love above all things as the mark of unity that manifests his glory and speaks to the inner life of the Trinity.

There are two passages in the Acts of the Apostles that are of particular relevance to our discussion. The first of these is the well-known passage from Acts 4.32–35:

Now the whole group of those who believed were of one heart and soul, and no one claimed private ownership of any possessions, but everything they owned was held in common.

With great power the apostles gave their testimony to the resurrection of the Lord Jesus, and great grace was upon them all. There was not a needy person among them, for as many as owned lands or houses sold them and brought the proceeds of what was sold. They laid it at the apostles' feet, and it was distributed to each as any had need.

This passage is fascinating not least because of questions about the historicity and factual nature of this assertion about the early church. Nonetheless, what we can definitively say is that the author was presenting a vision of the early church that was living out a very particular form of unity, that of the sharing of possessions. It is interesting that it is this – rather than doctrine[7] – that is used by the author to give an impression of how unity might be found visible.[8] It is an understatement to say that this kind of economic decision does not top the list of expected markers of visible unity in the contemporary church, and this is perhaps part of a bigger trend of shying away from economic justice as a marker of Christian witness (at least on a local or individual scale). Yet such a decision – to share – is a marker of the believers having 'one heart and soul', a practical out-working of Christian charity, and a mark of the unity bestowed by the Holy Spirit.

The second passage we might consider is the coming of the Holy Spirit at Pentecost (Acts 2). Familiarity with this passage can, perhaps, hide some of its more surprising aspects. The first of these is the unity in diversity of the multiple languages; the opposite of the Babel tower and a premonition of the mission to the Gentiles and the spreading of the Christian faith beyond typical or traditional boundaries. Yet here we do not find differences being obliterated in the work of the Holy Spirit, but rather there is a moment in which these differences are secondary to that work. This fact leads to the second important aspect: these differences are unified in baptism, in which they 'receive the gift of the Holy Spirit' (Acts 2.38). 'For the promise is for you, for your children, and for all who are far away, everyone whom the Lord our God calls to him', as St Peter says (Acts 2.39). 'So those who welcomed his message were baptized, and that day about three thousand persons were added. They devoted themselves to the apostles' teaching and fellowship, to the breaking of bread and the prayers' (Acts 2.41–42).

It is, therefore, through the Holy Spirit working in the sacrament of baptism that the diverse people in that place – and places after, through the generations – were brought to unity. Acts 2.43–47 further suggests the links between selling possessions and distributing proceeds to all, spending time in prayer and worship, and breaking bread. Peter's preaching speaks of the death and resurrection of Christ, of the salvific nature of his Passion and of the gift of the Holy Spirit in enabling people to see and hear this message. Peter's singular focus on the Christ event brings people to a unity of purposive love, grounded in the work of the Spirit, which reflects the love of Christ for his church.

Key in the Acts narrative on the necessity of circumcision were Paul and Barnabas, who 'had no small dissension and debate' with those who 'were teaching the brothers, "Unless you are circumcised according to the custom of Moses, you cannot be saved"' (Acts 15.1–2). It would be an understatement to say that Paul's writing – and that of the other Epistles – has been front and centre of 'biblical' approaches to ecclesiology and church order. As we discussed at the start of this chapter, there is a challenging balance between discipline and unity which we find throughout Paul's writing, and it is a historical fact that churches have resorted to excluding some people from church bodies in matters of doctrinal disagreement.[9] Paul's letters make clear that 'unity' is not something to be exploited and to allow a free-for-all. Yet for him, and his time, likewise for ours, the bounds of acceptability and professing the *same* faith are contentious but important. However, shining out of Paul's writing and his appearance in Acts is the importance of discussion, sometimes even fierce debate, on matters of faith, the importance of forgiveness, and of the primacy of love in listening to and seeking to truly understand one's opponents.

The most well-known example of Paul's writing on church discipline is found in the first letter to the church in Corinth. It is important to recognize the context of this letter, which

Paul himself outlines in chapter 1 by appealing to the church, 'by the name of our Lord Jesus Christ, that all of you be in agreement and that there be no divisions among you, but that you be knit together in the same mind and the same purpose' (1 Corinthians 1.10).[10] Paul chastises the Corinthians for their sectarian behaviour, and once again makes clear links with the sacrament of baptism. Paul's letter, much like Peter's preaching on the day of Pentecost, focuses on the Christ event, encouraging his readers to focus their attention on this rather than on their differences.

Yet in 1 Corinthians 5, Paul does appear to list some behaviours as putting someone outside the church (including sexual immorality, greed, swindling and idolatry). It is here that the line, 'Do not even eat with such a one' (5.11) is found, and Paul suggests that the church should be judging those inside the church, commanding them, 'Drive out the wicked person from among you' (5.13). In many ways, this short chapter lies at the heart of many of the debates in the Anglican Communion about matters of unity, not least given the suggestion among some that LGBTQIA Christians are sexually immoral and should therefore be driven out and not be table companions. This is not the place to debate this particular interpretation, save to state that positionality in debates on this are likely (at least in part) to determine perspectives on unity, not least the place of The Episcopal Church (USA) in the Anglican Communion.

What is clear, however, is that Paul does call for discipline for those who are *acting* in particular ways scandalous to the gospel and contrary to the Spirit (1 Corinthians 6.11) (note here that he does not make reference to doctrine per se, although it is of course argued that those calling for changes in doctrine are encouraging or enabling 'sexual immorality'), and that discipline is something undertaken by the whole church.[11] It is here that we must start to question the relevance of this passage to the contemporary situation in the Anglican Communion (or Church of England), given both that the interpretation of 'sexually immoral' is contested[12] (and hence not 'of the whole *Anglican* church', let alone the church catholic) and also that other issues Paul mentions are infrequently seen as a

cause for excommunication (for example, greed). Paul's underlying point, that 'a little yeast leavens all of the dough' (5.6)
remains, but surely applies primarily to where determined and
demonstrable wickedness is being undertaken by an individual
and where this is contaminating the wider church (something
clearly not applicable to matters of sexuality).

Indeed, in 1 Corinthians 6,[13] Paul addresses disagreements
and debates among believers, which appears to be much more
relevant to contemporary difficulties than the previous chapter.
'To have lawsuits at all with one another is already a defeat for
you' (1 Corinthians 6.7), states Paul, which has some reson-
ance in parts of the Church of England that appear keen to
control the bounds of unity through recourse to legal challenge,
however well intentioned, rather than through synodal and
generative discussion.[14] We frequently return to debates about
the meaning of 'sexual immorality' and hence the bounds of
'acceptability' as members of the church, yet in so doing we
fail to appreciate the fact that Paul's wider point is not specifically about this one (contested) facet of Christian ethics but
rather about Christian ethics as a whole. To put it another
way, not embodying the Christian ethic of love for God and
neighbour, and the implications of being a temple of the Holy
Spirit, is the cause of division and lack of unity, rather than
consensual homosexuality.[15] Paul makes this abundantly clear
in his response to abuses at the Lord's Supper in chapter 11.
Chastising the Corinthians for their lack of charity, their lack
of care for the hungry, and their 'contempt for the church of
God' (11.22), Paul reminds them that at the centre of their life
as a church is the new covenant proclaimed by Christ in the
institution of the Eucharist.

Towards the end of the Epistle, Paul speaks of the 'varieties
of gifts but the same Spirit' (1 Corinthians 12.4), once again
pointing towards the importance of unity in diversity and sacramental unity, a 'body [that] is one and has many members ...
For in the one Spirit we were all baptized into one body – Jews
or Greeks, slaves or free – and we were all made to drink of one
Spirit' (12.12–13). He goes on:

God has so arranged the body, giving the greater honour to the inferior member, that there may be no dissension within the body, but the members may have the same care for one another. If one member suffers, all suffer together with it; if one member is honoured, all rejoice together with it.

Now you are the body of Christ and individually members of it. (12.24–27)

Here, Paul is sketching out for a church in crisis what the landscape would need to look like for unity truly to be revealed. In chapter 13, he enters his paean to love, speaking of those characteristics of love that would show a community to be living as the one body into which it has been called. The previous chapters of discipline are not the centrepiece of this letter, but rather the preamble to this endlessly popular and deeply visionary understanding of how those in one body might best act towards one another in order not only to benefit the body but its individual members as well. 'Now faith, hope, and love remain, these three, and the greatest of these is love' (13.13), says Paul, reminding his readers that if the primacy is given to love, then communities can be built up in faith and hope. 'Let all that you do be done in love' (16.14).

The Epistle to the Romans shows similar themes in chapters 12 and 13. Paul writes once again of the importance of building up the whole body and the primacy of love in enabling this to happen, neatly summarizing that 'love is the fulfilling of the law' (Romans 13.10), and emphasizing the importance of pursuing 'what makes for peace and for mutual upbuilding' (14.19). We find a similar theme in Philippians 2, where the humility required to live the Christian life is grounded in the humility of Christ (2.5–11), and 'the same mind' is linked with 'having the same love' (2.2). Here, there is 'comfort in Christ … consolation from love … partnership in the Spirit … tender affection and sympathy' (2.1, NRSVUE), each of Paul's themes building to a climatic hymn to the kenosis of Christ.

Throughout Paul's relational and self-effacing language permeates his writing and provides a helpful biblical model for unity, as does his placing belief in Christ and baptism as central to a Christian identity, and hence a fundamental Christian unity. In Galatians 3.27–29 this is fleshed out:

> As many of you as were baptized into Christ have clothed yourselves with Christ. There is no longer Jew or Greek, there is no longer slave or free, there is no longer male and female; for all of you are one in Christ Jesus. And if you belong to Christ, then you are Abraham's offspring, heirs according to the promise.

Paul, or another if Paul were not the author, emphasizes the importance of Christ as originator and source of unity in Ephesians 2, and throughout the Epistle. He speaks of it being Christ 'our peace' who 'has made both groups into one', 'create[d] in himself one new humanity in place of the two, thus making peace', reconciling 'both groups to God in one body through the cross, thus putting to death that hostility through it' (Ephesians 2.13–16). Here, the writer makes reference to the division between Gentile and Jew, who are now 'built together spiritually into a dwelling-place for God' (2.22), 'built upon the foundation of the apostles and prophets, with Christ Jesus himself as the cornerstone' (2.20). The Ephesians are begged to walk with 'humility and gentleness, with patience, bearing with one another in love, making every effort to maintain the unity of the Spirit in the bond of peace' (Ephesians 4.2–3) because 'there is one body and one Spirit, just as you were called to the one hope of your calling, one Lord, one faith, one baptism, one God and Father of all, who is above all and through all and in all' (4.4–6).[16]

It is in Ephesians 4 that we specifically meet 'doctrine' as potentially being a risk to unity:

> We must no longer be children, tossed to and fro and blown about by every wind of doctrine by people's trickery, by their craftiness in deceitful scheming. But speaking the truth in love, we must grow up in every way into him who is the head, into Christ, from whom the whole body, joined and knit together by every ligament with which it is equipped, as each part is

working properly, promotes the body's growth in building itself up in love. (4.14–16)

The context of this passage (referring to 'no longer walk[ing] as the gentiles walk, in the futility of their minds', 4.17) suggests, however, that differences in Christian doctrine do not necessarily take a central role in disunity (or at least that this is not what the author is referring to), and similarly there is a recognition that we must 'all of us come to the unity of the faith and of the knowledge of the Son of God, to maturity, to the measure of the full stature of Christ' (4.13). The author then returns to the 'rules for new life' that are similar to those found in the (other) Pauline letters, relating to being 'members of one another' (4.25), walking 'in love, as Christ loved us' (5.2), and the renouncing of pagan ways (Ephesians 5), suggesting that the body is best 'built up in love' through living the new life in Christ.

Similar themes on unity are found in other Epistles by different authors. In 1 Peter 3, we hear of the encouragement to 'have unity of spirit, sympathy, love for one another, a tender heart, and a humble mind' (1 Peter 3.8).[17] Competing with 'the more excellent way' of 1 Corinthians 13 in its homage to love, 1 John 4.13–21 gives a compelling and important emphasis to love in the vertical unity through Trinity to humankind, and horizontally among humankind. Here we hear of the centrality of love of brother and sister in the discernment of those who truly love God, and once again find love at the centre of our call to unity.

In this brief discussion of unity and the church in the Bible, we have met a number of different themes, among them the primacy of love, the role of truth and holiness, the Trinitarian source and model of unity, the importance of lived-out Christianity as a locus of unity, and the emphasis given to unity as a visible and metaphysical reality by the biblical writers and by Christ himself. We now turn to see how these themes have been applied in Christian history, and to ask how this might help us in our search today for unity in our own church in crisis.

Notes

1 Church of England, 'Holy Communion Order One', https://www.churchofengland.org/prayer-and-worship/worship-texts-and-resources/common-worship/churchs-year/holy-week-and-easter-2 (accessed 10.1.24).

2 Charles Raven, 'Unity in the Anglican Church', GAFCON, 16 June 2020, https://www.gafcon.org/news/unity-in-the-anglican-church (accessed 16.1.24).

3 This is a deeply complex area. Readers may wish to consult Jeehei Park, *All Citizens of Christ: A Cosmopolitan Reading of Unity and Diversity in Paul's Letters* (Leiden: Brill, 2022).

4 This is relevant, too, when considering John 17.17: 'Sanctify them in the truth; your word is truth.' It is clear that truth and the preaching of the gospel cannot be neatly separated from conceptions of unity, but – of course – what that 'truth' entails is likely to be a matter of debate on contested issues! Yet it is *growth* in sanctification, truth and unity which appears to be the mark of the Christian community, each of these grounded in the overflowing love of the Trinity.

5 Readers may wish to consult David Ford, *The Gospel of John: A Commentary* (London: Baker, 2022), which addresses this in some detail.

6 Church of England Evangelical Council, 'Visibly Different', 26 July 2020, https://ceec.info/wp-content/uploads/2022/10/visibly_different_-_dated_26_july_2020.pdf (accessed 20.1.24).

7 Of course, we see debates in Acts 15 about circumcision and the forming of a council on this matter, which ultimately decides in favour of a diversity of practices. Yet what is most key here, perhaps, is that the diversity of practices already exists and that what is reported is an attempt to actively prevent something, which is already bearing fruit in the calling of new disciples (in the calling of the Gentiles). There are some contemporary echoes here, in which perceived doctrinal purity appears to be placed above the fruits of missional work with those for whom particular forms of doctrinal purity provide a stumbling block for faith in Christ.

8 Indeed, so important is this sharing of goods, and a refusal to do so is seen to be a 'lie to the Holy Spirit', that Ananias and Sapphira meet their ends in the next chapter (Acts 5).

9 Depending on the view of the reader, different examples of this may elicit different responses!

10 Here again 'purpose' is linked to 'mind', suggesting an active missional (not simply evangelistic) role for those professing unity.

11 Of course Paul revisits this in 2 Corinthians 2.5–11. Here the Corinthians are encouraged to 'forgive and console' the offender, to

'reaffirm [their]. love for him', suggesting that for Paul love endlessly retains the primacy.

12 Not least given Paul's own statement in chapter 12 that 'no one can say "Jesus is Lord" except by the Holy Spirit' (12.3). Many LGBTQI Christians say precisely that! We might think of the parallels with Acts 15.7–11 here: the Holy Spirit is given by God, so 'why are you putting God to the test by placing on the neck of the disciples a yoke that neither our ancestors nor we have been able to bear?'

13 Once again, this is not the place to address 1 Corinthians 6.9–11, except to say that these verses do not appear to have much relevance to our discussions of unity per se.

14 Francis Martin, 'Church organizations urge Bishops not to commend blessings for same-sex couples', *Church Times*, 15 July 2023, https://www.churchtimes.co.uk/articles/2023/7-july/news/uk/church-organisations-urge-bishops-not-to-commend-blessings-for-same-sex-couples (accessed 20.1.24).

15 It is unfortunate, perhaps, that the divisions within the Corinthian church were so focused on matters of sexual ethics. This has hugely skewed our interpretations of the purpose and context of Paul's writing.

16 Referred to in Ulrich Heckel, 'The Seven Marks of the Unity of the Church', *The Ecumenical Review* 73(4), pp. 566–80, as the seven marks of unity, to which we will return in Chapter 7.

17 Interestingly, this was the Epistle used for Bible study at the Lambeth Conference 2022.

6

Heresies and history:
Creeds, councils and the patristic era

From its earliest days (as we have seen in Acts), the history of
the church has been impacted and shaped by discussions over
belief and practice and their relationship to the unity of the
whole. For an institution – more so a metaphysical reality – that
was handed down by Christ to have as among its key markers
that of unity, it is not at all clear that the church has consistently lived into this calling. In each generation, there have been
matters of faith, or matters of practice, that have been placed
above 'unity' in importance, and each occasion has – to varying
degrees – been seen retrospectively as either a moment of tri-
umph and holiness for the church, or a moment of discord and
shame. We might think here of the suspension of the *Nederduitse Gereformeerde Kerk* and the *Nederduitsch Hervormde
Kerk* from the World Council of Churches during the grotesque
evils of apartheid,[1] the various churches' responses to Naziism,
yet also the Great Schism between East and West, the mono-
physite rejection at the Council of Chalcedon in AD 451, or
indeed, pertinent for our purposes, the Reformation.

Each of these cases led to a rejection by ecclesial bodies
(whether denominational or pan-denominational) of some
professing to be Christians, yet the results have not been uniform. In some cases the willingness of churches to consort with
(and sometimes even participate in the architecture of) cultural
anti-Christian norms has led to the inevitable destruction and
obliteration of these 'churches' once society has been brought
back (often violently) to its senses. In others, churches have continued despite these schisms and excommunications, and the
work of the ecumenical movement in finding ways of holding

these threads together has been a key part of twentieth- and twenty-first-century Christianity. Oftentimes, the ability and willingness to recognize each other as fellow workers in the Lord's vineyard has taken significant periods of time.

In our own age, there is much talk of capitulation and compromise to culture in the way that some Anglicans and some Anglican churches have responded to the 'challenge' of LGBTQIA Christians.[2] In many ways, this is an attempt to place current debates in the former of the above streams – to call out doctrinal developments as anti-Christian, and hence suggest that churches that take an affirming stand on same-sex relationships are embarking on a journey of decline, having lost something of the *esse* of the Christian faith.[3] Those who have come to believe that taking an affirming line is not only compatible with the gospel but is a gospel imperative will position themselves within the latter stream. Indeed, beyond schism and separation, there is a third dynamic, that of the intentionally affirming church that is founded on that basis.[4]

It is worth our returning to the idea of heresy (and its opponent, orthodoxy) when considering these opposing positions. Describing something as heresy is a significant charge, and one that has been applied to those who are affirming of same-sex relationships by 'orthodox' bishops.[5] Heresy might be best defined in the words of Alister McGrath: 'A heresy is *a doctrine that ultimately destroys, destabilizes, or distorts a mystery rather than preserving it.*'[6] McGrath argues against heresy as being either something corrupting from outside the church or something that doesn't gain majority approval in the church.[7] As he states:

> The process of marginalization or neglect of these 'lost Christianities' generally has more to do with an emerging consensus within the church that they are inadequate than with any attempt to impose an unpopular orthodoxy on an unwilling body of believers.[8]

The use of heresy and orthodoxy in our current situation appears, therefore, to be both premature and ill advised.

It does, therefore, seem out of place to make use of the language of heresy in current discussions about disunity in Anglicanism, but if such language is not used, then we might reasonably query whether and why our current disagreements are to be given priority over the unity of the church.[9] Individual Christians and theologians, even bishops, might indeed believe that the opposing view is indicative of heresy, according to the definition outlined above, but the personal opinion of a bishop is not the same as their episcopal presence, and surely nor should personal opinions be the basis on which schism is enacted in a synodal and episcopal church in such a period of 'reception' of doctrinal developments.[10] As the Bishop of Southwark, Christopher Chessun, puts it, 'reception gives context to the space we move into following change. In other words, moving from a proposition to the reality of lived experience.'[11] He makes reference to the Windsor Report, describing 'reception' as:

> a way of testing whether a controversial development arising within a province by legitimate processes, might gradually, over time, come to be accepted as an authentic development of the faith' and enable a settlement (Windsor Report, para. 68). In a church such as ours, shaped at the Reformation as it was in argument and conflict, reception is an important test. It is a principle that sets the boundaries of accommodation. All of this is to say that reception acknowledges that the Church itself is a living organism.

This appears to be a healthy and appropriate way of envisaging how proposed developments of doctrine might be engaged with, recognizing that unity relates to both belief *and* practice, and the importance of the lived experience of – in this case – LGBTQIA Christians in particular provinces in coming to a joint discernment of the way in which proposed developments destroy, destabilize or distort, or indeed build up, strengthen and clarify, the 'mystery' (which includes faith and holy living). In such a case, it is hard to see how unity is not given the primacy – a unity that does not pretend to uniformity, nor agreement, but a unity that allows ecclesial discernment on such important matters of human anthropology.

The challenge with such a vision, of course, is that some appear unwilling to allow debate or development on particular doctrinal issues that they describe as 'first order salvation issue'.[12] The determination of what is, and is not, a first-order issue is itself contested (as is the historical validity of describing issues as 'first order' in Anglicanism), yet for some, 'the discussion about human identity and sexuality' is 'an issue which is central to the Christian faith and on which there is no room for disagreement in the Church'.[13] The present reality is that whether or not there is an Anglican heritage to the idea of 'first order' issues, sexuality is considered to be one by large numbers of people within the Anglican Communion (and is professed to be one by some in the Church of England).[14] In many ways, this is the key challenge that lies at the heart of the debates in Anglicanism: should we countenance and employ the language of first-order issues, and, if so, how are they determined?[15] We will return to this in our concluding chapters.

It is interesting that during the General Synod debates of November 2023, an amendment raised by Jayne Ozanne, a prominent LGBTQIA campaigner, to ask bishops 'to consider whether sexual activity outside of marriage is a first-order creedal issue and publish that opinion' was rejected (including by the House of Bishops).[16] There was a curious addition of 'creedal' to 'first-order' in this amendment, and we can see even by this addition the complexities and contestations around what is 'salvific' in matters of belief (and practice). It is abundantly clear that sexual ethics per se are not part of the profession of faith in the Athanasian, Apostles' or Niceno-Constantinopolitan creeds, and yet the purpose of the creeds is not, in doctrinal terms, to outline what is required for salvation, but rather to profess a joint belief in the church's understanding of God.

As we have previously noted, there is an interesting tension between the role of faith and 'holy living' in different conceptions of 'that which is needed for salvation', the simplest argument being that faith leads to changed behaviour that conforms itself to an increasing growth in godliness. It is in this light that Paul's emphasis on holy living can be read, yet such a reading leaves open the possibility that there might be different manifestations of this Christian living based on different interpretations of the implications of belief in Christ and a commitment to the gospel. The challenge with describing any of these versions of lived-out gospel truth as first order means that we elevate an *implication* to the same level as a professed set of beliefs, and it is difficult to argue that this is in line with a vision of Anglicanism found in the Lambeth Quadrilateral.

As we have said, the creeds primarily speak of the nature of God and of ecclesially agreed understandings that were debated and discussed in the early years of the Christian faith. Scott Hahn's helpful book, *The Creed*, outlines the political and ecclesial debates, compromises and encounters that led to the creeds that we commonly use in the contemporary church.[17] The Nicene Creed, 'truly ecumenical' in that it was accepted as authoritative across the ecclesial spectrum (although the simplistic notion that it was simply promulgated in the Council of Nicaea of AD 325 is no longer the standard academic position), must therefore be read through the lens of the context and politics in which it was formulated and promulgated.[18]

It is this political landscape that helps explain the specific questions that the creed, as formulated, was created to address. This creed is therefore somewhat different from the Apostles' Creed, thought to be based on the baptismal creeds used in the churches of Rome in the third and fourth centuries, although of course there are key elements present in both which suggests the ongoing need to define the faith impacting on those things that people preparing for baptism might be expected to know and believe.[19] It is, of course, also interesting to note that the canon of Scripture was similarly being settled upon during this time,[20] and hence the relationships between creedal belief, Scripture and ecclesial authority were, and remain, complex and contested.

The Athanasian Creed, not mentioned in the Lambeth Quadrilateral yet found in the Book of Common Prayer, is the only creed that contains anathemas and similarly contains a link to good works, which is omitted from the other creeds:

At his coming all people will arise bodily
and give an accounting of their own deeds.
Those who have done good will enter eternal life,
and those who have done evil will enter eternal fire.

Yet once again we find no specific reference to what those good (or bad) deeds might entail, beyond what is presumably an expected reference to Scripture. That the creeds are not comprehensive is, therefore, not in doubt. Instead we return once again to the key question we have met in different guises in these pages, which might be formulated in the following way: does the absence of mention of sexual practice in the creed mean that it is *adiaphora*? *Adiaphora*, 'those things which are indifferent', are those elements in Christian belief 'which are neither specifically commanded nor specifically prohibited by God'.[21] Yet it is not entirely clear that those on either side of the current sexuality debate believe that this is strictly a matter of *adiaphora*, even if those in favour of same-sex relationships might argue that this contemporary matter is not specifically argued for or against in Scripture.[22] Instead, both those in favour and those opposed to same-sex relationships might argue that this is a thing anything but indifferent. However, this issue is also – in this stage of reception in the church – not one on which there must be a uniform belief or practice in order to permit the unity of the church. We return here, of course, to concepts of first order (and other order), which we might argue are singularly unhelpful in our conversations on doctrine.

Yet when we approach the creeds, we can discern from them something of the importance of unity in their various formulators' understandings of the church. Both creeds end with a commentary on the nature of the church. The Apostles' Creed has:

I believe in the Holy Spirit,
the holy catholic church,
the communion of saints,
the forgiveness of sins ...

While the Niceno-Constantinopolitan Creed has:

> I believe in one, holy, catholic and apostolic Church.
> I confess one Baptism for the forgiveness of sins ...

We see the common themes (indeed, marks[23]) of holiness and catholicity (universality),[24] apostolicity, oneness, the relationship with the Holy Spirit, and sacramentality (through baptism). These are themes that we have met throughout our survey of the meaning and practice of unity, and it is striking that they are found in the creedal statements that unite not only Anglicans but the vast majority of Christians worldwide. Yet as we have seen, while these creeds provide the basis for unity, the thorny issue of extra-creedal doctrine (or Christological-doctrinal implications) remains unsettled. This is not a new problem for the church.

Unity in the earliest days of the church focused on these creedal elements, yet the writers of the patristic era did not shy away from debates about right doctrine and the exclusion of heresy. Cyprian of Carthage[25] is somewhat typical in his highlighting the importance of unity and its relationship to the biblical texts we addressed in the previous chapter:

> He who breaks the peace and the concord of Christ, does so in opposition to Christ; he who gathers elsewhere than in the Church, scatters the Church of Christ. The Lord says, 'I and the Father are one' (John 10.30); and again it is written of the Father, and of the Son, and of the Holy Spirit, 'And these three are one.' (1 John 5.7) And does anyone believe that this unity which thus comes from the divine strength and coheres in celestial sacraments, can be divided in the Church, and can be separated by the parting asunder of opposing wills? He who does not hold this unity does not hold God's law, does not hold the faith of the Father and the Son, does not hold life and salvation.[26]

The degree to which baptism appears to be contingent on an ongoing relationship with the church for many of these important figures in the church's history is fascinating. Baptism in and of the church itself is key, as Cyprian of Carthage writes:

For as, in that baptism of the world in which its ancient in-
iquity was purged away, he who was not in the Ark of Noah
could not be saved by water, so neither can he appear to be
saved by baptism who has not been baptized in the Church
which is established in the unity of the Lord according to the
sacrament of the one ark.[27]

Augustine of Hippo writes in his *Against the Donatists*:

And just as baptism is of no profit to the man who renounces
the world in words and not in deeds, so it is of no profit to him
who is baptized in heresy or schism; but each of them, when
he amends his ways, begins to receive profit from that which
before was not profitable, but was yet already in him.[28]

Baptism, and the sacraments more generally, are necessary for
the Christian life, but the need to assent to common beliefs
(here primarily about the nature of Christ) and live a common
life are also determined to be essential if baptism is to grant its
gifts. Of course, Augustine is writing in the light of the Donatist
heresy (where faultless clergy – specifically those who had not
capitulated to the persecutions of Diocletian – were required for
ministry to be effective), and this is true of much if not most of
the Fathers' writing on heresy. We must also take into account
the different ecclesial landscape in which we now live. While
much of the Fathers' writing on the 'oneness' of the church has
been adopted by Roman Catholic writers through the years, the
growth of denominationalism and the ecumenical movement
calls us to question whether that oneness is truly situated – even
in an ideal situation – in a single institutional church. We will
return to such questions in our next chapter; for our purposes
here, we might instead think of the role of bishops in Anglican polity and of their positionality as 'focus of unity' in any
particular ecclesial communion.

For the Fathers, church order is also inseparable from unity,
and the bishop as central to the visible unity of the church, most
specifically in his role as proper minister of the Eucharist, is a
consistent theme during this period. Ignatius of Antioch made

it clear nothing should be done 'connected with the Church without the bishop',[29] stating that 'there is one flesh of our Lord Jesus Christ, and one cup to show forth the unity of His blood; one altar; as there is one bishop'.[30] The intimate union with the bishop reflected intimate union with Christ, and hence anything done 'apart from the bishop' was a marker of disunity and placed an individual outside the church. Similarly, the bishops' collegiality with one another was central to Cyprian of Carthage's understanding of episcopal ministry.[31]

Baptism – and active association with the church – is also central to the Fathers' delineation of heresy and schism. Jerome suggests:

> The difference between heresy and schism is that heresy contains perverse doctrine, schism separates from the church on account of episcopal dissension. To be sure this can be understood this way to some extent in the beginning. However that may be, no schism fails to concoct some heresy for itself, so that it may appear to have withdrawn from the Church rightly.[32]

Augustine concurs:

> But heretics, in holding false opinions regarding God, do injury to the faith itself; while schismatics, on the other hand, in wicked separations break off from brotherly charity, although they may believe just what we believe.[33]

We see here the joint opposition of the Fathers to both forms of division in the church. In our contemporary situation, we must surely be attentive to both, yet careful with our language when considering them. It is easy to accuse others of one, while becoming a perpetrator of the other. Irenaeus, in particular, speaks powerfully of the importance of avoiding both schisms and heresies in his *Against Heresies*. Concerning those fomenting schisms, he states (with echoes of Matthew 12.25):

> He shall also judge those who give rise to schisms, who are destitute of the love of God, and who look to their own spe-

cial advantage rather than to the unity of the Church; and who for trifling reasons, or any kind of reason which occurs to them, cut in pieces and divide the great and glorious body of Christ, and so far as in them lies, (positively) destroy it – men who prate of peace while they give rise to war, and do in truth strain out a gnat, but swallow a camel.

There were, of course, debates about the importance and meaning of catholicity itself, and this unsurprisingly made reference to matters of doctrine or dogma, often in the context of the four marks of the church described at the First Council of Constantinople and described in the creed (one, holy, catholic, apostolic). Tertullian linked the importance of doctrine to the apostolicity of the church,[34] and St Vincent of Léris, gave the following definition of catholicity:

> All possible care must be taken, that we hold that faith which has been believed everywhere, always, by all. For that is truly and in the strictest sense Catholic, which, as the name itself and the reason of the thing declare, comprehends all universally. This rule we shall observe if we follow universality, antiquity, consent. We shall follow universality if we confess that one faith to be true, which the whole Church throughout the world confesses; antiquity, if we in no wise depart from those interpretations which it is manifest were notoriously held by our holy ancestors and fathers; consent, in like manner, if in antiquity itself we adhere to the consentient definitions and determinations of all, or at the least of almost all priests and doctors.[35]

These are hard words for those who seek to justify the development of doctrine or practice in any matter at all. We might think of slavery, of the role of women, of the legitimacy of the death penalty, and of many other matters where legitimate doctrinal developments have not only occurred but have secured widespread support. Yet we must be careful not to mistake, once again, the implications of doctrine for the core of the doctrine itself. Determining what is central to the faith and what is peripheral is itself a question of theological interpretation,[36] yet it is surely a misinterpretation of catholicity if we hold to an understanding of the Christian faith as lacking any dynamic expression, or of being able to speak afresh to each generation. We return here, of course, to a discussion of *adiaphora* and of the centralities and peripheries, implications and essentials of the faith. It is perhaps reassuring to see that such problems are not new.

As we have said, the Fathers are writing in a time that has similarities to our own, yet has some fundamental differences too. Their words on schism relate not to denominations but are situated in a context of a nascent and developing church that faces challenges from within and without, and which – with exceptions – can be seen to be mostly at least one organism, if with different and disagreeing manifestations.[37] Their focus on 'the church', then, has nuances different from our own, and their oneness speaks differently to ours. We shall return to this in our next chapter, but for now it is important for us to remember that, as Anglicans, our internal unity is only part of the story of Christian unity. Yet their focus on the four marks of the church does speak into our situation, reminding us that if we are to seek that oneness, it must be as a church that is growing in holiness, is situated in apostolicity, and seeks to find its place and identity in the church catholic.

Thus as we meet the thinking of the early church in this brief journey, we meet a number of ways in which their concerns are our own concerns, and yet we must also be aware of the different contexts in which we find ourselves, and the different challenges that face us. What is striking, however, is that, while we might usually think of the Fathers' opposition primarily to heresy, they also have strong and uncompromising opposition to schism per se. Heresies are to be avoided, yet the breaking away from other Christians is not to be done lightly (even if their context is somewhat different, as we have described). In the contemporary Church of England, and in wider Anglicanism, we are not talking about a negligible minority who hold affirming views on matters of sexuality, but rather a wide stream that is becoming increasingly represented in other communions.[38]

To call such a stream 'heresy' and to simply disregard or reject it as compromise or capitulation to culture, and to formulate a schism on this basis, would surely have risked facing the disapproval of the Fathers. There is, perhaps, something here of the call to holiness requiring Christians to embark on any such conversation in good faith, echoing the words of Cyprian of Carthage: 'It behooves the sons of God to be peacemakers, gentle in heart, simple in speech, agreeing in affection, faithfully linked to one another in the bonds of unanimity.'[39]

A willingness to argue and debate theologically has been sorely lacking, and yet it is this (along with the inevitable political scrapping) that was so key to the formulation of the creeds in their current state. Doctrine has developed over time without the inevitability of schism, and if the church is to grow in holiness, truth and unity, and not merely its members, then surely we are called to learn from the mistakes – as well as the positive lessons – of the history of the church.

Similarly, Clement of Rome asks the church of his day:

Why are there quarrels and ill will and dissensions and schism and fighting among you? Do we not have one God and one Christ, and one Spirit of grace poured out upon us? And is there not one calling in Christ? Why do we wrench and tear apart the members of Christ, and revolt against our own body, and reach such folly as to forget that we are members of one another?[40]

The same questions might easily be raised in the contemporary church, in Anglicanism and beyond. The aphorism, 'in essentials, unity; in non-essentials, liberty; in all things, charity',[41] may be challenging to implement (not least due to our failure to agree on the essential and the non-essential, as discussed above!), but is surely the aim of our journeying together as Christians. It is to the lessons learnt from other Christian denominations and the ecumenical movement that we now turn.

Notes

1 An interesting discussion of the relationship between apartheid and heresy is found here: Neville Richardson, 'Apartheid, Heresy and the Church in South Africa', *The Journal of Religious Ethics* 14(1), 1986, pp. 1–21.

2 Church of England Evangelical Council, 'CEEC calls for action and offers the Church of England a better way forward', Church Society, 30 January 2023, https://www.churchsociety.org/resource/ceec-statement/ (accessed 20.1.24).

3 An example might be Ian Paul, 'Does allowing same-sex marriage result in church decline? Here's what the numbers show', *Premier Christianity*, 17 June 2022, https://www.premierchristianity.com/opinion/does-allowing-same-sex-marriage-result-in-church-decline-heres-what-the-numbers-show/13282.article (accessed 10.1.24). The statistics, and just as importantly the interpretation of the statistics, are contested and often appear misused, and debates in this arena do often fall into a reminder of the causation-correlation fallacy.

4 For example, the Metropolitan Community Churches: https://www.mccchurch.org/landing.html (accessed 20.1.24).

5 Here we find the work of the self-professed Anglican bishops in the Anglican Network in Europe, the Anglican Convocation Europe, and the Anglican Mission in Europe: Christian Today, 'Orthodox Anglicans grieved over "disastrous decision" to commend same-sex blessings', 12 October 2023, https://www.christiantoday.com/article/orthodox.anglicans.grieved.over.disastrous.decision.to.commend.same.sex.blessings/140886.htm (accessed 20.1.24).

6 Alister McGrath, *Heresy: A History of Defending the Truth* (London: HarperCollins, 2010), p. 31, italics original.

7 McGrath, *Heresy*, p. 34.

8 McGrath, *Heresy*, pp. 81–2.

9 For clarity, what is meant here is not whether such disagreements should be allowed to be aired but whether their airing is enough to cause schism.

10 For an interesting discussion of the importance of reception, see Ormond Rush, 'Reception Hermeneutics and the "Development" of Doctrine: An Alternative Model', *Pacifica* 6(2), 1993, pp. 125–40.

11 Christopher Chessun, 'Bishop Christopher's Presidential Address to Synod', The Diocese of Southwark, 20 November 2023, https://southwark.anglican.org/bishop-christophers-presidential-address-to-synod/ (accessed 20.1.24).

12 Peter Saunders, 'Sexual immorality is a first order salvation issue. It is time for the Church of England to go under the surgeon's knife', Anglican Mainstream, 15 February 2017, https://anglicanmainstream.

org/sexual-immorality-is-a-first-order-salvation-issue-it-is-time-for-the-church-of-england-to-go-under-the-surgeons-knife/ (accessed 26.1.24); and James Paice, 'Letter to Church Times about Living in Love and Faith', Anglican Mainstream, 26 January 2024, https://anglican-mainstream.org/letter-to-church-times-about-living-in-love-and-faith/ (accessed 26.1.24).

13 Evangelical Group on General Synod, 'Is Human Sexuality a First Order Issue?', https://www.eggscofe.org.uk/uploads/5/5/6/3/55636 32/1._is_human_sexuality_a_first_order_issue.pdf (accessed 20.1.24).

14 Marcus Throup, *All Things Anglican: Who We Are and What We Believe* (London: Canterbury Press, 2018).

15 Mark Chapman, Martyn Percy and Sathianathan Clarke, eds, *The Oxford Handbook of Anglican Studies* (Oxford: Oxford University Press, 2016), p. 12.

16 Church of England, 'General Synod Order Paper IV, Tuesday 14 November 2023', https://www.churchofengland.org/sites/default/files/2023-11/op-iv-final-1.pdf (accessed 20.1.24).

17 Scott Hahn, *The Creed: Professing the Faith through the Ages* (London: Darton, Longman and Todd, 2017).

18 A good discussion is found in David E. Henderson and Frank Kirkpatrick, *Constantine and the Council of Nicaea: Defining Orthodoxy and Heresy in Christianity, 325 C.E.* (Chapel Hill, NC: University of North Carolina Press, 2016).

19 Harry R. Boer, *A Short History of the Early Church* (Grand Rapids, MI: Eerdmans, 1976), pp. 73–8.

20 Details can be found in Edmon L. Gallagher and John D. Meade, *The Biblical Canon Lists from Early Christianity* (Oxford: Oxford University Press, 2017); and discussed further in F. F. Bruce, *The Canon of Scripture* (Westmont, IL: InterVarsity Press, 2018).

21 Malcolm Duncan, *One for All: The Implications* (Oxford: Lion Hudson, 2017), pp. 105–11.

22 There is not the space to interrogate this issue here, but Jonathan Tallon's *Affirmative: Why You Can Say Yes to the Bible and Yes to People Who are LGBTQI+* (Marlow: Richardson Jones, 2023) is a good place to start.

23 Angelo Di Berardino, ed., *Ancient Christian Doctrine 5: We Believe in One Holy Catholic and Apostolic Church* (Westmont, IL: InterVarsity Press, 2018), pp. 1–15.

24 The inclusion of the Communion of Saints is interesting here. I cannot here include a full engagement with this but it is certainly interesting to think about unity in the context of a church that is both militant and triumphant (and penitent). Here, perhaps, we look primarily to metaphysical unity rather than visible, but it is notable that the Communion is included in the Apostles' Creed as being central to the authors' understanding of the church.

25 The selection of Fathers here is by no means comprehensive but attempts to represent the key themes of the era.

26 Cyprian of Carthage, 'Treatise 1', https://www.newadvent.org/fathers/050701.htm (accessed 10.1.24).

27 Cyprian of Carthage, 'Epistle 73', https://www.newadvent.org/fathers/050673.htm (accessed 10.1.24).

28 Augustine, 'On Baptism, Against the Donatists' (Book IV), https://www.newadvent.org/fathers/14084.htm (accessed 11.1.24).

29 Ignatius, 'The Epistle of Ignatius to the Smyrnaeans', https://www.newadvent.org/fathers/0109.htm (accessed 20.1.24).

30 Ignatius, 'The Epistle of Ignatius to the Philadelphians', https://www.newadvent.org/fathers/0108.htm (accessed 20.1.24).

31 Church of England, *Episcopal Ministry: The Report of the Archbishops' Group on the Episcopate* (London: Church House Publishing, 1990), p. 308.

32 Jerome, *Commentary on Titus* (3.10–11), in *St. Jerome's Commentaries on Galatians, Titus, and Philemon* trans. Thomas P. Scheck (Notre Dame, IN: University of Notre Dame Press, 2010), p. 346.

33 Augustine, 'Of Faith and the Creed', https://www.newadvent.org/fathers/1304.htm (accessed 11.1.24).

34 Tertullian, 'Prescription Against Heretics', https://www.newadvent.org/fathers/0311.htm (accessed 11.1.24).

35 Vincent of Lerins, 'Commonitory', https://www.newadvent.org/fathers/3506.htm (accessed 11.1.24).

36 One which is best conceived as the 'result of an ecclesial process', of which more in our penultimate chapter: William J. Byron, *One Faith, Many Faithful: Short Takes on Contemporary Catholic Concerns* (Mahwah, NJ: Paulist Press, 2012), p. 227.

37 Related, in no small part, to those things happening in civil society, as discussed in Michael Root, 'Once More on the Unity We Seek: Testing Ecumenical Models', in Jeremy Morris and Nicholas Sagovsky, eds, *The Unity We Have and the Unity We Seek* (London: T&T Clark, 2003), pp. 174–6.

38 Almost unthinkable even a decade ago, these conversations are now coming into the open in the Roman Catholic Church. See Vatican News, 'Doctrinal declaration opens possibility of blessing couples in irregular situations', 18 December 2023, https://www.vaticannews.va/en/vatican-city/news/2023-12/fiducia-supplicans-doctrine-faith-blessing-irregular-couples.html (accessed 20.1.24).

39 Cyprian of Carthage, 'Treatise 1', https://www.newadvent.org/fathers/050701.htm (accessed 10.1.24).

40 Clement, 'Letter to the Corinthians', https://www.newadvent.org/fathers/1010.htm (accessed 10.1.24).

41 Commonly but likely erroneously attributed to Augustine of Hippo.

7

Dwelling together in unity: Ecumenism and relationship

It is easy to forget quite how remarkable the period since the mid-twentieth century has been for inter-church relationships and changes in attitude towards the ecumenical venture. Relations between Anglicans and Roman Catholics, for example, have changed beyond recognition. As we discussed in Chapter 4, in 1896 Pope Leo XIII issued the encyclical *Apostolicae Curae*, describing Anglican orders as 'absolutely null and utterly void', and yet in the Week of Prayer for Christian Unity in January 2024, the Pope and the Archbishop of Canterbury joined together at the tomb of the Apostle Paul to send out pairs of bishops, one Roman Catholic and one Anglican, to 'continue to testify to the unity willed by God for his church'.[1]

During the event, Pope Francis spoke about love. Reflecting on the Lukan biblical question, 'Who is my neighbour?', the Pope responded:

> This question attempts to divide, to separate people into those we should love and those we should shun. This kind of division is never from God; it is from the devil.
>
> Only a love that becomes gratuitous service, only the love that Jesus taught and embodied, will bring separated Christians closer to one another. Only that love, which does not appeal to the past in order to remain aloof or to point a finger, only that love which in God's name puts our brothers and sisters before the ironclad defence of our own religious structures, will unite us.[2]

At the same ecumenical service, the Archbishop of Canterbury – invited to speak by the Pope – spoke of how 'our rivalry or dislike of our brothers and sisters cuts us off from the freedom that God offers his church'. There is some irony, too, to this service – a sign of a commitment to greater visible unity – taking place in the light of the ongoing calls for 'visible differentiation' within the Church of England and the wider Anglican Communion.

It is not hyperbole to suggest that this visible ecumenism would have been unthinkable several generations previously. At the coronation of Queen Elizabeth II, Roman Catholics were still not permitted to attend non-Catholic services, with the Cardinal Archbishop remaining outside the ceremony; yet at the coronation of King Charles III in Westminster Abbey, at the heart of the English church, the Cardinal Archbishop of Westminster gave a blessing.[3] Similarly, the oil of chrism used for the anointing of the new King was consecrated in Jerusalem by the Patriarch of Jerusalem, His Beatitude Patriarch Theophilos III, with the participation of the Anglican Archbishop in Jerusalem.[4] The ecumenical venture has become front and centre in the ecclesial landscape, most particularly since the changes brought about in the Roman Catholic Church's self-understanding in the light of the Second Vatican Council, and – while challenges most particularly on church order remain (themselves erring into the doctrinal, for example on holy orders, the Eucharist, and so on) – the era of churches viewing each other with suspicion and hatred, at least on an institutional level, is surely coming to an end.

The invitation to Anglicans and to other non-Roman Catholics, including the Ecumenical Patriarch, to take part in the vigil prayer service for the opening of the Synod on synodality is another example of how attempts are being made to show visible, if imperfect, unity not only in the context of grand gestures but in the nuts and bolts of Christian life and worship.[5] Yet it is not only in liturgical or institutional events, but in doctrinal conversation that much fruit has been borne. The International Anglican–Roman Catholic Commission for Mission and Unity (IARCCUM, the source of the pairs of bishops commissioned by Pope Francis and the Archbishop of Canterbury at St Paul's outside the Walls), exists alongside the Anglican–Roman Catholic International Commission (ARCIC, now in its third phase). IARCCUM's role is to 'facilitate the development of strategies for translating the degree of spiritual communion that has been achieved into visible and practical outcomes', while strengthening relationships, encouraging dialogue, and promoting joint witness and mission of Roman Catholics and Anglicans.[6] ARCIC, meanwhile, has published theological reports on the Eucharist, ministry, authority, salvation, communion, moral theology, and the Virgin Mary, with its current manifestation examining matters of right ethical teaching.[7]

In seeking to find common ground, the role of these ecumenical partnerships is to reveal unity where it already exists and to address those areas where honest disagreement might be laid out and engaged with. These organizations do not exist in a vacuum, and the issue of homosexuality has previously led to significant challenges within these conversations (although with the release of *Fiducia Supplicans*, it is unlikely that this would continue to be the case).[8] These partnerships exist across the ecclesial spectrum. The Anglican–Reformed dialogue has been ongoing since 1984, and most recently has produced a very helpful report on *koinonia* (communion), described as 'God's gift for the life of the Church, to be lived out responsibly in God's world', 'grounded in life of the Triune God, in which we are invited to participate together'.[9]

The Church of England is a founding member of the World Council of Churches (WCC), established in 1948. Created to further the cause of ecumenism, the WCC today aims to provide a space for its member churches to 'reflect, speak, act, worship and work together, challenge and support each other, share and debate with each other'.[10] It is notable that the Anglican Communion, as an entity, is not a member of the WCC, but rather its individual constituent churches are free to join if they wish to do so. The description of Anglicanism in WCC documentation makes reference to the Chicago-Lambeth Quadrilateral, the centrality of the Eucharist, the importance of baptism, the sacramental rites of confirmation, reconciliation, marriage, anointing of the sick and ordination, and refers to the 'common worship' 'at the heart of Anglicanism', with a 'comprehensiveness found within the churches, which seek to chart a via media in relation to other Christian traditions'.[11] The description explains that 'Anglican and Episcopal churches uphold and proclaim the Catholic and Apostolic faith, proclaimed in the scriptures, interpreted in the light of tradition and reason'. The churches that form the Communion are 'all in communion with the see of Canterbury, and thus the archbishop of Canterbury, in person and ministry, is the unique focus of Anglican unity'.[12] They are 'held together by bonds of affection and common loyalty', which are expressed in the Instruments of Communion. Given our exploration of the breadth of understanding of Anglican identity, it is interesting that no mention is made here of first-order issues, or – interestingly – explicitly of the Reformed nature of the Church of England (although the Reformation is mentioned).

Given the extensive involvement of the Church of England, and the wider Anglican Communion, in ecumenical conversations, it is important for us to be clear on what positionality the church owns when engaging in these encounters. Here, once again, we are brought back to Anglican self-understanding and identity. Does the Church of England see itself as free to enter into ecumenical conversations, or does it feel some kind of loyalty to a wider Anglican understanding? What oversight and governance is required by the Anglican Communion Office on ARCIC and IARCCUM engagements, as relationships of Rome with constituent Anglican churches?

While, historically, the Church of England may have presented itself as the English church, and hence merely a geographical expression of the church catholic, this was not accepted by the Roman Catholic Church and is similarly strained by the global presence of the Anglican Communion. The existence of Anglican churches across the world effectively competing (or at least operating) in a denominational landscape means that while the Church of England may not see itself as a denomination in the purest sense, and indeed some Anglicans worldwide may also hold to such a perspective, nonetheless its engagement in the ecumenical domain means that it is inevitably received at least in a denominational way, even if that denominational identity is one that accentuates its *mere* membership of the church catholic.

In matters of ecumenism (particularly when viewed as receptive ecumenism), it is recognized – to varying degrees – that different churches each contribute distinct gifts to the wider ecclesial enterprise (cf. 2 Corinthians 4.7–9).[13] These gifts may take the form of histories, or doctrinal understandings, or polities, or relationships, or ways of expressing the faith differently in different situations or contexts. The Anglican Communion, and the Church of England, have perhaps been slow to recognize that there might be distinct gifts of Anglicanism for the wider church catholic. Much is made of recent decisions on sexuality 'distinguishing' the Church of England from 'being part of the one, holy, catholic, and apostolic church',[14] and yet this fails to recognize not only the variety of views and the streams of theological development in the wider church catholic and the episcopal and synodal way that the Church of England has come to a mind on these issues, but it also fails to recognize that, as part of the church catholic, the Church of England or other parts of the Anglican Communion may – by virtue of its history and model of theological engagement – offer a prophetic voice to the remainder of this church.

This is a challenging tension, of course, and there is doubtless a line between offering a prophetic witness and being found to be so far outside the stream of mainstream Christian belief that such a witness cannot be heard. It is deeply unfortunate that words such as 'orthodox' and 'revisionist' have been used as powerful weapons in ecclesial dialogue on matters of sexuality and gender, as these do appear (beyond being simply dishonest in their terminology) to limit the possibility of listening, so key to any process of reception. While the old adage that the church moves in centuries may carry some weight, nonetheless – as we shall see in our next chapter – on matters of sexuality and gender, there is a need not only for the church to respond to wider society but also to recognize that real people (and the church's mission towards them), including Christians, are hurt, ostracized and damaged by a focus on finding consensus (not least with the church catholic). It is also somewhat absurd to suggest that, after many decades of reports, debates and delayed decisions, the Church of England's decision to commend prayers for God's blessing for same-sex couples in December 2023 was a rapid and hastily made one.

Yet debates within the Anglican Communion and the Church of England have also been deeply dishonest in the way that the church catholic has been represented, as we intimated in Chapter 1 with regard to the issue of women's ordination. The Church of England, for example, is a member of the Porvoo Communion, which is an active communion of northern European churches with intercommunion and recognition of ministry. Many of the churches in this communion permit and celebrate same-sex marriages,[15] yet this communion is little heard about when debates about same-sex relationships take place in the Church of England. Similarly, the arrangement and agreement between Old Catholics in Europe and the Anglican Church is longstanding, the Bonn Agreement having been in place since 1931.[16] This agreement specifically stated:

> Intercommunion does not require from either Communion the acceptance of all doctrinal opinion, sacramental devotion, or liturgical practice characteristic of the other, but implies that each believes the other to hold all the essentials of the Christian faith.

Incidentally, this statement appears to be a helpful way of imagining communion where there is disagreement about some matters of doctrine or practice, which may prove helpful within Anglicanism itself. The Old Catholic churches, similarly to the churches of Porvoo, permit a variety of blessings (for civil unions or for marriages), implying that – at least at present and in practice – Anglicans do indeed believe this not to be an 'essential' of the Christian faith (and hence certainly not first order). The importance of these unions is significantly under-recognized in the Church of England, despite its having a diocese in Europe, yet their existence and the ongoing relationships do put pay to the idea that there is a single, unified position on matters of sexuality across the wider church.

Indeed, the Church of England's refusal to move on this issue has led to challenges in its local ecumenical partnerships (LEPs). Here, there is a formal agreement for the Church of England and another denomination to work together in a particular place, sharing buildings or congregations. Several of the denominations that form these partnerships with the Church of England (for example the Methodists and the United Reformed Church) permit same-sex marriages in church, and yet they have been prevented from doing so in the context of many LEPs with the Church of England. Similarly, the Methodist Church's move towards affirming same-sex marriage appears to mean that the hope of a reconciliation between that church and the Church of England is increasingly difficult to envisage.

The key issue, of course, is that while these extant ecumenical partnerships and communions are important on a local or in an institutional sense, some of the largest churches on the global stage continue to hold to a conservative view on sexuality. The perspective of these large churches is then presented as the 'majority view' (by numbers) of the church. Thus, until there is a change in majority view (which, of course, will require prophetic voices from a *minority*), any change or development in the doctrine of marriage, or of the understanding of the human person in the light of the contemporary context or scientific developments, is presented as being uncatholic. We have already addressed the challenge of developing doctrine in a church that claims continuity through time, but here we specifically face the difficulty of approaching a worldwide church that is so frequently defined in terms of numbers and hence authority lies in the hands of the majority.

Yet as we intimated in Chapter 1, the scale of numbers does not necessarily suggest either a uniformity of belief or any involvement of the laity – who make up the vast majority of Christians worldwide – in the formulation of belief. The Church of England, as a church that split with the Roman church on a doctrinal issue *in the face of* majority opposition, is surely one that can recognize that while majority opinion must hold some weight, there is a need to properly interrogate and engage with the forces that produce such an opinion, and recognize that there is often a diversity of belief and practice that is found beneath official positioning.

A good example, which we have referred to a number of times, is the recent development in the Roman Catholic Church on precisely these matters, and the publication of *Fiducia Supplicans*. The sheer pace of change in the Roman Catholic Church[17] is somewhat staggering, and yet for a church that places such authority in the Magisterium and particularly in the person of the Pope (and their work through the curial departments), it is not necessarily so surprising. While the recommendations from the Church of England and from the Roman Catholic Church in terms of blessings are not – in terms of content – the same, nonetheless the entire approach to LGBTQIA people has clearly and visibly shifted in recent years to the extent that the Roman Catholic position today is much closer to the majority (affirming) position in the Church of England than it is to the Roman Catholic position of 20 years ago. In short, it is not at all clear that matters of human sexuality are uniquely unlikely to experience developments in doctrine.

Yet this highlights another challenge for the Anglican Communion in the way that it engages in the ecumenical venture. To return to ARCIC, these conversations have primarily focused on matters of doctrine, and have released common statements on a variety of aspects. These statements from ARCIC I were given a mixed reception, with the Roman Catholic response making clear that 'further clarification or study is required before it is said that the statements made in the Final Report correspond fully to Catholic doctrine on the Eucharist and on Ordained Ministry'.[18] Such a response may be expected from a church with a central doctrinal authority. Yet the response from the Anglican Communion is equally fascinating.

The key response is found in Resolution 8 of the 1988 Lambeth Conference.[19] It is clear here that while there was (quite remarkably, given the variety of perspectives across the Communion) general agreement, particularly on the statements on the Eucharist, ministry and ordination, nonetheless there were questions raised 'about a number of matters, especially primacy, jurisdiction and infallibility, collegiality, and the role of the laity'.

While this is not necessarily surprising given the lack of a central doctrinal authority and the different theological strands of thinking across a worldwide Communion, it does nonetheless open up a number of questions.

The first of these is determining what precisely it is that can hold Anglicans together doctrinally in order to enter into such attempts at theological resolution as ARCIC. That is not to denigrate the significant effort and impressive output, but rather to question what precisely is meant by 'Anglican' in the title of the commission. The fact that there was widespread agreement and yet some dissention about the final report suggests that within Anglicanism there is a diversity of theological and doctrinal opinion, and hence the positioning of what is 'Anglican' is likely to be different depending on which thread of opinion is followed. There were doubtless similar informal responses from those within the Roman Catholic Church, yet for that communion there is a clear centralized doctrinal authority that can speak on behalf of Roman Catholics. In Anglicanism, this does not exist, and while the Lambeth Conference is also not an authority, the ambivalence of the resolution makes clear that there is divergence of thought even among the bishops.

This is not in and of itself problematic, but it does lead us to question what appears to be an implicit assumption in Anglicans as 'official Anglicans' engaging in such dialogue, which is that there is a defined Anglican doctrinal position on matters such as the Eucharist, ministry and authority from which such conversations can take place. It is not at all clear that this is the case – unless there is to be a reliance on the Book of Common Prayer and the Ordinal (and developments since), which appear to focus the 'Anglicanism' primarily on the Church of England. Yet even if we were to accept that there were such a position on these central elements of church identity, as conversations move beyond these to wider issues of the role of Mary, the doctrine of salvation, and most particularly in the third phase of ARCIC towards ethical teaching, it is simply no longer feasible to suggest that there is any single Church of England, let alone Anglican, doctrinal position on these matters.

What may, then, be suggested is that those from the Anglican delegation were seeking to represent the breadth and diversity of Anglican theology and not present a single perspective. Once again, this may be the case, but in doing so it is not clear to what extent any conclusions reached would truly relate to Anglicans as a body. It is much more likely that there would be agreement reached between the Roman Catholic Church and 'some Anglicans'. While this is not in itself problematic, it is not quite in line with what the aims and objectives of these initiatives are, and runs the risk of producing a nominal unity of belief between two official entities (although it is hard to know what the 'entity' is in the case of the Anglican Communion) that ultimately serves little purpose in practical change.

Indeed, because of the sheer variety of understanding of what it is to be an Anglican and what it means to do Anglican theology (or rather, theology in an Anglican way), even were the statements to outline matters of agreement on doctrine (that is, doctrinal proclamations or specific understandings of beliefs), that does not mean that there is agreement on the method used to arrive at that destination. Of course, this is likely to be the case when comparing Roman Catholic and Anglican methodology (and perhaps it would be a more interesting meeting if that were the focus rather than doctrinal assertions), yet if there remains a lack of clarity on what it means to do theology in an Anglican way, then there are limits to the utility of such a doctrinal discussion. Given the ongoing debate about what constitutes first-order and essential matters in Anglicanism, it is not clear that Anglicans would even agree that 'each believes the other to hold all the essentials of the Christian faith' in the context of Old Catholics, let alone Roman Catholics.

We return, then, to the problems posed in Part 1 of this book, whereby there is a fundamental crisis in forming an agreed identity as Anglicans, which will inevitably play out in any ecumenical relationships. This poses the question: how should Anglicans engage with ecumenism if we are to do so in a way that shows integrity to our identity? Can we really do so if we have not undertaken the hard work beforehand of working out our identity as a church in the twentieth-first century? Is there really such a thing as Anglican doctrine that can be taken to a doctrine commission? And what is our relationship with other ecclesial bodies when our key identity marker is simply to be part of the one, holy, catholic and apostolic church?

It is striking that in conversations about unity in the Anglican Communion, there appears to be less interest shown in the wider unity of the church catholic than of intra-Communion unity. We have noted here how such conversations often include concerns about the impact of 'doctrinal change' placing Anglicans without the church catholic, but this often appears in abstract concerns rather than in conversations around wider visible unity. On occasion, it appears that a commitment to being a particular 'type' of church is more important than wider concerns about unity – and this type of church is one that gathers around particular interpretations (and modes of interpretation) of Scripture (including those things thought to be first order) rather than anything beyond this. Where other communions agree on doctrinal issues, then the fact of their agreement is used to increase the validity of this particular perspective, but this model of being the church does not open itself to the possibility of diversity of perspective or approach (and is often in significant disagreement with other parts of the church catholic on the nature of the sacraments, church order and other key issues that have been addressed by the ecumenical movement).

It is in such an approach that phrases like 'the biblical understanding' are found, belying a belief that only one such *correct* understanding exists.[20] It is from this approach that a statement such as that of John Dunnett, the National Director of the Church of England's Evangelical Council, can be launched, in which he asserts that 'it appears that the Church of England no longer sees scripture as our supreme authority', linking this to 'the final blow to the unity of the Anglican Communion'. Dunnett bewails the lack of 'faithfulness to biblical teaching, which would deepen the unity for which Jesus prayed in John 17', echoing the words of Phil Ashey of the American Anglican Council, who stated that adopting an alternative interpretation to that favoured by those who oppose same-sex relationships 'forever breach[es] the limits of Anglican diversity'.

Yet this is ultimately to make a single way of interpreting

Scripture, and the particular interpretation that is reached on the question of same-sex relationships (and the associated questions of human anthropology), the locus for unity throughout the church catholic, which is entirely without any historical precedent and runs in direct contradiction to the ecumenical movement. Indeed, part of the fruitfulness of ecumenical dialogue and encounter has been to identify elements of commonality in method and outcome without the need to create a uniform version of either. The exploration of the diversity of scriptural interpretation around a set of commonly held beliefs is one of the gifts of the ecumenical movement, and to ignore this or seek to suggest that a conservative evangelical interpretative method and outcome is central to the Church of England's ability to be part of the church catholic is simply not viable. There is much useful space within the ecumenical sphere for discussion and debate about both the method of coming to the varied positions on same-sex relationships and the outcome itself. To close down such conversations before they can start in the name of unity, making agreement on this the keystone of Christian identity, is as audacious as it is absurd.

Indeed, because this form of confected unity is not even found within Anglicanism itself, one of the Anglican Communion's gifts to the ecumenical movement is surely its own ecclesial model of achieving unity within diversity, based on its identity as being a part of the church catholic (as outlined in the Quadrilateral) without further doctrinal requirements. As a church that values and upholds the centrality of a collegial episcopate without recourse to a central authority, the Anglican Communion may indeed favour shades of doctrinal understanding within certain bounds, yet also offer those bounds and its commitment to the Quadrilateral as its own understanding of what it means to be the church (indeed, such was the intention of the Quadrilateral when first formulated). Anglicanism can therefore be seen to be ecumenical in its essence because its identity is primarily simply to be part of, rather than a distinct section of, the church catholic. Attempts to privilege a particular scriptural understanding rather than recognize a theology *in via*[21] thus reduces, rather than expands, the possibility of such a church engaging with and enrichening the ecumenical venture, and ultimately the cause of genuine unity.

Anglicanism's claim to being a part of the church catholic does bring some questions into sharp relief, and most particularly when there are disagreements about the four strands of the Quadrilateral. We have seen already the difficulties posed when interpretations rather than Scripture itself are prioritized, and similarly when doctrinal requirements beyond the 'sufficient statement of the Christian faith' found in the creeds are demanded. Anglicanism's commitment to baptism (including infant baptism), and common practice thereof, has been relatively undisturbed compared to other issues in church unity, although questions occasionally arise about the validity of infant baptism, or the need to be baptized to receive the sacrament of the Eucharist. As we have described earlier in this book, eucharistic doctrine within the Anglican Communion is boundaried but mixed. Yet it is the commitment to the historic episcopate that has provided the most recent controversy.

Two examples here show the difficulty. The first is the ordination of women to the episcopate. Given the diversity of perspectives across the Anglican Communion (and to a lesser extent within the Church of England), the ordination of women to be bishops means that there is now the potential that bishops are no longer bishops 'to the whole church' but only to those parts that have received this as an appropriate development in doctrine and church order. This may be institutional in nature (i.e., a province of the Anglican Communion that through its episcopal and synodal deliberations does not recognize this – as yet – as a valid development), or it could be individual, where believers or groups of believers (for example 'The Society under the patronage of Saint Wilfred and Saint Hilda', in England) refuse to do so despite a church-wide decision to accept such ministry.

The second example was highlighted in the episcopal ordination of Bishop Gene Robinson, a gay man, in 2003. The Primates at their meeting stated:

In most of our provinces the election of Canon Gene Robinson would not have been possible since his chosen [sic] lifestyle [sic] would give rise to a canonical impediment to his consecration as a bishop ... In this case, the ministry of this one bishop will not be recognized by most of the Anglican world, and many provinces are likely to consider themselves to be out of Communion with the Episcopal Church (USA).[22]

It is noteworthy that this issue of church order – the reception of the ministry of a bishop – was ultimately formulated in doctrinal terms rather than ecclesiological ones, in contrast to the debates over women's episcopal ministry (as we saw in an earlier chapter). Yet in both cases, it does appear that a break – or a perceived break – in episcopal order risks the Anglican model of unity as outlined in the Quadrilateral. In other words, if a bishop is appointed to have responsibility to the whole church, then how is this possible if the whole church does not accept them either by virtue of their sex or their sexuality (and 'lifestyle')?

The Quadrilateral, however, does offer the hint of a solution with its inclusion of the words 'locally adapted'. Here we return to our discussions about the limits of Anglicanism. We must surely acknowledge that if we do recognize the autonomy (if also the interdependence) of different Provinces, then we must also recognize that it is up to them to determine what this 'locally adapted' might look like, whether that is the episcopal ordination of women or of LGBTQIA people. Individuals, groupings and provinces may wish to abstain from receiving sacramental ministry at their hands, but this does not make them in any way less a bishop. It is in the managing of these complex relationships, and our willingness to accept the messiness and imprecise living out of our identity, that the future of Anglican unity is likely in part to lie; we will address this in our final chapter. For now, however, it is important to note that merely rejecting an individual's episcopal ministry (who has been validly ordained through agreed processes) does not, in any concrete way within a historic understanding of Anglicanism, stop them from being a bishop to the whole church. What is at question is whether the whole church is willing to receive their ministry.

In Chapter 5, we made mention of Ephesians 4.1–6, which the German Protestant theologian Ulrich Heckel has described as containing the 'seven marks of the unity of the church':[23]

> I therefore, the prisoner in the Lord, beg you to lead a life worthy of the calling to which you have been called, with all humility and gentleness, with patience, bearing with one another in love, making every effort to maintain the unity of the Spirit in the bond of peace. There is one body and one Spirit, just as you were called to the one hope of your calling, one Lord, one faith, one baptism, one God and Father of all, who is above all and through all and in all. (Ephesians 4.1–6)

Heckel described these seven – the one body, one Spirit, one hope, one Lord, one faith, one baptism, and one God and Father of all[24] – as 'an excellent basis for arriving at mutual understanding … within worldwide ecumenism'. Heckel notes the unity of the body as proceeding from the unity of the Trinity:

> The *unity* of the church as the body of Christ in Ephesians is thus grounded in the unity and diversity of the Trinity: one Spirit (4.4), one Lord (4.5), one God (4.6). The Letter to the Ephesians lists these seven characteristics as marks of the unity of the church – nothing more is required.

This may be an optimistic outlook, yet it does offer a credible and biblical basis for the unity that the churches profess to seek. These seven, too, provide a model for churches like the Anglican Communion that are going through periods of disagreement and division. Heckel makes mention of the personal – relational – character of unity, the importance of it taking a visible form in the coming together of the community for worship, and the grounding of this unity in the sacrament of baptism.

Baptism, from an Anglican perspective, is not the work of the individual being baptized but of the grace of God, which 'brings people into relationship with Christ and his Church':

For both infants and adults the service has the same inner logic, a movement from welcome and renunciation through to an identification with the people of God in their dependence on God, their profession of the saving name, and the common activities of prayer, eucharist and mission.[25]

It is in baptism that we as Christians find our common identity, however much we might disagree about the finer points or the implications of our faith in God, our trust in the holy Scriptures, and our reliance on grace. It is in baptism that our identity begins – and it is in recognizing God's inclusion and God's authority and grace that baptism brings that we might properly start to seek answers to the thorny questions of Anglican identity and unity across our churches. In the final part of this book, we try to do just that.

Notes

1 Devin Watkins, 'Pope at Ecumenical Vespers: "Christian journey to unity rooted in prayer"', *Vatican News*, 25 January 2024, https://www.vaticannews.va/en/pope/news/2024-01/pope-francis-ecumenical-vespers-week-prayer-christian-unity.html (accessed 27.1.24).

2 Cindy Wooden, 'Love is the only path to Christian unity, pope says', United States Conference of Catholic Bishops, 25 January 2024, https://www.usccb.org/news/2024/love-only-path-christian-unity-pope-says (accessed 27.1.24).

3 Christopher Lamb, 'A first since the Reformation: Catholic bishops will take part in the coronation', Religion Media Centre, 5 May 2023, https://religionmediacentre.org.uk/news/a-first-since-the-reformation-catholic-bishops-will-take-part-in-the-coronation/ (accessed 20.1.24).

4 Royal Family, 'The consecration of the Coronation Oil', 3 March 2023, https://www.royal.uk/news-and-activity/2023-03-03/the-consecration-of-the-coronation-oil (accessed 10.1.24).

5 Hannah Brockhaus, 'Pope Francis calls silence "essential" at prayer vigil for Synod on Synodality', Catholic News Agency, 30 September 2023, https://www.catholicnewsagency.com/news/255530/pope-francis-calls-silence-essential-at-prayer-vigil-for-synod-on-synodality (accessed 10.1.24).

6 Details on the Anglican–Roman Catholic Dialogue are available here: https://iarccum.org/.

7 Anglican Communion, 'ARCIC Anglican–Roman Catholic International Commission', https://www.anglicancommunion.org/ecumenism/ecumenical-dialogues/roman-catholic/arcic.aspx (accessed 20.1.24).

8 Jonathan Petre, 'Church unity talks fail over gay bishop', *The Telegraph*, 1 December 2003, https://web.archive.org/web/20040306153216/http://www.telegraph.co.uk/news/main.jhtml?xml=%2Fnews%2F 2003%2F12%2F01%2Fnchur01.xml (accessed 20.1.24). It is interesting that, responding to the ordination of women to the episcopate in the Church of England, the then President of the Pontifical Council for Promoting Christian Unity, Walter Cardinal Kasper, stated not only that this 'signified a breaking away from apostolic tradition and a further obstacle for reconciliation between the Catholic Church and the Church of England', but also suggested that the legislation to provide alternative episcopal oversight in the Church of England for those opposed to women's ordination was the 'unspoken institutionalism' of 'an existing schism'. This is a fascinating comment, not only because of the somewhat limited vision of the Anglican Communion that this belies (women had already been ordained as bishops in the Communion before this date, yet it appears that Kasper's focus is on the Church of England and Roman unity), but also because of the focus on schism, which may not have been received well by those agitating to keep women from being ordained bishops in the Church of England. The story is reported here: William Oddie, 'Now the Church of England has decided on women bishops, ARCIC III is futile. As the CDF says, it is the Ordinariate now which is "ecumenism in the front row"', *Catholic Herald*, 17 July 2014, https://catholicherald.co.uk/now-the-church-of-england-has-decided-on-women-bishops-arcic-iii-is-futile-as-the-cdf-says-it-is-the-ordinariate-now-which-is-ecumenism-in-the-front-row/ (accessed 20.1.24).

9 International Reformed–Anglican Dialogue, '*Koinonia*: God's Gift and Calling', Anglican Consultative Council 2020, https://www.anglicancommunion.org/media/421992/irad_koinonia-gods-gift-and-calling-nov2020.pdf (accessed 20.1.24).

10 World Council of Churches, 'What is the World Council of Churches?', https://www.oikoumene.org/about-the-wcc (accessed 20.1.24).

11 World Council of Churches, 'Anglican churches', https://www.oikoumene.org/church-families/anglican-churches (accessed 20.1.24).

12 It is perhaps this reference to the Archbishop's 'ministry' which is the reasoning for his not officiating at the blessings of same-sex couples. This, however, is a rather diluted understanding of the meaning of ministry.

13 Margaret O'Gara, 'Receiving Gifts in Ecumenical Dialogue', in Paul Murray, ed., *Receptive Ecumenism and the Call to Catholic Learning: Exploring a Way for Contemporary Ecumenism* (Oxford: Oxford University Press, 2008), pp. 26–38.

14 Ian Paul, 'Why is sexuality such a big deal?', Psephizo, 22 June

2023, https://www.psephizo.com/sexuality-2/why-is-sexuality-such-a-big-deal/ (accessed 12.1.24).

15 Indeed, to the apparent chagrin of the Church of England as reported here: The Presbyterian Outlook, 'Church of England warns Swedish church on same-sex marriage', 24 July 2009, https://pres-outlook.org/2009/07/church-of-england-warns-swedish-church-on-same-sex-marriage/ (accessed 20.1.24).

16 AOCICC, 'Anglicans and Old Catholics together in Europe', 2017, https://www.anglicancommunion.org/media/307411/AOCICC-Brochure-2017.pdf (accessed 25.1.24).

17 This article from 2011 shows quite how far the dial has moved: Brian Mullady, OP STD, 'Pope Benedict XVI on the Priesthood and Homosexuality', *Linacre Quarterly* 78(3), 2011, pp. 294–305.

18 Dicastery for Promoting Christian Unity, 'Response to the First Anglican/Roman Catholic International Commission – The Catholic Church's Response to the Final Report of ARCIC I, 1991, http://www.christianunity.va/content/unitacristiani/en/dialoghi/sezione-occidentale/comunione-anglicana/dialogo/arcic-i/risposte-ai-lavori-di-arcic-i/testo-in-inglese2.html (accessed 24.1.24).

19 Anglican Communion, 'Resolution 8 – Anglican–Roman Catholic International Commission (ARCIC)', 1988, https://www.anglicancommunion.org/resources/document-library/lambeth-conference/1988/resolution-8-anglican-roman-catholic-international-commission-(arcic)?author=Lambeth+Conference&year=1988 (accessed 10.1.24).

20 Church of England Evangelical Council, 'CEEC responds to General Synod decision', 15 November 2023, https://ceec.info/ceec-responds-to-general-synod-decision/ (accessed 20.1.24).

21 Sarah Coakley develops a striking understanding of the importance of this intentional journeying to our theology, describing orthodoxy as 'a goal', 'a project, the longed-for horizon of personal transformation in response to divine truth'. Sarah Coakley, *God, Sexuality, and the Self* (Cambridge: Cambridge University Press, 2013), p. 89. There is much to commend this understanding of the theological quest, and Anglican engagement with doctrine would benefit hugely from recognizing the contingent nature not only of our own theological journeying but of the contingency of the unity which we now seek alongside fellow Christians in the ecumenical adventure.

22 Primates' Meeting, 'A Statement by the Primates of the Anglican Communion meeting in Lambeth Palace', Anglican Communion News Service, 16 October 2003, https://www.anglicannews.org/news/2003/10/a-statement-by-the-primates-of-the-anglican-communion-meeting-in-lambeth-palace.aspx (accessed 20.1.24).

23 Ulrich Heckel, 'The Seven Marks of the Unity of the Church', *The Ecumenical Review*, 73(4), pp. 566–80.

24 Heckel later also includes the role of the 'apostles and prophets',

offering a link to the apostolicity and even the 'historic episcopate, locally adapted', of the Quadrilateral.

25 Church of England, 'Christian Initiation: Commentary by the Liturgical Commission', https://www.churchofengland.org/prayer-and-worship/worship-texts-and-resources/common-worship/christian-initiation/commentary#mm097 (accessed 20.1.24).

PART 3

The search for Anglican unity

8

Rediscovering our common threads

In these pages, we have begun an exploration of the context in which we might seek our unity, and of the grounds for and loci of unity both within and beyond this Anglican tradition and identity. We have identified the Trinitarian and the various Christological understandings of unity's wellspring. Here we have found reference to the *kenotic* nature of unity, poured out by Christ on the church; yet here too we see the language of Christ's 'abiding' in and with the disciples, the action of the Holy Spirit and the primacy of love. As Christians – and as Anglicans – we cannot afford merely to ignore Christ's call to unity, but nor can we seek to manufacture it or use it for our own ends as a political tool.[1]

We face a number of significant challenges. Despite our friendship and loyalty as Anglicans, we appear not only to have stopped listening to one another but even found that our language, assumptions and basic facets of our identity seem no longer to be the same. This is much more than a divorce of the Church of England from the wider Communion: within the Church of England there are deep divisions in understanding and belief, in practice and liturgy. While it is politically useful to describe there being a simple dividing line between the Global South and the Global North, this is not necessarily the truth. In debates about same-sex relationships, it is not at all clear whether this as presenting issue is fundamental, or whether it is a playing out of other disagreements over our common identity – or both.

Talk of the 'rupture' of the Communion infrequently appears without blame being in some way apportioned or at least hinted at. In the Church of England, the Anglican Communion has frequently been portrayed as a single organism that has to suffer the aberrations of 'liberals' seeking a place at the table for LGBTQIA Christians. Even the Archbishop of Canterbury, at the Anglican Consultative Council following the General Synod vote of February 2023, appeared to suggest that the English church simply didn't care about the wider Communion:

> In the last few weeks, as part of our discussions about sexuality and the rules around sexuality in the Church of England, I talked of our interdependence with all Christians, not just Anglicans, particularly those in the global south with other faith majorities.
>
> As a result, I was summoned twice to Parliament and threatened with parliamentary action to force same-sex marriage on us, called in England 'equal marriage'.
>
> When I speak of the impact that actions by the Church of England will have on those abroad in the Anglican Communion, those concerns are dismissed by many. Not all, but by many in the General Synod.[2]

This weaponization of the Anglican Communion, combined with an unwillingness by those in leadership positions to speak clearly, openly, consistently and unambiguously – all under the guise of 'unity' – is itself a huge wound in the side of our ecclesial relationships. The racist and colonial attitudes that imbued much of the history of the development of the Anglican Communion take on new forms in our contemporary church, including the oft-presented idea that Black Christians – most particularly but not only from the continent of Africa – are virulently homophobic and that this places them in direct competition with white 'liberals'. Across the Communion, we seem to show a deep scepticism about listening – listening not necessarily to change our minds, but to understand where the other's perspective and positioning comes from.

Our Communion's politics are filled with statements of condemnation, with an unwillingness to recognize the face of Christ in the other, and – we must add – with the victimization and objectification of LGBTQIA Christians across the globe, who are used endlessly in Anglican Communion games. Reference to the 1998 Lambeth Conference Resolution I.10 is endless,[3] yet the Archbishop of Canterbury and the other Instruments of Communion appear at best reticent and at worst entirely unwilling publicly and in a timely way to combat the homophobia and encouragement to violence that Anglican bishops have called for in the sponsoring of draconian anti-LGBTQIA legislation.[4] There appears to be a consistent focus on this one issue – on which we disagree – in Communion debates, rather than the huge areas on which we agree and areas of urgent global need, much to the detriment of the Anglican Communion's voice on the global stage and of our development of a wider call to unity.[5]

Yet as it currently stands there appears to be no willingness to 'park' this issue and recognize it as something on which, as Christians and specifically as Anglicans, we can disagree. We have met talk here of first-order salvation issues, and the inclusion, however ahistorical, of these issues in matters that can shake or destroy our unity and 'impair' our communion. On other issues of theology (justification, the Eucharist) or church order (women's ordination),[6] the Communion has held together. Yet our positioning on same-sex relationships[7] – affecting a minority of already oppressed people around the globe, even if some Primates wish to suggest that they have no LGBTQIA people in their jurisdiction – appears to leave the Communion in a place that, at best, sees unity as a far-off dream.

While it is doubtless the case that many across the globe have come to their conclusions on matters of sexuality following roughly the same hermeneutic, it has been the end result – total opposition to same-sex relationships – that has become the marker of 'orthodoxy'. While many will talk about following the 'clear meaning of Scripture', their ways of determining that this is the 'clear meaning' will vary in their complexity, methodology and aetiology. Thus what becomes clear is that it is the doctrinal (if that is the right word) position that matters, that sex (undefined) is for marriage, and marriage is between one man and one woman (for life – although this, it appears, is optional)[8] – which is the rallying call for orthodoxy, and indeed because of this it has been raised to take on almost a creedal importance.

There are, of course, differing reasons for why this 'doctrine' has taken on such a position. One of these is that it speaks to something fundamental about human anthropology and associated theological understandings of createdness and human purpose. Another is that this is the marker of 'believing in the Bible', and that its rejection shows a commitment to ignore Scripture (this, of course, is contested). Another is that it is the belief of the 'church catholic' (which we have engaged with earlier in this book). Another, as we saw in the case of the Roman Catholic Church, is the role of culture, albeit one that is far too infrequently challenged. Yet while all or some of these, and other reasons, may be accepted by differing groups across the Communion, what has become the totem is the statement itself. We see this in the extraordinarily frequent references to Lambeth I.10 (which has no legal, binding or even contemporary standing), in the fact that this Resolution (and content) was included yet again in the 2022 Lambeth Conference's 'Call on Human Dignity',[9] and in the reference to the Anglican formularies in relation to 'marriage and sexuality' in a statement from the Global South Fellowship of Anglican Churches.[10]

Our key question, then, is whether this doctrinal positioning is in keeping with what has been historically understood to be Anglican polity and identity, and if not – given it is now being proposed as central to Anglican identity and the future of the Anglican Communion – what might be done to rediscover unity in Anglicanism. Unity in Anglicanism, indeed, is not precisely the same as Anglican unity, and we will return to this below. We must recognize that, while visible unity and metaphysical unity are not necessarily one and the same, our Anglican heritage has left us with organically developed structures that express this visible unity but appear no longer to be able to do so.

It has been our contention here that these structures need to be re-examined and reinterpreted in any case, even were the Communion to be at peace over matters of sexuality. It is surely no longer acceptable in a postcolonial world that so much of the Communion relies on an English bishop to be the 'focus for unity', given the vastly different contexts in which Anglicans live, and the historical association of the English church with its having been the church of a colonial force. This is a complicated business. While there remain 'bonds of affection' for Canterbury in some of the Communion, there is deep discomfort about 'meddling with the internal affairs' of former colonies by the Archbishop, reminding him that 'Africa is no longer a colony of the "British Empire"'.[11] Statements such as those made by the Chair of the GAFCON Primates Council are typical and, while understandable, there is a level of dishonesty in suggesting that the 'spiritual head' of the Communion (whom they reject) or, indeed, any other bishop should not offer an opinion or even a censure on laws that are so clearly in opposition to basic human rights for LGBTQIA people.

Herein lies the difficulty, as the dynamic is clearly uncomfortable, and the prospect of a white English archbishop being seen to speak down to and lecture African bishops on matters of sexual morality (not least given the history of colonial laws) is one that quite reasonably raises hackles on the side of the African episcopal hierarchy, and nervousness and reticence on the part of the English archbishop. Yet it is surely not a healthy church when bishops cannot debate with one another and where the 'spiritual head' cannot at least seek to provide some kind of moral guidance on such matters (the complexities of competing moralities notwithstanding). The fact that the Archbishop of Canterbury inhabits this role by virtue of being Archbishop of Canterbury is surely at the heart of the problem, as this inevitably sets up the deeply uncomfortable power imbalance that we find expressed here. For the holder of that position, too, the tensions involved in being Primate of All England and 'spiritual leader' of the Anglican Communion are surely too much to bear, and it appears inhumane for any ecclesial body to expect a bishop to inhabit such a position.

We will address some of the structural issues later, as while unity is not merely a matter of institutions and structures, it is naive to pretend that they do not have a role in the manifestation of visible unity. For now, however, let us return to some of those elements that we addressed in Part I of this book, and highlight those things that appear central to Anglican identity and possible paths to unity.

Our first key proposition was that Anglicanism is not, at least in its own self-conception, a denomination; instead, it sees itself as primarily part of the church catholic (indeed, the church, one, holy, catholic and apostolic). In its original manifestation in England, this takes the form of an Established church, and hence a church that was, at least in its original conception and proclaimed self-belief, if not in actuality, there as 'church' for all those who were seeking church. This is more challenging in jurisdictions where the church is not Established, and yet it remains a key part of the identity of (and the formation of) Anglican churches worldwide. For Anglicans, it is more important in the first instance to understand how the church, one, holy, catholic and apostolic, is defined rather than how Anglicanism itself is defined. The clearest and most long-lasting definition of this has been codified in the Chicago-Lambeth Quadrilateral, which is really a description of what it is to belong to this church catholic.

It is not at all clear whether this initial Anglican identity marker is still universally recognized or agreed to, not only by members of churches in the Anglican Communion beyond England but in the Church of England itself. That there is not a shared understanding of what it means to be Anglican is not in dispute; we need merely read the statements arising from different parties within the national and global church to recognize that this is the case. In many ways, the question that then arises is what is to be done about this fact. Is it, for example, worth fighting for this conception of Anglicanism, one that is embedded in the DNA of the church and yet may no longer be the majority conception of 'Anglicanism'? To what degree does the present erase the past, or conversely to what degree can a contemporary Anglicanism that bears little resemblance to the Anglicanism of the past lay claim to being Anglican?

This appears to be a somewhat anachronistic and semantic argument at first glance, but it is anything but. If those for whom Anglicanism is an attempt (albeit limited) at comprehensiveness, and finds its identity as merely being part of the church catholic in that particular place and time, with no claims to exclusivity, are unwilling to see such a tradition and ecclesial expression die at the hands of increasing denominationalism and doctrinal purity, then it is not unreasonable to see the current debates about unity as revealing a much deeper and existential fight for the meaning and life of Anglicanism itself. If, for example, plans to enable 'structural differentiation' within the Church of England are put in place in order to retain 'unity' and avoid open schism,[12] and these plans include proposals to embed structures of doctrinal purity and create a church within a church that no longer sees itself as merely a part of the church catholic (as historically understood within Anglicanism), then at that stage the Church of England as historically formulated and expressed will cease to exist.

The same is true across the Anglican Communion. The increasing centralization of the Communion, including a quasi-papal role for the Archbishop of Canterbury, the professed willingness and ability of the Primates' Meeting (quite against the reality of their role, as we have discussed) to attempt to anathematize and exclude provinces on the basis of scriptural interpretation, the attempted according of binding status to Lambeth Conference Resolutions, and the growth of doctrinal denominationalism, ultimately leads to a Communion that behaves more like a church than a communion of churches, and hence becomes something that is fundamentally different in character to that which has previously either been envisaged or existed. This development (or at least some version of it, with or without Canterbury at the helm) may be favoured by the 'majority' of Anglicans worldwide (again, a contested phrase), but in taking this step the Communion may lose touch with what it has historically meant to be Anglican. If this is a decision made episcopally and with the consent of the constituent churches, then while regrettable it is understandable. However, as we find ourselves now, these kinds of moves appear to be happening by default or at least without the proper debate being had, and often in the name of 'unity'. As we have discussed, unity constructed in this way is not unity at all, and is certainly not Anglican.

As we have described, the Chicago-Lambeth Quadrilateral outlines the key elements that Anglicans traditionally might expect to find in the church catholic. These remain central to Anglican self-identity and as we discussed in the previous chapter, provide an important basis for ongoing ecumenical engagement. Among them is a commitment to the historic episcopate, locally adapted, as a visible form of the apostolicity of the church (and, indeed, its one-ness and catholicity). We have addressed matters of catholicity in the episcopate in the previous chapter, yet here it is important to return to idea of the bishop as 'focus of' or 'focus for' unity that we first met in Part I.

As we described, this phrase has been misused and misinterpreted, leading to a situation where bishops feel that they ought not to express their position on matters of doctrinal disagreement in order to retain 'unity'. In the Church of England, male ordinands who do not accept women's ordination (whether for reasons of church order or complementarian theology) are permitted to receive ordination at the hands of a selected male bishop (who themselves have not ordained women to the priesthood or laid on hands at the ordination of women to the episcopate, and who, at their own episcopal ordination, did not have hands laid upon them by bishops who had ordained women), whereas women cannot take part in a 'pick-and-choose' model of episcopacy (thus if a woman has a diocesan bishop who does not believe she is a priest, there is no model of 'alternative episcopal oversight' for her). While this situation has arisen as a way to try to hold different parts of the church together,[13] most particularly those who oppose women's ordination (again, an appeal to 'unity'), what it has ultimately achieved is a breakdown in the meaning of the catholicity of episcopal ministry, and ultimately challenged the conception of episcopal ministry as historically received.

Thus in the Church of England while there remain geographical dioceses and (at present) a commitment to such an arrangement, priests (based on particular understandings of church order or theology, or a combination of both) can opt out of these diocesan structures for 'oversight' purposes with either a Provincial Episcopal Visitor or others providing alternative episcopal oversight (which might include ordinations, confirmations, eucharistic presidency, 'spiritual oversight'). The original thinking behind the plan (which was as much political, in order to get legislation through the General Synod, as it was theological) was to enable 'traditionalists' and 'conservative evangelicals' to continue to flourish within the Church of England's structures. While this is a laudable aim, nonetheless it is fascinating that the historic understanding of episcopacy (both geographical, in terms of diocesan bishops, and catholic) was suspended – in large part for those whose commitment to being catholic required them not to have women bishops because of loyalty to the church catholic (in this case, primarily in the form of the Roman Catholic Church).[14]

The Church of England's positioning on this issue, in which structural provision was made that fundamentally changed the nature of the episcopate, was different from that found in other Reformed churches, whose positions have included requiring uniformity on matters of church order, and others who have allowed those who disagree to continue in ministry and be given sacramental provision but have not permitted the ordination of new clergy who will not agree to episcopal and synodal decisions on matters of church order. We meet here – as with matters of sexuality – the challenge of synodal government, and the role of the bishop-in-synod (as an expression of conciliarity), meaning that decisions can be made that are politically expedient but increasingly change the nature of the ecclesial body itself.

While these structures for women's ministry can be significantly deleterious to ordained women (of which more below), they are nonetheless somewhat different from changes to the outward-facing pastoral provision of the church as might occur in 'structural differentiation' for those opposed to same-sex relationships. This latter form of provision seeks to legitimize a branch or even province of an Established church in which narrow doctrinal interpretative methods or interpretations (well beyond the historically Anglican) can legitimately be used to forbid or permit membership, and whose members are allowed to say that other clergy of that same Established church are leading people to hell. Yet it is hard to see how both structural elements, catering for people whose explicit grounds for requiring such structural change is a commitment to the Church of England as historically understood, do not significantly impact upon one of these historical understandings of Anglicanism.

To return to our concept of the bishop as focus of or for unity, it is clear that there is an urgent need for us to develop a useful and workable understanding of this phrase. It appears necessary that there be some commonality of faith with those with episcopal authority, yet Anglicanism does provide the model of bishop-in-synod, which we appear to have been prone to under-appreciate or see defined in purely political ways. It is clear that the current model of General Synod is moving increasingly towards a politicized and polarized form, which started with the debates about the ordination of women and has reached a zenith in debates on same-sex relationships. The most recent sessions of Synod have been anything but edifying; they have primarily involved those with opposing, long-held and immovable views speaking about those views to one another in phlegmatic speeches that are often more akin to preaching, with no intention (or possibility, given the mode and content of delivery) of listening, and bishops engaging in the debates but mostly – until recently – voting en bloc.

In the 2023 rounds of Synod, there was a welcome level of dissention among the bishops, which suggests that the other unfortunate facet of 'focus for unity' is losing its grip, which has been an unwritten and often unspoken assumption that bishops should speak with one voice on (almost) all matters. This has led to a deep level of distrust in the House and College of Bishops in England. It is different to there being an agreed statement and is more akin to 'Cabinet responsibility', which does not have a historical grounding in matters of faith or order in Anglicanism. The focus on 'speaking with one voice' has meant that individual bishops are known to think one thing but are forced not only to defend the opposite but to pretend that – following discussion – it is now their view. It is curious that for many years it was the bishops who were in favour of same-sex relationships who held their tongue in order to maintain unity; it was those opposed who openly dissented within the House of Bishops when the majority view was revealed to be against them.[15]

This 'speaking with one voice' has been a most regrettable and damaging innovation of recent years, and its lazy association with 'unity' and most particularly with 'collegiality' has been entirely without precedent. As we have discussed a number of times, unity cannot be manufactured, and any attempt to do so will be seen as the dishonest approach that it is. Collegiality, properly expressed, is a gift to the church,[16] and grounded in patristic understandings of episcopal ministry.[17] Yet it is quite a different thing from bishops pretending unanimity where there is none, and denying any dissent. Instead it is a process of 'mutual responsibility and accountability', which works to build up the church and enables different views to be expressed and discernment to be undertaken. 'Speaking collegially does not mean speaking in full agreement on every subject', but, as the Church of England's own work puts it, has a role in 'helping the Church to discern the tolerable limits to diversity in issues of faith, order and morals by giving moral and spiritual leadership'.[18] In fact, it is in collegiality that a 'focus for unity' might best be found, rather than in any individual bishop. This is a model that is entirely Anglican in nature, envisaging unity as inherently embodying diversity, yet with a shared directionality of purpose, nature and function in the episcopate.

The tension between this and diocesan leadership may well be pronounced, but it is important to recognize that open discussion of diversity of opinion on such matters is much more likely to lead to trustworthiness in any process of collegiality, and aid in the expression of episcopal ministry in any particular geographical location. The level to which decisions should and can be made at a national level is important,[19] most particularly on issues of clergy discipline. It is perhaps in matters of discipline (which in many cases are applied doctrine) that the role of the College is to set bounds and for individual bishops to steward these in their own diocese.[20] For Anglicans, bishops-in-synod join in a process of discernment of faith, and in so doing are called to be 'attentive to the ecclesial nature of the interpretation of Scripture', with the 'unity of faith' being 'viewed most of all as the result of an ecclesial process' that utilizes 'creeds, dialogue, the exercise of a variety of charisms and ministries, recourse to sacred Scripture and guidance by those charged with leadership in the church'.[21]

Returning to the Synod chamber, it is clear that while the bishop-in-synod model is important, much more attention needs to be paid as to how this might be put in place in our contemporary church (and indeed across the Communion, where in some Provinces there is effectively rule by episcopal *fiat*, once again entirely in contradiction of the history of Anglicanism). There may need to be more emphasis placed on diocesan synods, with the elected clergy and people of the diocese gathering around the bishop. Indeed, this may also mean there has to be more attention paid to the way that bishops are appointed and the involvement of the diocese in selecting (or even electing) their Ordinary. The form of discussion and decision-making in the General Synod, that of debates resembling parliamentary democracy, also needs significant revision, as does the way that Synod members are elected. At present, the General Synod claims to speak as representative of the Church of England, but it is abundantly clear that it is no such thing and, hence, while the political drivers to pass legislation may be necessary to command a majority (or indeed two-thirds majority) in General Synod, this does not necessarily lead to satisfactory or consensual decisions across the whole church.

Indeed, the idea of bishop-in-synod is primarily a theological idea representing something metaphysical, which is then expressed visibly in the institutions and structures of the church. While it is understandable that the General Synod (following the Church Assembly) took its current form in the way that it did, and that the Crown Nominations Commission works the way it does, the outward form is not that which is central to its Anglican identity. The local adaptation of the episcopate is dynamic and must surely be undertaken in order to best allow consensual episcopal ministry to be expressed in any particular place or time. Synodal involvement does not necessarily mean that the bishop is at the behest of the synod that gathers around them, and there will be occasions when the bishop should be making use of their teaching authority (most particularly when considering the essentials, historically understood, of the Anglican expression of Christianity).[22] Synodality, effectively expressed, does enable a church that fosters 'inclusion, participation, discipleship and shared responsibility', in an 'atmosphere of prayer ... structured by worship and Bible study ... evinc[ing] a constant quest for integrity in debate, consensus and unity'.[23]

The historic episcopate, locally adapted, must also be allowed to be one of the loci of unity across the Anglican Communion, and not merely the Archbishop of Canterbury. We see this in the meeting of the Lambeth Conference and the Primates' Meeting (of which more in the final chapter), yet both of these bodies – at least in their output – appear not to have recognized the importance of the synodal in the expression of the episcopal ministry. While bishops across the Communion may disagree with one another and wish to censure one another (such as in the Primates' Meeting), they need to be cognisant that the bishops with whom they disagree (if rightly ordering their episcopal ministry) are disagreeing with them with the authority of a bishop-in-synod, and thus cannot be easily dismissed (nor, indeed, dismissed as a *personal* entity, but rather must be engaged with as an ecclesial one). The top-down model of episcopal ministry (where, for example, the Archbishop of Canterbury is seen to be the 'boss' of other bishops) flies in the face of this normative expression of Anglican episcopacy, and the whole Anglican Communion would benefit from its deconstruction.

The fundamental importance of the historic episcopate has not generally been challenged in debates and discussions about unity in the Church of England or the Anglican Communion, but this has recently changed in the development, by the Church of England Evangelical Council, of 'non-consecrated overseers' for those opposed to same-sex relationships.[24] This is a fundamental break with Anglican ecclesiology, made more concerning given the involvement in the selection panels of currently serving honorary assistant bishops. To date no concern has been publicly expressed about this plan by serving bishops, which is somewhat astonishing given what appears not only to be schismatic in origin but also fundamentally un-Anglican.

There are similar concerns of fundamental ecclesiology relating to the 'planting' of churches by self-professed Anglican breakaway churches, such as the 'Anglican Mission in England'.[25] While these churches themselves have no relationship with the See of Canterbury, nonetheless they are recognized by other groups claiming to represent Anglicanism globally (for example GAFCON), despite their engaging in such ahistorical behaviours. This outlines the tensions (which may or may not be felt as such) that now exist for those who define Anglicanism on doctrinal grounds; by determining Anglicanism in one particular way, they appear drawn to shedding those parts of Anglicanism that would have been historically understood to be central to its identity. Destroying our basic ecclesiology in the name of 'unity' is entirely without any serious historical consideration of Anglican polity.

We have noted, too, the importance of the Scriptures (but not any particular mode of interpretation), sacraments and creeds as lying at the heart of Anglican understandings of the church catholic, and we have also discussed the challenges of making elements of doctrinal purity of particular doctrinal interpretative methods central to Anglican identity, or raising particular elements of doctrine to be peri-creedal. As we stated in our introduction to the Church of England, there is no one Anglican (the polity not the strand within the Church of England) model of doing theology or scriptural interpretation, even though there may be bounds within which interpretative methods have historically sat. Yet there has – at least in theory, if not in practice in the wider Communion – been some level of common practice, worship or liturgy within the Church of England. At the present time, that is no longer the case. It is possible that a refocus on wide, generous but shared liturgical provision (not dissimilar to that conceived of in the production of *Common Worship*), at least in principal services, would be beneficial in recapturing something of the unity expressed through public worship. Clergy commit to this in Section B of the Canons of the Church of England, but there is a practiced laxity that is deleterious to the visible unity of the church.[26]

It is also a prescient time for authorized work to be done

to try to outline the bounds of theological method, scriptural interpretation, doctrinal understanding and applied teaching that have been undertaken in the name of Anglicanism, both historically and in the present day. This is not a simple task, nor would it be without controversy, yet it would be helpful in providing a genuine attempt to celebrate and respect the streams of theological development and thinking that have taken place within the Established church and the wider Communion. While this might initially be a process that focused on the Church of England, there is nonetheless the need, too, to expand this beyond England, asking what forms of belief and practice have germinated and flourished under the Anglican banner. This is not to suggest that there then become only certain agreed ways of doing theology, but it is to suggest that such a project might put pay to the idea that diversity is alien to the Church of England and the wider Anglican Communion. Exploring the relationship between teaching and doctrine, applied and contextual understandings of particular teachings, would help enormously in seeking to develop a genuine understanding of what Anglicanism has looked like in reality, rather than merely in principle – of course, much work has been done already in this area (we have made reference to such work throughout this book) but the key element that is missing is its study and engagement on an ecclesial level. This might, for example, be a key task for reinvigorating synodal discussion; it is lamentable how little is known about Anglicanism by active members, both lay and ordained, of the Church of England (and wider Communion).

Before we turn to concerns on a wider Communion basis, let us briefly consider what might be described as the 'risks' of unity. So far, we have identified unity as a dominical imperative, as something central to traditional understandings of the church and as ecclesially expressed in distinctive ways in the Anglican tradition. However, we must be clear that unity – or rather, the use of 'unity' as an absolute imperative – can also have dark and somewhat nefarious uses. Unity in its truest sense is a theological and metaphysical reality expressed in visible forms, but, as we have seen, it is entirely possible to focus on these visible forms (such as in the 'speaking with one voice' of episcopal bodies) and in so doing lose touch with the underlying reality. In such cases, people become means to an end, rather than ends in themselves, with consequences not only for them but for the whole body. A focus on unity without remembering that it is a unity of the body with many members, where, rather than recognizing the indispensability of the weaker members, the eye says to the hand 'I have no need of you', is deeply dangerous for ecclesial health (cf. 1 Corinthians 12.14–26). 'If one member suffers, all suffer together with it,' as St Paul reminds us.

Such a commitment to unity at all costs risks often unintended (but occasionally quite intended) consequences, in which vulnerable or minority voices, and those on the margins of the church and society (for example women, people of colour, disabled people, LGBTQIA people) are silenced. These dynamics are far too often ignored by those at the centre of the church, and hence the most vulnerable are asked to shoulder burdens or bear yokes that the majority would not need to do. This can lead to institutional violence and repression of minorities: for example, in the requirement of celibacy for gay and lesbian clergy in the Church of England in the name of 'unity', and the willingness by those in authority to delay updated guidelines in order to appease those who will not accept an episcopal and synodal decision.[27] Such decisions of delay and stasis may be beneficial for institutional survival or politics, but there is a consistent failure among those who do not fall into more vulnerable groups to recognize the human cost of such decisions.

Similarly, while provision was made for those who oppose the ordination of women (as we have described), little attention appears to have been paid to those for whom this 'disagreement' is a matter of personal identity and calling (namely women). As we have seen, the ecclesial dial is usually set towards the inherited, which remains normative, leading to 'opt-in' use of prayers for same-sex blessings, and the arrangements on women bishops as outlined above (with consequent implications for the theological underpinnings). The normative in the church thus becomes white, male, cis-heterosexual, non-disabled, conservative and static, and others are expected to accept the status of aberration from the norm. There are questions of catholicity here, as we have previously addressed, yet there are questions of justice, too – which cannot be shied away from in discussions of unity. If 'unity' is merely a tool to push those who don't agree with, or don't form part of, the majority out of the church, then we are mistaking it for uniformity and failing to live into our calling as the church.

It is to that calling, and the way we might live it as a Communion, that we turn in our final chapter. Anglican unity offers many questions, and perhaps fewer answers, but we cannot simply turn away if we are to live out the desire of Jesus in John's Gospel and be the place of mission, ministry and witness that the church is called to be.

Notes

1 This is not, of course, the first time such questions have been asked, and the Virginia Report (available here: https://www.anglican-communion.org/media/150889/report-1.pdf (accessed 16.5.24)) was an early attempt to ask some similar questions to those outlined in response to the 1988 Lambeth Conference. It is notable that while this report addressed unity, belonging and communion in a distinctive Anglican context, its contribution to how these might be lived out in the structures of the Communion posed more questions than answers (and it appears to address structural issues without much of a decolonizing lens). While more descriptive than necessarily prophetic, this report is worth re-engaging with in the light of the changed dynamics in the Communion since it was first formulated. Few of its questions appear to have been engaged with in a way that might move beyond the abstract to the lived out.

2 Archbishop of Canterbury, 'Archbishop of Canterbury's Presidential Address at ACC-18', 12 February 2023, https://www.archbishopof canterbury.org/speaking-writing/speeches/archbishop-canterburys-presidential-address-acc-18 (accessed 26.1.24).

3 Anglican Communion, 'Section I.10 – Human Sexuality', https://www.anglicancommunion.org/resources/document-library/lambeth-conference/1998/section-i-called-to-full-humanity/section-i10-human-sexuality (accessed 20.1.24).

4 Statements, when they eventually come, are routinely only from the Archbishop and not the other Instruments of Communion, for example: Archbishop of Canterbury, 'Archbishop of Canterbury's

statement on Ghana's anti-LGBTQ+ Bill', https://www.archbishopof
canterbury.org/news/news-and-statements/archbishop-canterburys-
statement-ghanas-anti-lgbtq-bill (accessed 24.1.24).

5 Stephen Bates, 'African cleric breaks ranks on gay issue', *The
Guardian*, 8 September 2003, https://www.theguardian.com/world/2003/
sep/08/gayrights.religion (accessed 20.1.24).

6 As we have described, the episcopal ordination of Gene Robinson
was described as a matter of both church order and doctrine.

7 Posited as *the* proxy for whether we 'believe the Bible' or give
Scripture primacy, it is problematic as an assertion for many reasons, as
we have already discussed.

8 Anglican Communion, 'Resolution 26 – Church and Polygamy',
https://www.anglicancommunion.org/resources/document-library/
lambeth-conference/1988/resolution-26-church-and-polygamy?sub
ject=Marriage (accessed 20.1.24). This makes it clear that while doctrine
may not have changed, there was openness to some pastoral accommodation to address specific concerns in the Communion.

9 George Conger, 'Changes made to the Lambeth Call: Human
Dignity', Anglican Ink, 26 July 2022, https://anglican.ink/2022/07/26/
changes-made-to-the-lambeth-call-human-dignity/ (accessed 10.1.24).

10 Mark Michael, 'GSFA Demands Anglican Communion Reset', The
Living Church, 23 February 2023, https://livingchurch.org/2023/02/23/
gsfa-demands-anglican-communion-reset/ (accessed 11.1.24).

11 Laurent Mbanda, 'Gafcon Response to Archbishop of Canterbury', GAFCON, 14 June 2023, https://www.gafcon.org/news/gafcon-
response-to-archbishop-of-canterbury (accessed 10.1.24).

12 *Church Times*, 'LLF bishops respond to fears of schism over
same-sex relationships', 25 January 2024, https://www.churchtimes.
co.uk/articles/2024/26-january/news/uk/llf-bishops-respond-to-fears-of-
schism-over-same-sex-relationships (accessed 27.1.24).

13 This was not, of course, the only option – and might be justified
as being a messy but necessary way of maintaining 'greatest possible
unity'. However, it is notable that the approach taken was arguably less
'Anglican' than the alternative, where those who opposed the Church of
England taking this step nonetheless would accept the outcome of the
decision once the church had discerned the way forward.

14 The Roman Catholic Church here took centre stage because of
the identification of many 'traditionalists' of the Church of England
as being the English branch of the Western Church, the majority of
which is found in the Roman Catholic Church, meaning there is a particular focus on the 'restoration of complete communion of faith and
sacramental life between Anglicans and Roman Catholics'. More on
this is available from The Society's website: https://www.sswsh.com/
Our-Commitments.php (accessed 20.1.24).

15 Francis Martin, 'Bishops go public with their rift over blessings

for same-sex couples', *Church Times*, 12 October 2023, https://www.churchtimes.co.uk/articles/2023/13-october/news/uk/bishops-go-public-with-their-rift-over-blessings-for-same-sex-couples (accessed 10.1.24).

16 Indeed, the Church of England has produced resources on this point in the past: House of Bishops, 'Bishops in Communion: Collegiality in the Service of the Koinonia of the Church' (London: Church House Publishing, 2000).

17 Sarah Roland Jones, 'Episcopé and Leadership', in Mark Chapman, Sathianathan Clarke and Martyn Percy, eds, *The Oxford Handbook of Anglican Studies* (Oxford: Oxford University Press, 2015), p. 451.

18 House of Bishops, 'Bishops in Communion: Collegiality in the Service of the Koinonia of the Church' (London: Church House Publishing, 2000), p. 28.

19 For example, the way that *Issues in Human Sexuality* has been implemented across the Church of England, and the status of whatever replaces it. *Issues in Human Sexuality: A Statement by the House of Bishops*, London: Church House Publishing, 1991, https://www.church ofengland.org/sites/default/files/2018-07/issues-in-human-sexuality.pdf (accessed 15.5.24).

20 This raises questions, for example, about the legitimacy and possibility of enforcing 'guidance' issued by the House of Bishops on clergy entering same-sex marriages: Church of England, 'House of Bishops Pastoral Guidance on Same Sex Marriage', 15 February 2014, https://www.churchofengland.org/sites/default/files/2017-11/house-of-bishops-pastoral-guidance-on-same-sex-marriage.pdf (accessed 20.1.24). At present, collegiality might be best expressed in discerning to what extent these matters should be 'national policy' and to what extent they should be at the discretion of the local bishop, rather than on the policy itself, about which there are significant disagreements although a clear majority are in favour of change.

21 William J. Byron, *One Faith, Many Faithful: Short Takes on Contemporary Catholic Concerns* (Mahwah, NJ: Paulist Press, 2012), p. 227.

22 During recent debates on the Living in Love and Faith project, it has not been entirely clear why bishops have not made use of their authority, for example to issue guidance for discipline (removing *Issues in Human Sexuality* and releasing the new pastoral guidance for clergy). A closer attention being paid to what is rightly reserved to bishops collegially and individually, and what would benefit from synodical discussion, would be beneficial, and the Canons can assist in delineating this. This may, of course, vary between different churches in the Communion.

23 Paul Avis, 'Synodality and Anglicanism', *Ecclesiology* 19(2), 2023, pp. 133–40.

24 Church of England Evangelical Council, 'Alternative Spiritual

Oversight', https://ceec.info/alternative-spiritual-oversight/ (accessed 28.1.24).

25 Anglican Mission in England, 'Planting', https://www.anglican-missioninengland.org/join/planting/ (accessed 28.1.24).

26 It is curious that so many of those who have so opposed the introduction of liturgy through Section B of the Canons of the Church of England for same-sex couples not infrequently make use of forms of service that are neither authorized nor allowed by Canon. The proposal here is not necessarily to limit the forms of service but rather to recapture something of the common thread that might run through those forms.

27 Helen-Ann Hartley and Martyn Snow, 'Living in love, faith – and reconciliation', *Church Times*, 25 January 2024, https://www.churchtimes.co.uk/articles/2024/26-january/comment/opinion/living-in-love-faith-and-reconciliation (accessed 28.1.24).

9

Walking together and walking apart: Anglican unity in a time of crisis

Unity is no simple matter. Throughout this book we have addressed not only the Church of England, currently facing threats of schism and allegations of disunity over same-sex blessings, but also the wider Anglican Communion. In the last chapter, we focused primarily on the issues of the Church of England, yet the same principles can be applied to the wider Communion: a renewed focus on understanding the history of Anglicanism in any particular place, including its teaching, interpretative methods, liturgy, contextual expression, episcopal presence and synodal nature; a recognition that the model of bishop-in-synod and bishop-in-college requires ongoing theological and institutional commitment, engagement and renewal; and a commitment to being part of the church catholic at a particular moment, in a particular place, with an openness to those who are seeking a church that is built within the contours of an Anglican understanding of the church catholic.[1]

While it would be simpler to focus only on the Church of England, especially given its current in-fighting and deeply challenging present (there is enough material there!), that would be to do damage to the historical and present reality that inextricably links the Church of England to the wider Anglican Communion. While there remains a deep discomfort – rightly – about the nature of this relationship (as we saw in our discussion of the role of the Archbishop of Canterbury in the last chapter), nonetheless this relationship exists, and surely needs transforming rather than pretending out of existence. It is simply a fact that what happens in the Church of England has implications and ramifications elsewhere in the Communion, which helps explain the sheer anger expressed and stated need for 'impaired communion' by some provinces in the face of changing teaching on matters of sexuality in England. There is much talk of doctrine, and of the changes being un-Anglican, yet there is also a contextual and cultural element to the opposition to the English plans.

This is both spoken and unspoken. We have met mention of homosexuality being 'un-African' earlier in these pages, there are concerns about growing conservative church groups (often Pentecostal) in parts of the world that Anglicans are 'competing' with and losing ground,[2] and it is a matter of fact that changes in England could have significant impacts on the safety of Christians worldwide.[3] Yet this places the Church of England in a difficult position: should it focus on doing what it believes is right in England for LGBTQIA people, or should it look to its global role and retain stasis for the 'common good'? We have seen earlier in this book how the current Archbishop of Canterbury has accused General Synod members of 'dismissing' his concerns about 'the impact that actions by the Church of England will have on those abroad in the Anglican Communion'.[4] The evidence from the General Synod debates themselves clearly do not back up this assertion, and in the Archbishop's remarks he refers to the 'interdependence' of Anglican churches, without a clear recognition that the relationship is more complex than this, not least given the history of colonialism and the continued role of the Archbishop of Canterbury.

This is something that the Church of England – and the wider Communion – needs to face head on if we are to make progress towards a fairer and more peaceable Communion. Many in England (possibly including the current Archbishop of Canterbury) do not wish to accept the responsibility of their current positionality in the Communion, yet we must also recognize that if nothing is done then this will inevitably remain the case. Similarly, even if structural change does occur, there remains the impression and historical reality: the actions of the English church will likely continue to have an impact beyond its shores in some parts of the Communion. This is the complex dilemma in which the Church of England finds itself, and has been one of the key drivers to 'unity' in the past half century.

It appears, however, that the Church of England, in its development of liturgies for same-sex couples, has now moved beyond this paradigm. In doing so, it has responded not only to the clear need to engage with English culture – with whichever outcome – from a place of being the Established church, but it has also responded to the missional and pastoral imperative of LGBTQIA Christians in England looking for moral and spiritual warmth and guidance. Interestingly, talk of a third province or structural changes in England to enable those who oppose same-sex relationships to maintain a pure church suggests, perhaps, that their words about the impact on the Anglican Communion were more rhetorical than genuine.[5] We now find ourselves, therefore, in a place where as the Church of England begins to tilt back to its central calling to be the church for England, its other role – that of focus of unity for the Communion – is being placed under significant strain. Similarly, it is important not to lose sight of the genuine impact that decisions made in England, rightly or wrongly, will have on other Anglican churches and, rather than use this as a matter for stasis, to seek to understand and ameliorate this in a collegial way as much as possible.[6]

In our previous chapter, we considered the difficulty of maintaining the current role of the Archbishop of Canterbury in the modern postcolonial era; here, we might also consider the difficulty of maintaining the role where the 'focus of unity' across the Communion is also expected to lead the English church. This is no longer feasible, and the role has become effectively impossible to undertake. Thus, looking to the future of the Anglican Communion, if the role of 'focus of unity' is to be retained in the 'person and ministry' of an individual bishop holding some kind of – as yet undefined – primacy, then there is an urgent need to separate this from the role of Primate of All England.[7]

This is not a new idea but is increasingly becoming an urgent one.[8] However, what needs to be addressed, beyond merely the decoupling of this role, is whether imbuing any individual bishop with this authority and role (and responsibility) continues to serve not only the Anglican Communion but its ecclesiology. We have noted previously the increasing centralization of the Anglican Communion and the quasi-papal role of the Archbishop of Canterbury, neither of which allow a focus on the shared episcopal communion that sits at the heart of the Anglican model. Bishops in communion with one another are, perhaps, best represented at the Lambeth Conference, which itself, as we have noted, might benefit from a clearer sense of purpose, and might focus on relationship building and finding common voice on mission and witness[9] rather than on disputed doctrinal matters that inevitably lead to uncomfortable and damaging power-play. That bishops from across the Communion are invited to a meeting inevitably held in England is also problematic from a postcolonial perspective, and it is notable that GAFCON, for example, has held its conferences primarily in the Global South.

Alongside these two Instruments we find the Primates' Meeting, which also appears to run the risk of being a model of centralization (not least in the content of its communiqués) and an attempt at representation, despite the fact that on its own terms it is neither of these things. A meeting of provincial metropolitan archbishops is not in itself problematic, and may indeed aid in enabling difficulties (and not merely theological) to be aired and conversation to take place, but the Primates' Meeting has increasingly become a place of grandstanding and media management rather than a serious expression of collegiality. A reset in, and refocusing of the roles of, both the Primates' Meeting and the Lambeth Conference to make this collegiality and communion, and the global nature of the Communion, more visible would be a significant step in moving forwards as a communion of churches. Indeed, there did appear to be attempts to do this with the most recent Lambeth Conference, including the meeting of bishops from around the world in advance of the conference, using video technology, the intentional focus on Bible study, the use of Calls rather than Resolutions, and – in a very welcome move – a focus on Anglican identity continuing into Part III of the Conference.[10] There is, of course, much more to be done.

One key missing element in the Anglican Communion's polity at present seems to be synodality. The Anglican Consultative Council (ACC) includes non-episcopal members among it, although its work is primarily facilitation, exchange and co-ordination.[11] While the Anglican Communion Office describes this body as 'the most representative' body, it is not entirely clear what that means or how this representative nature is expressed in the work of the ACC. The ACC appears to do good work in highlighting particular concerns from across the Communion and enabling lay and priestly voices to be heard in the activity and actions of the Anglican Communion, and of all the Instruments of Communion it does appear to be the most clearly defined. That said, the ACC is not, in and of itself, a reflection of the underlying ecclesiology of Anglicanism; it is primarily institutional, yet serves that purpose in what appears to be a reasonably effective and useful way.

Which brings us back to the need – or otherwise – for a single bishop to take on the role of 'focus of unity' that would be vacated by the Archbishop of Canterbury. Such a need could be met by an election of a bishop by the Primates' Meeting, for example, or a recommendation from the ACC, and the role could be held for a short, limited period on a rotating basis. Yet before determining this, it is key to identify what role it is that this new Primate-of-Primates would be expected to play. Would it be primarily about leadership and organization of an institution? Given the Anglican Communion is not an entity but rather a Communion of churches, to what extent is this either practical or ecclesiologically coherent? Does the Communion, indeed, need such leadership? If the role is to be a 'focus of unity', to what degree is that role best inhabited by a single bishop rather than set within the collegial episcopate across the Communion? In other words, is there a benefit to having an individual bishop – imbued with episcopal authority – hold this kind of role? Is this really Anglican? We do not seek to answer that here, except to note that these kinds of questions are required when approaching the future of what remains in many ways a vestige of colonial power and authority, however spiritualized.

Let us return briefly to the question of synodality in the Communion. As we have noted, that is not the role of the ACC, and it is interesting that for a church that places so much focus on collegial bishop-in-synod, there is no such model at the centre of the Communion. However, given the role of the Communion as a group of churches in communion with one another, rather than as a single church, this does fit with the wider ecclesiology. The bishops' communion with one another is the sign of unity, and the bishops are sent out from their dioceses having exercised their episcopal ministry in a synodal fashion. While at the provincial level (or at the level of the Church of England, in an unusual formulation) there is then the need for another synodal process at the level of the church, when bishops from different churches meet together such a model is not necessarily required and indeed may erroneously suggest that the Anglican Communion is a single church and not a collection of churches. That said, there may indeed be benefit to considering whether lay (and priestly) voices are heard effectively from across the communion (not least given the preponderance of men in episcopal roles).

This brings us back to the fundamental ecclesiology of the Communion, the way that agreements may or may not be found on matters of doctrine, and the importance of such agreement on the maintenance of communion (and hence unity). As we have seen, the bishop-in-synod (together with rightly exercised episcopal authority[12]) is the Anglican model for agreeing matters of teaching (including teaching contexualized to any particular place or time), debating doctrinal matters, and determining local polity.[13] At the level of a church, there is the opportunity (and often the imperative) to undertake such discussions in wider synodal gatherings such as the General Synod. It is then the bishops of these individual churches who meet together at the Lambeth Conference in an act of visible communion – bishops who may have their own doctrinal understandings, teachings and applications, but who carry these alongside their role and function as a bishop in the constituent church from which they hail.

Because the Communion is a meeting of churches and not an entity, such decision-making bodies rightly do not exist within the Communion. It thus becomes problematic (and, as we have shown, out of line with the Anglican tradition) when matters of doctrine, and, in particular, teaching,[14] become matters on which the 'Communion' wishes to opine. This is quite simply not the role of the Communion. This doesn't resolve the issue where some provinces state that others have broken with what they see as fundamental doctrine (even if their assertion that such doctrine is un-Anglican is faulty), but it is to say that much of what has been asked of the central bodies of the Communion is simply not within their gift. This has either led to the overstepping of the bounds of their authority, as with the Primates' Meeting, or total stasis and strange decision-making relating to English synodal outcomes, as with the Archbishop of Canterbury. In many ways, the refusal to attend the Lambeth Conference is the most honest and Anglican of actions – even if done for reasons that sit outside classical Anglican understandings of the nature of the church.

There is, however, something interesting and inconsistent about the suggestion that any church can be 'out of communion' with another. While this may indeed be true in visible form, it is not at all clear that it is within the gift of humankind to determine whether or not one is in communion with another, whether or not one believes them to have the right doctrine, or even to be a Christian. If we see *koinonia* as a 'gift to be received, not only personally but as one within the Body, a fellowship in Christ across time in the communion of saints', then our perspective must surely switch from being those who decide who else is welcome at God's table to being those who are invited to eat at the table alongside whoever else God has chosen to invite.[15] Such *koinonia* is 'revealed in mutual sharing, mutual recognition, mutual respect, and mutual belonging', a 'relational way of being together in Christ', which seems to be a good way of describing the ultimate aim and purpose of the Anglican Communion.

Thus, while we may furiously disagree with one another over matters of doctrine, there does appear to be a gospel imperative to break bread together, and to come to a table that belongs to neither conservative nor liberal. Indeed, in Anglicanism, congregations and clergy approach the same table with varying beliefs about what the sacrament itself entails or means, yet still they approach. While Paul's command, 'Do not even eat with such a one' (1 Corinthians 5.9–13), may provide justification for a refusal to approach the table with those we might consider to be 'sexually immoral', it appears that the imperative to come to the table that is Christ's, to which 'he is always inviting his friends to share his meal with him in joy and love',[16] supersedes this command when it comes to Christ's meal and not our own. Indeed, given the Eucharist is primarily a metaphysical and ecclesial reality, it appears that even if we wanted to we could not 'not receive' alongside others. 'For as often as you eat this bread and drink the cup, you proclaim the Lord's death until he comes', says Paul in the same letter (1 Corinthians 11.26), and in so doing we join with all Christians in Christ's feast that he entrusts to his whole church, whether or not we exclude them or excuse ourselves from a celebration at any particular place and time. God's primacy is paramount.

This perspective on communion also plays out when considering 'structural' provisions suggested for those seeking separation yet continued membership of the Church of England. It is not at all clear how we might claim to remain members of the same church if we cannot receive communion alongside one another, which is surely one of the clear markers not only of visible unity but of ecclesial cohesion. Indeed, for those who claim that approaches to same-sex relationships are a first-order salvation issue, it is entirely incoherent to wish to remain part of a church with those who – in this conception – are denying others their salvation and ultimately closing the doors to eternal life. Once again, it is theologically more consistent for churches to walk away from 'communion with Canterbury' if they believe this to be the case, and it does appear to be an extremely confused ecclesiology to wish to remain in the same church (in the case of the Church of England) but with separate structures, such as a diocese or province.

In a book about unity, it might be reasonable to ask why there has been such a focus on institutions. In part, this is because of the nature of Anglicanism, and the inevitable formation of institutions when a key marker of identity and communion is the episcopate. In part, too, it is because the Anglican Communion is not fit for purpose in its current state, which has emphasized not only the disunity that exists but also the inability of our current structures and institutions to act as loci for unity in the way that is required, not least because of their failure to embody the ecclesiology that underlies Anglicanism. In many ways, the crisis of unity that we are facing – both in the Church of England and in the wider Anglican Communion – is a crisis of confidence in our ecclesiology.

In her excellent book, *The Anglican Tradition from a Post-colonial Perspective*, the theologian Kwok Pui-lan considers the possible positive role for conflict and crisis in our current situation. She quotes the American ethicist Kyle Lambelet, who argues that we should embrace 'a more positive, theological reception of agonism, or struggle, in the church' and suggests that 'celebrating such struggle might enable a more faithful practice of Christian unity'.[17] She makes clear the absolutely essential nature of undertaking postcolonial analysis of our structures to ensure that we are truly creating a Communion that reflects and respects the diversity of the global nature of our Communion, and calls us to a serious reflection on the intersection between race, gender and sexuality both in the discord within the Communion and more widely. 'Lambeth', she reminds us, 'no longer serves as a symbol of unity where bishops meet, but as a reminder of division,' and yet there remains significant stasis in even recognizing this fact, let alone seeking to resolve the problem. She points to the need to recognize complexity in the current debates around sexuality, stating unambiguously that being postcolonial in approach does not mean being anti-LGBTQIA. She offers us some helpful questions:

How can we avoid reinscribing the cultural superiority of the West on the one hand and uncritical acceptance of biblical literalism and cultural authenticity of formerly colonized peoples on the other?

How can we promote genuine dialogue and mutual understanding that both learn from and go beyond the colonial past, which for some is just a generation or two away?[18]

Kwok's analysis is helpful because it moves us away from the simplistic binaries that have plagued debates on unity and the Anglican Communion for generations. She approaches the Communion as it is now, but demands that we listen to the unheard voices who are so often missing from discussions on Anglicanism, and learn from the different expressions, liturgies and experiences of Anglicanism around the globe. She calls our attention to the relationship of Anglicanism with the global order and considers the role of mission in different global contexts. Kwok's analysis reminds us not to mistake Anglican for English, and that remains key in our reimagining the future – a future that will include institutions, but one in which those institutions must serve the ecclesiology and reality of global Anglican life.

It is not about ceding power from North to South, Kwok tells us, but rather an opportunity to grow – as a Communion and as individual churches within it. It is for this reason that talk of the 'average Anglican' as being 'a woman in her 30s living in sub-Saharan Africa on less than four dollars per day'[19] is both helpful and yet also unhelpful – helpful, because it reminds us in the Global North of our privilege and requires us to resituate ourselves, re-engaging with those bonds of unity and of the reality of God's world, but unhelpful because it suggests that there is something that can be called an 'average' Anglican. What would be more helpful is to say that this woman in her 30s living in sub-Saharan Africa is *Anglican* in just the same way we are, requiring us to do the work to reveal the implications of such a simple statement. All of this, and more, is required if we are to truly rediscover the variety within Anglicanism globally that does not boil down to different opinions on same-sex relationships. Such a future is possible, but only if we are willing to do the work to make it happen.

Throughout these pages, we have made a case for what it means to be Anglican, or at least how Anglican identity has been envisaged traditionally and into the present day. We must be honest that part of our difficulty in the contemporary church is that there is not a shared understanding of what being Anglican is, and our challenge is what we do with that fact. This is a more fundamental problem than disagreements on doctrine or scriptural interpretation, because it impacts on the way we might address and seek to resolve these disputes. We have seen the failure of the Anglican Covenant and the ongoing failure of the Instruments of Communion either to manufacture or to reveal unity, yet there does remain hope that something of a joint understanding remains. When Anglicans worship together, or when we happen to find ourselves in an Anglican polity beyond our own,[20] we do so using liturgy that contains 'features ... essential to the safeguarding of our unity',[21] such as 'the use of scripture and creeds, baptism, confirmation, communion, and the ordinal'.[22] In so doing, we continue to show unity in Anglicanism, if not full-fat and neatly packaged Anglican unity.

In our most fruitful relationships, and in our joint mission and witness, across the Communion with one another on a personal level, we see evidence of the Ten Principles of Partnership: local initiative, mutuality, responsible stewardship, interdependence, cross-fertilization, integrity, transparency, solidarity, meeting together, and acting. In this on-the-ground activity, there are many examples of where the 'common life' of churches joined in friendship and communion is embodied in much more than approaches to pastoral provision or discipline of clergy in the Global North. For all the talk of a crisis in institutional unity, there is often an inability to see the fruits of this common life among ordinary Anglicans from very different contexts, working together for the common good. These Anglicans may well not agree on matters of sexuality – indeed, they may vehemently disagree – and yet their commitment to building the Kingdom of God together remains.[23]

The Church of England and the wider Communion are now in a place where developing a serious, debated theological narrative of unity is well overdue. It would be naive to suggest that it will be simple to find consensus on this, yet rather than seeking to tinker with structures and use sticking plasters, attention to the underlying theological and ecclesiological questions is much more likely to lead to a long-term, sustainable, defensible and ultimately holy outcome as the church seeks to be one, catholic and apostolic. The benefits of doing this work of theology, influenced as it must be with attention to the colonial past and the postcolonial present, will be present not only within Anglicanism but may prove to be a gift to the wider church.

Anglicanism has far too frequently shied away from finding and expressing its distinct identity. Even if it does not wish to make exclusive claims of denominationalism it nevertheless has distinct gifts to offer to the church catholic. Among these is that lack of exclusivity, a wide and generous stream of doctrine and teaching, a deep commitment to the Scriptures and the sacraments, a consensual vision of the bishop-in-synod, and a commitment to mission and witness despite difference. These things are what has held us together when we have been living into our calling at our best, and they have the possibility to do so again today. There *is* a distinctive Anglican charism, even if this is not described in denominational terms, and it is a charism that has much to say to the wider church catholic at this particular moment in history.[24]

For too long, the Church of England and the Anglican Communion have been riven by divisions, arguments, anger and even hatred, leading our witness to the wider world fractured and unconvincing. In our fears over numbers and lack of growth in the Church of England, we have sought to find easy reasons – such as being overly progressive on sexuality or too 'traditional' in our parochial expression – rather than do the hard work of proper analysis, prayer and Anglican expressions of mission and witness. In the Church and Communion, we have sought to pretend away division, sacrificing prophecy on the altar of unity, saying one thing and doing another, and refusing to grapple with our differences, leading either to violent outbursts of fury and frustration or reducing us to the blancmange of the lowest common denominator. We have failed to recognize that our journey towards truth is not at its end but *in via*, and we have fallen back on silence and stasis in vain attempts to secure a confected 'unity' that remains out of reach. It needn't be this way.

In his concluding address to the Lambeth Conference of 2008, the then Archbishop Rowan Williams said about Christian unity:

First and above all, this is union with Jesus Christ; accepting his gift of grace and forgiveness, learning from him how to speak to his Father, standing where he stands by the power of the Spirit. We are one with one another because we are called into union with the one Christ and stand in his unique place – stand *in* the Way, the Truth and the Life. Our unity is not mutual forbearance but being summoned and drawn into the same place before the Father's throne. *That* unity is a pure gift – and something we can think of in fear and trembling as well as wordless gratitude; because to be in that place is to be in the light of absolute Truth, naked and defenceless. St John's Gospel has been reminding us that the place of Jesus is not a place where ordinary, fallen human instinct wants to go. Yet it's where we belong, and where God the Father and Our Lord Jesus Christ want us to be, for our life, our joy and our healing.

That's the unity which is inseparable from truth. It's broken not when we simply disagree but when we stop being able to see in each other the same kind of conviction of being called by an authoritative voice into a place where none of us has an automatic right to stand. Christians divided in the sixteenth century, in 1930's Germany and 1980's South Africa because they concluded, painfully as well as (often) angrily, that something had been substituted for the grace of Christ – moral and ritual achievement, or racial and social pride, as if there were after all a way of securing our place before God by something other than Jesus Christ.[25]

Such a vision of unity is surely what must lie at the heart of any theological vision for the Anglican Communion. The gift of unity, intertwined with truth and holiness, empowered and initiated through and by love, flowing from its Trinitarian source, and finding its visibility not only in our structures and institutions but in our relationships and lives of Christian service, witness and mission. Unity as gift and imperative sits above our disagreements, requiring us not to contort ourselves into pseudo-agreement, but instead to recognize that metaphysical unity precedes our disagreements and will be revealed in different visible ways as we journey on together.

We may believe our fellow Christians are wrong, and are even getting parts of the gospel wrong, but surely we cannot believe that disagreement on matters of sexual ethics means that we are preaching the wrong gospel in its entirety. Our failure to believe in the work of the Spirit and the power of prayer, and our endless human need to be in control surely does damage not only to our communion with one another but to our own faith and ability to live Christian lives to the full. Our willingness to anathematize and demean, to misrepresent and approach discussions in bad faith – indeed, even to approach discussions refusing to believe the other's commitment to Christ – is not maintaining the unity of the Spirit in the bond of peace.

The churches of the Anglican Communion are held together by bonds of affection and common loyalty. The members of the Church of England are held together by just the same. The phrase 'walking together' has become increasingly commonly used in Anglican circles in recent years, and for good reason. Our Anglican lives are journeys, in which we pray for increase in holiness, truth, love and unity, despite occasionally taking the wrong turn. The reason we journey together is because then our companion can help us find the path again – and the other way around. Yet it is neither our path nor theirs: it is God's. It is neither our table nor theirs: it is God's. It is neither our communion nor theirs: it is God's.

We have a choice whether to go on that journey together or not. The Anglican journey is well defined, even if it is just a well-defined way of walking along the road of the church catholic. We may not have 'perfect unity', and sometimes the messiness will be needed to help us on our way. Sometimes we will only ever be able to look towards the greatest degree of unity. Yet this is our calling as Anglicans, as Christians, as human beings: we are called to communion and relationship. Our Anglican identity lays out the path for us if we would only but look for it. It is up to us whether we choose to live into that calling.

Love unity; avoid divisions; be the followers of Jesus Christ, even as He is of His Father.[26]

Notes

1 Unfortunately, the recent proposals brought to the Primates' Meeting in May 2024 by Archbishop Justin Welby seem to have been less grounded in a detailed analysis than they might otherwise have been. The substantive output, 'the prospect of an elected primate who might serve alongside the Archbishop of Canterbury and the other Instruments of Communion as chair of the Primates' Meeting', and potentially as president of the Anglican Consultative Council, does not show any serious engagement with the structural or postcolonial critiques outlined in this book, and in any case was rejected by the Primates. All that is left is a 'recasting' of the 'description' of the Anglican Communion, which is hardly a root-and-branch reform. See the Communiqué available here: Anglican Communion, 'Primates' Meeting Communiqué, Rome, 2 May 2024', https://www.anglicancommunion.org/media/515756/Primates-Meeting-2024-Communique-02052024.pdf (accessed 15.5.24).

2 The complex relationship between theology and politics is engaged with in detail in Ezra Chitando and Adriaan van Klinken, eds, *Christianity and Controversies over Homosexuality in Contemporary Africa* (Oxford: Routledge, 2016).

3 *BBC News*, 'Welby: Backing gay marriage could be "catastrophic" for Christians elsewhere', 4 April 2014, https://www.bbc.com/news/uk-26894133 (accessed 28.1.14).

4 Archbishop of Canterbury, 'Archbishop of Canterbury's Presidential Address at ACC-18', 12 February 2023, https://www.archbishopofcanterbury.org/speaking-writing/speeches/archbishop-canterburys-presidential-address-acc-18 (accessed 26.1.24).

5 An example of the language often employed in appeals to the 'unity' of the Anglican Communion when English churches object to same-sex blessings might be: 'the readiness of the House of Bishops to trample, imperialistically, in White, Western boots, over the biblical convictions of the vast majority of Anglicans worldwide'. From a letter from St Helen's Bishopsgate: William Taylor, 'St Helen's Bishopsgate breaks with the Bishop of London and will uphold the Bible's teaching on marriage and sex', Anglican Ink, 1 March 2023, https://anglican.ink/2023/03/01/st-helens-bishopsgate-breaks-with-the-bishop-of-london-and-will-uphold-the-bibles-teaching-on-marriage-and-sex/ (accessed 20.1.24). The complexity of the colonial inheritance and relationship to matters of sexuality is infrequently engaged with in such rhetoric.

6 Of course, it is also not a reasonable argument to suggest that churches shouldn't stand for what they believe to be true in case it leads to lack of popularity or political difficulty. That is not to minimize the genuine risk to life in this case, but to make clear that theology should

not only be done based on what is popular or culturally acceptable, in whatever context.

7 Not least in order to allow the Archbishop of Canterbury to focus on the Church of England.

8 James Walters, 'Anglican Communion requires a rotating presidency', *Church Times*, 29 January 2022, https://www.churchtimes. co.uk/articles/2022/28-january/comment/opinion/anglican-communion-requires-a-rotating-presidency (accessed 22.1.24).

9 As exemplified in the Five Marks of Mission, for example.

10 Lambeth Conference, 'Anglican Identity set to be the next theme in Lambeth Call discussion series', 6 November 2023, https://www. lambethconference.org/anglican-identity-set-to-be-the-next-theme-in-lambeth-call-discussion-series/ (accessed 20.1.24).

11 Anglican Communion, 'Anglican Consultative Council', https:// www.anglicancommunion.org/structures/instruments-of-communion/ acc.aspx (accessed 11.1.24).

12 Church of England, 'Canons of the Church of England: Section C', https://www.churchofengland.org/about/leadership-and-governance/ legal-resources/canons-church-england/section-c (accessed 10.1.24).

13 There is an interesting debate to be had about the difference between doctrine, teaching and contextual application of that teaching, for which there is not space here. Similarly, there are important questions here about the role of conscience and subsidiarity, and the place of synodal discernment in setting their bounds and engaging with disputes.

14 For example, it is not at all clear that the matter of same-sex relationships is doctrinal (even if marriage might be – if not creedal). The practice as relates to same-sex relationships appears to be more a question of applied doctrine and teaching. The relationship with canon law will be different in different jurisdictions, but even within the Church of England it is not at all clear that 'doctrine' is coterminous with canon law, despite a focus on Canon B30 (see Canon A5).

15 International Reformed–Anglican Dialogue, '*Koinonia:* God's Gift and Calling', Anglican Consultative Council, 2020, https://www. anglicancommunion.org/media/421992/irad_koinonia-gods-gift-and-calling-nov2020.pdf (accessed 20.1.24).

16 Jaci Maraschin's 'Worship and the Excluded', in Marcella Althaus-Reid, ed., *Liberation Theology and Sexuality* (Aldershot: Ashgate, 2006), is a helpful reminder of the scandal of eucharistic separation. The quote here is from p. 127.

17 Kwok Pui-lan, *The Anglican Tradition from a Postcolonial Perspective* (New York: Seabury Books, 2023), p. 223.

18 Kwok, *The Anglican Tradition from a Postcolonial Perspective*, p. 15.

19 Jeff Walton, 'As bishops meet, Anglican future is already written',

Anglican Ink, 2 August 2022, https://anglican.ink/2022/08/02/as-bishops-meet-anglican-future-is-already-written/ (accessed 20.1.24).

20 For example in the Anglican Centre in Rome, which makes use of liturgy from across the Communion.

21 The Lambeth Conference 1958's Resolution 74, as quoted in Kwok, *The Anglican Tradition from a Postcolonial Perspective*, p. 104.

22 Kwok, *The Anglican Tradition from a Postcolonial Perspective*, p. 104.

23 This is not to ignore the very real difficulties that certain theological positions can cause to, for example, LGBTQIA people on the ground. Queer people in parts of the world where both culture and church discriminate against them face significant challenges, and hence it is important for church leaders to be able to disagree with one another on this (while appreciating the difficulties of perceived or real power imbalances in such dialogue).

24 We might think, for example, of the increased interest in synodality within the Roman Catholic Church.

25 Rowan Williams, 'Concluding Presidential Address to the Lambeth Conference', 3 August 2008, http://rowanwilliams.archbishopofcanterbury.org/articles.php/1350/concluding-presidential-address-to-the-lambeth-conference.html (accessed 20.1.24).

26 Ignatius, 'The Epistle of Ignatius to the Philadelphians', https://www.newadvent.org/fathers/0108.htm (accessed 20.1.24).

Bibliography

ACI Africa, 'No Blessing for "same-sex couples" in Africa, Catholic Bishops Declare, Vatican Agrees', ACI Africa, 11 January 2024, https://www.aciafrica.org/news/9998/no-blessing-for-same-sex-couples-in-africa-catholic-bishops-declare-vatican-agrees (accessed 11.1.24).

Anglican Consultative Council, *The Report of the Inter-Anglican Theological and Doctrinal Commission* (The Virginia Report) (London: Anglican Consultative Council, 1997.

Sam Allberry, 'Why Homosexuality is an Issue of First Importance', *The Village Church*, 9 April 2015, https://www.thevillagechurch.net/resources/articles/why-homosexuality-is-an-issue-of-first-importance (accessed 10.1.24).

Marcella Althaus-Reid, ed., *Liberation Theology and Sexuality* (Aldershot: Ashgate, 2006).

Anglican Church in North America, 'What is Anglicanism?', https://anglicanchurch.net/anglicanism/ (accessed 10.1.24).

Anglican Communion, 'Anglican Communion Office', https://www.anglicancommunion.org/structures/anglican-communion-office.aspx (accessed 11.1.24).

Anglican Communion, 'Anglican Consultative Council', https://www.anglicancommunion.org/structures/instruments-of-communion/acc.aspx (accessed 11.1.24).

Anglican Communion, 'Archbishop of Canterbury', https://www.anglicancommunion.org/structures/instruments-of-communion/archbishop-of-canterbury.aspx (accessed 10.1.24).

Anglican Communion, 'ARCIC Anglican–Roman Catholic International Commission', https://www.anglicancommunion.org/ecumenism/ecumenical-dialogues/roman-catholic/arcic.aspx (accessed 20.1.24).

Anglican Communion, 'Canon Law', https://www.anglicancommunion.org/structures/canon-law.aspx (accessed 10.1.24).

Anglican Communion, 'Presence at the United Nations', https://www.anglicancommunion.org/mission/at-the-un.aspx (accessed 11.1.24).

Anglican Communion, 'Primates' Meeting', https://www.anglicancommunion.org/structures/instruments-of-communion/primates-meeting.aspx (accessed 11.1.24).

Anglican Communion, 'Resolution 8 – Anglican–Roman Catholic International Commission (ARCIC)', 1988, https://www.anglicancommu

nion.org/resources/document-library/lambeth-conference/1988/res olution-8-anglican-roman-catholic-international-commission-(arcic)? author=Lambeth+Conference&year=1988 (accessed 10.1.24).

Anglican Communion, 'Resolution 26 – Church and Polygamy', https:// www.anglicancommunion.org/resources/document-library/lambeth-conference/1988/resolution-26-church-and-polygamy?subject= Marriage (accessed 20.1.24).

Anglican Communion, 'Section I.10 – Human Sexuality', https://www. anglicancommunion.org/resources/document-library/lambeth-conference/1998/section-i-called-to-full-humanity/section-i10-human-sexuality (accessed 20.1.24).

Anglican Communion, 'The Anglican Communion Covenant', https:// www.anglicancommunion.org/media/99905/The_Anglican_Coven ant.pdf (accessed 10.1.24).

Anglican Communion, 'The Lambeth Conference: Resolutions Archive from 1968', https://www.anglicancommunion.org/media/127743/ 1968.pdf (accessed 10.1.24).

Anglican Communion, 'What is the Anglican Communion?', https:// www.anglicancommunion.org/structures/what-is-the-anglican-com munion.aspx (accessed 10.1.24).

Anglican Consultative Council, 'Articles of Association', https://www. anglicancommunion.org/media/39479/the-constitution-of-the-angli can-consultative-council.pdf (accessed 20.1.24).

Anglican Mission in England, 'Planting', https://www.anglicanmission inengland.org/join/planting/ (accessed 28.1.24).

AOCICC, 'Anglicans and Old Catholics together in Europe', 2017, https:// www.anglicancommunion.org/media/307411/AOCICC-Brochure-2017.pdf (accessed 25.1.24).

Archbishop of Canterbury, 'Archbishop of Canterbury's Presidential Address at ACC-18', 12 February 2023, https://www.archbishopof canterbury.org/speaking-writing/speeches/archbishop-canterburys-presidential-address-acc-18 (accessed 26.1.24).

Archbishop of Canterbury, 'Archbishop of Canterbury's Statement on Ghana's Anti-LGBTQ+ Bill', https://www.archbishopofcanterbury. org/news/news-and-statements/archbishop-canterburys-statement-ghanas-anti-lgbtq-bill (accessed 24.1.24).

Archbishop of Canterbury, 'Lambeth Call on Human Dignity: Read Archbishop Justin's remarks', https://www.archbishopofcanterbury. org/speaking-writing/speeches/lambeth-call-human-dignity-read-arch bishop-justins-remarks (accessed 10.1.24).

Archbishop of Canterbury, 'Living in Love and Faith: Statement by the Archbishop of Canterbury', 16 November 2023, https://www. archbishopofcanterbury.org/news/news-and-statements/living-love-and-faith-statement-archbishop-canterbury (accessed 10.1.24).

Don S. Armentrout and Robert Boak Slocum, eds, *An Episcopal Dic-*

tionary of the Church: A User Friendly Reference for Episcopalians (New York: Church Publishing Inc., 2000), https://www.episcopal church.org/glossary/via-media/ (accessed 2.1.24).

Pat Ashworth, 'Draft Lambeth Conference 'call' threatens to reignite 1998 row over homosexuality', *Church Times*, 22 July 2022, https://www.churchtimes.co.uk/articles/2022/29-july/news/world/draft-lambeth-conference-call-threatens-to-reignite-1998-row-over-homosexuality (accessed 2.1.24).

Pat Ashworth, 'Lambeth 2022: Global South Bishops press for re-affirm ation of Resolution 1.10', *Church Times*, 29 July 2022, https://www.churchtimes.co.uk/articles/2022/5-august/news/world/lambeth-2022-global-south-bishops-press-for-re-affirmation-of-resolution-110 (accessed 2.1.24).

Justin Badi Arama, 'Global South archbishops question Welby's "fitness to lead" the Anglican Communion following synod vote on gay blessings', Anglican Ink, 9 February 2023, https://anglican.ink/2023/02/09/global-south-archbishops-question-welbys-fitness-to-lead-the-angli can-communion-following-synod-vote-on-gay-blessings/ (accessed 10.1.24)

Augustine, 'Of Faith and the Creed', https://www.newadvent.org/fathers/1304.htm (accessed 11.1.24).

Augustine, 'On Baptism, Against the Donatists (Book IV), https://www.newadvent.org/fathers/14084.htm (accessed 11.1.24).

Paul Avis, 'Synodality and Anglicanism', *Ecclesiology* 19(2), 2023, pp. 133–40.

Paul Avis, *The Anglican Understanding of the Church: An Introduction* (London: SPCK, 2013).

Stephen Bates, 'African cleric breaks ranks on gay issue', *The Guardian*, 8 September 2003, https://www.theguardian.com/world/2003/sep/08/gayrights.religion (accessed 20.1.24).

BBC News, 'Welby: Backing gay marriage could be "catastrophic" for Christians elsewhere', 4 April 2014, https://www.bbc.com/news/uk-26894133 (accessed 28.1.24).

Charles Bell, *Queer Holiness* (London: Darton, Longman and Todd, 2022).

Charles Bell, 'The Eucharistic Feast: Participation, representation and sacramental integrity in the time of social distancing', Anglicanism.org, https://anglicanism.org/the-eucharistic-feast-participation-represen tation-and-sacramental-integrity-in-the-time-of-social-distancing (accessed 10.1.24)

Harry R. Boer, *A Short History of the Early Church* (Grand Rapids, MI: Eerdmans, 1976).

Gerald Bray, *The Faith We Confess: An Exposition of the Thirty-Nine Articles* (London: The Latimer Trust, 2009).

BIBLIOGRAPHY

Christopher Craig Brittain and Andrew Mackinnon, *The Anglican Communion at a Crossroads* (Philadelphia, PA: Penn State University Press, 2018).

Hannah Brockhaus, 'Pope Francis calls silence "essential" at prayer vigil for Synod on Synodality', Catholic News Agency, 30 September 2023, https://www.catholicnewsagency.com/news/255530/pope-francis-calls-silence-essential-at-prayer-vigil-for-synod-on-synodality (accessed 10.1.24).

Andrew Brown, 'The latest hate speech from the Church of Nigeria', *The Guardian*, 13 March 2009, https://www.theguardian.com/comment isfree/andrewbrown/2009/mar/13/religion-anglicanism-akinola-nigeria (accessed 12.1.24).

F. F. Bruce, *The Canon of Scripture* (Westmont, IL: InterVarsity Press, 2018).

Kaya Burgess, 'Behold the Bishop of Brexit as church models itself on politics', *The Times*, 7 February 2022, https://www.thetimes.co.uk/article/bishop-of-brexit-church-models-itself-politics-vd8mv2fgg (accessed 20.1.24).

Stephen Burns, Bryan Cones and James Tengatenga, eds, *Twentieth-Century Anglican Theologians* (London: Wiley, 2021).

Antony Bushfield, 'Tense primate meeting on LGBT Christians gets underway', Premier Christian News, 11 January 2016, https://premier christian.news/en/news/article/tense-primate-meeting-on-lgbt-christians-gets-underway (accessed 10.1.24).

William J. Byron, *One Faith, Many Faithful: Short Takes on Contemporary Catholic Concerns* (Mahwah, NJ: Paulist Press, 2012).

Mark Chapman, *Anglican Theology* (London: T&T Clark, 2012).

Mark Chapman, *Anglicanism: A Very Short Introduction* (Oxford: Oxford University Press, 2006).

Mark Chapman, Martyn Percy and Sathianathan Clarke, eds, *The Oxford Handbook of Anglican Studies* (Oxford: Oxford University Press, 2016).

Christopher Chessun, 'Bishop Christopher's Presidential Address to Synod', The Diocese of Southwark, 20 November 2023, https://south wark.anglican.org/bishop-christophers-presidential-address-to-synod/ (accessed 20.1.24).

Ezra Chitando and Adriaan van Klinken, eds, *Christianity and Controversies over Homosexuality in Contemporary Africa* (Oxford: Routledge, 2016).

Christian Today, 'Orthodox Anglicans grieved over "disastrous decision" to commend same-sex blessings, 12 October 2023, https://www.christiantoday.com/article/orthodox.anglicans.grieved.over.disastrous.decision.to.commend.same.sex.blessings/140886.htm (accessed 20.1.24).

Church of England, 'Canons of the Church of England: Section B', https://www.churchofengland.org/about/leadership-and-governance/legal-services/canons-church-england/section-b (accessed 10.1.24).

Church of England, 'Canons of the Church of England: Section C', https://www.churchofengland.org/about/leadership-and-governance/legal-resources/canons-church-england/section-c (accessed 10.1.24).

Church of England, 'Christian Initiation: Commentary by the Liturgical Commission', https://www.churchofengland.org/prayer-and-worship/worship-texts-and-resources/common-worship/christian-initiation/commentary#mm097 (accessed 20.1.24).

Church of England, 'Common Worship Ordination Services', https://www.churchofengland.org/prayer-and-worship/worship-texts-and-resources/common-worship/ministry/common-worship-ordination-0 (accessed 20.1.24).

Church of England, 'Crown Nominations Commission', https://www.churchofengland.org/about/leadership-and-governance/crown-nominations-commission (accessed 20.1.24).

Church of England, 'Funerals', https://www.churchofengland.org/life-events/funerals (accessed 10.1.24).

Church of England, 'GS2253: Consultation on Proposed Changes to the Membership of the Crown Nominations Commission for the See of Canterbury', February 2022, https://www.churchofengland.org/sites/default/files/2022-01/gs-2253-consultation-on-proposed-changes-to-the-canterbury-cnc.pdf (accessed 10.1.24).

Church of England, 'GS2307: National Church Governance Report and Recommendations from the National Church Governance Project Board', June 2023, https://www.churchofengland.org/sites/default/files/2023-06/gs-2307-national-governance-review-synod-july-2023-final_0.pdf (accessed 10.1.24).

Church of England, 'GS2328 *Living in Love and Faith*: Setting out the progress made and work still to do', February 2023, https://www.churchofengland.org/sites/default/files/2023-10/gs-2328-llf-nov-2023.pdf (accessed 10.1.24).

Church of England, 'General Synod', https://www.churchofengland.org/about/general-synod (accessed 5.1.24).

Church of England, 'General Synod Order Paper IV, Tuesday 14 November 2023', https://www.churchofengland.org/sites/default/files/2023-11/op-iv-final-1.pdf (accessed 20.1.24).

Church of England, 'Holy Communion Order One', https://www.churchofengland.org/prayer-and-worship/worship-texts-and-resources/common-worship/churchs-year/holy-week-and-easter-2 (accessed 10.1.24).

Church of England, 'Holy Communion Service', https://www.churchofengland.org/prayer-and-worship/worship-texts-and-resources/common-worship/holy-communion-service (accessed 10.1.24).

Church of England, 'House of Bishops', https://www.churchofengland.org/about/general-synod/structure/house-bishops (accessed 9.1.24).

Church of England, 'House of Bishops meeting: 29 November', 29 November 2023, https://www.churchofengland.org/media/press-releases/house-bishops-meeting-29-november (accessed 10.1.24).

Church of England, 'Leadership and governance', https://www.churchofengland.org/about/leadership-and-governance (accessed 10.1.24).

Church of England, 'National Church Institutions', https://www.churchofengland.org/sites/default/files/2024-01/nci-structure-chart-january-2024.jpg (accessed 12.1.24).

Church of England, 'No ordinary ministry', https://www.churchofengland.org/life-events/vocations/no-ordinary-ministry (accessed 24.1.24).

Church of England, 'Parents' guide to christenings', https://www.churchofengland.org/life-events/christenings/parents-guide-christenings (accessed 11.1.24).

Church of England, 'The Anglican Communion', https://www.churchofengland.org/about/building-relationships/anglican-communion (accessed 11.1.24).

Church of England, 'The Declaration of Assent', https://www.churchofengland.org/prayer-and-worship/worship-texts-and-resources/common-worship/ministry/declaration-assent (accessed 10.1.24).

Church of England, 'The Five Guiding Principles', https://www.churchofengland.org/sites/default/files/2017-10/the_five_guiding_principles.pdf (accessed 20.1.24).

Church of England, *Episcopal Ministry: The Report of the Archbishops' Group on the Episcopate* (London: Church House Publishing, 1990).

Church of England Evangelical Council, 'Alternative Spiritual Oversight', https://ceec.info/alternative-spiritual-oversight/ (accessed 28.1.2024).

Church of England Evangelical Council, 'CEEC calls for action and offers the Church of England a better way forward', Church Society, 30 January 2023, https://www.churchsociety.org/resource/ceec-statement/ (accessed 20.1.24)

Church of England Evangelical Council, 'CEEC responds to General Synod decision', 15 November 2023, https://ceec.info/ceec-responds-to-general-synod-decision/ (accessed 20.1.24).

Church of England Evangelical Council, 'Visibly Different', 26 July 2020, https://ceec.info/wp-content/uploads/2022/10/visibly_different_-_dated_26_july_2020.pdf (accessed 20.1.24).

Church Times, 'LLF bishops respond to fears of schism over same-sex relationships', 25 January 2024, https://www.churchtimes.co.uk/articles/2024/26-january/news/uk/llf-bishops-respond-to-fears-of-schism-over-same-sex-relationships (accessed 27.1.24).

Church Times, 'Leader comment: Key limiting factors', 9 July 2021, https://www.churchtimes.co.uk/articles/2021/9-july/comment/leader-comment/leader-comment-key-limiting-factors (accessed 16.1.24).

Civicus, 'LGBTQI+ Rights in the Commonwealth: Time for Change', Civicus Lens, 21 June 2022, https://lens.civicus.org/lgbtqi-rights-in-the-commonwealth-time-for-change/ (accessed 2.1.24).

Clement, 'Letter to the Corinthians', New Advent, https://www.new advent.org/fathers/1010.htm (accessed 10.1.24).

Sarah Coakley, *God, Sexuality, and the Self* (Cambridge: Cambridge University Press, 2013).

George Conger, 'Changes made to the Lambeth Call: Human Dignity', Anglican Ink, 26 July 2022, https://anglican.ink/2022/07/26/changes-made-to-the-lambeth-call-human-dignity/ (accessed 10.1.24).

Communiqué from the Primates' Meeting 2016, Anglican Communion New Service, 15 January 2016, https://www.anglicannews.org/features/2016/01/communique-from-the-primates-meeting-2016.aspx (accessed 10.1.24).

Graham Cray, ed., *Mission-Shaped Church* (London: Church House Publishing, 2012).

Cyprian of Carthage, 'Epistle 73', New Advent, https://www.newadvent.org/fathers/050673.htm (accessed 10.1.24).

Cyprian of Carthage, 'Treatise 1', New Advent, https://www.newadvent.org/fathers/050701.htm (accessed 10.1.24).

Randall T. Davidson, *The Five Lambeth Conferences* (London: SPCK, 1920).

Madeleine Davies, 'Anglican Catholic Future raises concerns about Methodist proposals', *Church Times*, 4 July 2019, https://www.church times.co.uk/articles/2019/5-july/news/uk/anglican-catholic-future-raises-concerns-about-methodist-proposals (accessed 10.1.24).

Madeleine Davies, 'Clarification: Not 10,000 but 20,000 new lay-led churches; not a strategy but a vision', *Church Times*, 9 July 2021, https://www.churchtimes.co.uk/articles/2021/16-july/news/uk/clarifi cation-not-10-000-but-20-000-not-a-strategy-but-a-vision (accessed 16.1.2024).

Matthew Davies, 'England: Anglican Covenant defeated in majority of dioceses', Episcopal News Service, 26 March 2012, https://www.episcopalnewsservice.org/2012/03/26/england-anglican-covenant-defeated-in-majority-of-dioceses/ (accessed 20.1.24).

Angelo Di Berardino, ed., *Ancient Christian Doctrine 5: We Believe in One Holy Catholic and Apostolic Church* (Westmont, IL: Inter-Varsity, 2018).

Dicastery for Promoting Christian Unity, 'Response to the First Anglican/Roman Catholic International Commission – The Catholic Church's Response to the Final Report of ARCIC I, 1991, http://www.christian unity.va/content/unitacristiani/en/dialoghi/sezione-occidentale/comunione-anglicana/dialogo/arcic-i/risposte-ai-lavori-di-arcic-i/testo-in-inglese2.html (accessed 24.1.24).

Dicastery for the Doctrine of the Faith, 'Declaration: *Fiducia Supplicans*,

On the Pastoral Meaning of Blessings', 18 December 2023, https://www.vatican.va/roman_curia/congregations/cfaith/documents/rc_ddf_doc_20231218_fiducia-supplicans_en.html (accessed 10.1.24).

Diocese of London, 'Bishop of London joins 650 bishops from 165 countries at Lambeth Conference', https://bishopoflondon.org/news/bishop-of-london-joins-650-bishops-from-165-countries-at-lambeth-conference/ (accessed 10.1.24).

Diocese of London, 'New Charitable Status for the Gregory Centre for Church Multiplication (CCX), 6 April 2023, https://www.london.anglican.org/articles/new-charitable-status-for-the-gregory-centre-for-church-multiplication-ccx/ (accessed 16.1.24).

Brian Douglas, *The Anglican Eucharist in Australia* (Leiden: Brill, 2022).

Malcolm Duncan, *One for All: The Implications* (Oxford: Lion Hudson, 2017).

Ecclesiastical Law Commission, 'The Principles of Canon Law Common to the Churches of the Anglican Communion (Second Edition)', 2022, https://www.anglicancommunion.org/media/483121/UFO_Principles-of-Canon-Law_Second-Edition_2022.pdf (accessed 10.1.24).

Encyclopaedia Britannica, 'Lambeth Conference', https://www.britannica.com/topic/Lambeth-Conference (accessed 11.1.24).

Episcopal News Service, 'Bishops who support full LGBTQ+ inclusion release statement from Lambeth Conference', 3 August 2022, https://www.episcopalnewsservice.org/2022/08/03/bishops-who-support-full-lgbtq-inclusion-release-statement-from-lambeth-conference/ (accessed 10.1.24).

Episcopal News Service, 'Justin Welby's Presidential Address to the General Synod', 5 February 2016, https://www.episcopalnewsservice.org/2016/02/15/archbishop-justin-welby-unpacks-primates-communique/ (accessed 10.1.24).

Evangelical Group on General Synod, 'Is Human Sexuality a First Order Issue?', https://www.eggscofe.org.uk/uploads/5/5/6/3/5563632/1._is_human_sexuality_a_first_order_issue.pdf (accessed 20.1.24).

David Ford, *The Gospel of John: A Commentary* (London: Baker, 2022).

GAFCON, 'About GAFCON', https://www.gafcon.org/about (accessed 10.1.24).

GAFCON, 'GAFCON IV – The Kigali Commitment', 21 April 2023, https://www.gafcon.org/news/gafcon-iv-the-kigali-commitment (accessed 11.1.24).

GAFCON, 'Global Movement', https://www.gafcon.org/about/global-movement (accessed 10.1.24).

GAFCON, 'History', https://www.gafcon.org/about/history (accessed 11.1.24).

Edmon L. Gallagher and John D. Meade, *The Biblical Canon Lists from Early Christianity* (Oxford: Oxford University Press, 2017).

Global South Fellowship of Anglican Churches, 'GSFA brings hope and builds orthodox unity in the Anglican Communion', https://www. thegsfa.org/news/gsfa-brings-hope-and-builds-orthodox-unity-in-the-anglican-communion (accessed 10.1.24).

Global South Fellowship of Anglican Churches, 'Who we are', https:// www.thegsfa.org/about-us (accessed 10.1.24).

Gloucester Diocese, 'A statement from 44 bishops on LLF', https:// gloucester.anglican.org/2023/a-statement-from-44-bishops-on-llf/ (accessed 4.1.24).

Scott Hahn, *The Creed: Professing the Faith through the Ages* (London: Darton, Longman and Todd, 2017).

Enze Han and Joseph O'Mahoney, *British Colonialism and the Criminalization of Homosexuality: Queens, Crime and Empire* (London: Routledge, 2018).

Hansard, 'National Institutions Measure', https://hansard.parliament. uk/Commons/1998-06-18/debates/ad2c352e-b388-4b59-9e75-5a10 e414f489/NationalInstitutionsMeasure (accessed 23.1.2024).

Helen-Ann Hartley and Martyn Snow, 'Living in love, faith – and reconciliation', *Church Times*, 25 January 2024, https://www.church times.co.uk/articles/2024/26-january/comment/opinion/living-in-love-faith-and-reconciliation (accessed 28.1.24).

Ulrich Heckel, 'The Seven Marks of the Unity of the Church', *The Ecumenical Review* 73(4), pp. 566–80.

David E. Henderson and Frank Kirkpatrick, *Constantine and the Council of Nicaea: Defining Orthodoxy and Heresy in Christianity, 325 C. E.* (Chapel Hill, NC: University of North Carolina Press, 2016).

House of Bishops, 'Bishops in Communion: Collegiality in the Service of the Koinonia of the Church' (London: Church House Publishing, 2000).

House of Bishops, 'Suffragan Bishops', 2004, https://www.churchof england.org/sites/default/files/2023-01/gs-misc-733-suffragan-bishops. pdf (accessed 10.1.24).

House of Bishops, 'The Nomination Process for Suffragan Bishops', 2016, https://www.churchofengland.org/sites/default/files/2017-11/nom ination-process-for-suffragan-bishops.pdf (accessed 20.1.24).

Ignatius, 'The Epistle of Ignatius to the Philadelphians', New Advent, https://www.newadvent.org/fathers/0108.htm (accessed 20.1.24).

Ignatius, 'The Epistle of Ignatius to the Smyrnaeans', New Advent, https://www.newadvent.org/fathers/0109.htm (accessed 20.1.24).

International Reformed-Anglican Dialogue, '*Koinonia:* God's Gift and Calling', Anglican Consultative Council, 2020, https://www.anglican communion.org/media/421992/irad_koinonia-gods-gift-and-calling-nov2020.pdf (accessed 20.1.24).

International Anglican–Roman Catholic Commission for Unity and Mission, 'Global Anglican Communion given greater voice in choosing future Archbishops of Canterbury', 12 July 2022, https://iarccum.

org/2022/global-anglican-communion-given-greater-voice-in-choos ing-future-archbishops-of-canterbury/ (accessed 20.1.24).

Jerome, *Commentary on Titus* (3:10–11), in *St. Jerome's Commentaries on Galatians, Titus, and Philemon*, trans. Thomas P. Scheck (Notre Dame, IN: University of Notre Dame Press, 2010).

Kwok Pui-lan, *The Anglican Tradition from a Postcolonial Perspective* (New York: Seabury Books, 2023).

Christopher Lamb, 'A first since the Reformation: Catholic bishops will take part in the coronation', Religion Media Centre, 5 May 2023, https://religionmediacentre.org.uk/news/a-first-since-the-reformation-catholic-bishops-will-take-part-in-the-coronation/ (accessed 20.1.24).

Lambeth Conference, 'Anglican Identity set to be the next theme in Lambeth Call discussion series', 6 November 2023, https://www.lambethconference.org/anglican-identity-set-to-be-the-next-theme-in-lambeth-call-discussion-series/ (accessed 20.1.24).

Lambeth Conference, 'The Lambeth Calls', https://www.lambethconference.org/phase-3/the-lambeth-calls/ (accessed 11.1.24).

Pope Leo XIII, '*Apostolicae Curae* (Apostolic letter on Anglican Ordinations)', 13 September 1896, https://iarccum.org/doc/?d=622 (accessed 10.1.24).

Diarmaid MacCulloch, 'The Anglican church can start afresh', *The Guardian*, 25 March 2012, https://www.theguardian.com/commentisfree/2012/mar/25/anglican-covenant-bishops-division (accessed 20.1.24).

Malines Conversations, 'Sorores in Spes', 15 December 2021, https://www.malinesconversations.org/sorores-in-spe/ (accessed 10.1.24).

Francis Martin, 'Bishops' divisions over same-sex marriage exposed', *Church Times*, 26 October 2023, https://www.churchtimes.co.uk/articles/2023/27-october/news/uk/bishops-divisions-over-same-sex-marriage-exposed (accessed 20.1.24).

Francis Martin, 'Bishops go public with their rift over blessings for same-sex couples', *Church Times*, 12 October 2023, https://www.churchtimes.co.uk/articles/2023/13-october/news/uk/bishops-go-public-with-their-rift-over-blessings-for-same-sex-couples (accessed 10.1.24).

Francis Martin, 'Church organizations urge Bishops not to commend blessings for same-sex couples', *Church Times*, 5 July 2023, https://www.churchtimes.co.uk/articles/2023/7-july/news/uk/church-organisations-urge-bishops-not-to-commend-blessings-for-same-sex-couples (accessed 20.1.24).

Laurent Mbanda, 'Gafcon Response to Archbishop of Canterbury', GAFCON, 14 June 2023, https://www.gafcon.org/news/gafcon-response-to-archbishop-of-canterbury (accessed 10.1.24).

Alister McGrath, *Heresy: A History of Defending the Truth* (London: HarperCollins, 2010).

Sarah Meyrick, 'Five global regions to have reps on CNC for Archbishop Welby's successor', *Church Times*, 22 November 2023, https://

www.churchtimes.co.uk/articles/2023/24-november/news/world/ five-global-regions-to-have-reps-on-crown-nominations-commission-for-archbishop-welby-s-successor (accessed 16.1.24).

Mark Michael, 'GSFA Demands Anglican Communion Reset', The Living Church, 23 February 2023, https://livingchurch.org/2023/02/23/gsfa-demands-anglican-communion-reset/ (accessed 11.1.24).

Alison Milbank, *The Once and Future Parish* (London: SCM Press, 2023).

Mission Issues and Strategy Advisory Group II, 'Towards Dynamic Mission: Renewing the Church for mission', 1993, https://www.anglican communion.org/media/108031/MISAG-II-Towards-Dynamic-Mission-1992.pdf (accessed 10.1.24).

Jeremy Morris, *A People's Church: A History of the Church of England* (London: Profile Books, 2022).

Jeremy Morris, 'Unashamed Integrity: Stephen Sykes and the "crisis" of Anglican Ecclesiology and Identity', *Ecclesiology* 15(1), pp. 62–80.

Jeremy Morris and Nicholas Sagovsky, eds, *The Unity We have and the Unity We Seek* (London: T&T Clark, 2003).

Thabo Msibi, 'The Lies We Have Been Told: On (Homo) Sexuality in Africa, *Africa Today* 58(1), 2011, pp. 55–77.

Brian Mullady, OP STD, 'Pope Benedict XVI on the Priesthood and Homosexuality', *Linacre Quarterly* 78(3), 2011, pp. 294–305.

Paul Murray, ed., *Receptive Ecumenism and the Call to Catholic Learning: Exploring a Way for Contemporary Ecumenism* (Oxford: Oxford University Press, 2008).

William Oddie, 'Now the Church of England has decided on women bishops, ARCIC III is futile. As the CDF says, it is the Ordinariate now which is ecumenism in the front row', *Catholic Herald*, 17 July 2014, https://catholicherald.co.uk/now-the-church-of-england-has-decid ed-on-women-bishops-arcic-iii-is-futile-as-the-cdf-says-it-is-the-ordin ariate-now-which-is-ecumenism-in-the-front-row/ (accessed 20.1.24).

Primates Meeting of the Anglican Communion, 'A Statement by the Primates of the Anglican Communion meeting in Lambeth Palace', https://www.fulcrum-anglican.org.uk/wp-content/uploads/2016/01/ primates2003lambeth.pdf (accessed 20.1.24).

Jeehei Park, *All Citizens of Christ: A Cosmopolitan Reading of Unity and Diversity in Paul's Letters* (Leiden: Brill, 2022).

Ian Paul, 'Does allowing same-sex marriage result in church decline? Here's what the numbers show', *Premier Christianity*, 17 June 2022, https:// www.premierchristianity.com/opinion/does-allowing-same-sex-marriage-result-in-church-decline-heres-what-the-numbers-show/13282.article (accessed 10.1.24).

Ian Paul, 'Why is sexuality such a big deal?', Psephizo, 22 June 2023, https://www.psephizo.com/sexuality-2/why-is-sexuality-such-a-big-deal/ (accessed 12.1.24).

David Paulsen, 'Archbishop of Canterbury's remarks on human dignity lift up traditional and progressive marriage beliefs', Episcopal News Service, 2 August 2022, https://www.episcopalnewsservice.org/2022/08/02/at-lambeth-conservative-bishops-work-the-sidelines-to-re affirm-majority-opposition-to-same-sex-marriage/ (accessed 10.1.24).

Catherine Pepinster, 'CofE's "transformation" with 10,000 lay-led communities angers clergy fearing the end of the parish', Religion Media Centre, 9 July 2021, https://religionmediacentre.org.uk/news/cofes-transformation-with-10000-lay-led-communities-angers-clergy-fearing-the-end-of-the-parish/ (accessed 16.1.24).

Catherine Pepinster, 'Evangelicals Fear LGBT Blessings Proposal Would Split the Church of England', Christianity Today, https://www.christianitytoday.com/news/2023/february/church-of-england-synod-lgbt-blessings-marriage-evangelical.html (accessed 20.1.24).

Kirk Petersen, 'Bishops in Ghana Endorse Anti-Gay Bill', The Living Church, 20 October 2021, https://livingchurch.org/2021/10/20/bishops-in-ghana-endorse-anti-gay-bill/ (accessed 10.1.24).

Kirk Petersen, 'GAFCON Rejects Archbishop Justin Welby's Leadership', The Living Church, 21 April 2023, https://livingchurch.org/2023/04/21/gafcon-rejects-archbishop-justin-welbys-leadership/ (accessed 15.1.24).

Jonathan Petre, 'Church unity talks fail over gay bishop', The Telegraph, 1 December 2003, https://web.archive.org/web/20040306153216/http://www.telegraph.co.uk/news/main.jhtml?xml=%2F-news%2F2003%2F12%2F01%2Fnchur01.xml (accessed 20.1.24).

David Pocklington, 'Bishops: From announcement to installation', Law & Religion UK, 20 April 2016, https://lawandreligionuk.com/2016/04/20/bishops-from-announcement-to-installation/ (accessed 5.1.24).

Primary Christian News, 'US Episcopal Church defiant on primates meeting: "Nothing will change"', Premier Christian News, 17 January 2016, https://premierchristian.news/en/news/article/us-episcopal-church-defiant-on-primates-meeting-nothing-will-change (accessed 15.1.24).

Primates Meeting, 'A Statement by the Primates of the Anglican Communion meeting in Lambeth Palace', Anglican Communion News Service, 16 October 2003, https://www.anglicannews.org/news/2003/10/a-statement-by-the-primates-of-the-anglican-communion-meeting-in-lambeth-palace.aspx (accessed 20.1.24).

Michael Ramsey, The Gospel and the Catholic Church (Peabody, MA: Hendrickson, 2009).

Charles Raven, 'Unity in the Anglican Church', GAFCON, 16 June 2020, https://www.gafcon.org/news/unity-in-the-anglican-church (accessed 16.1.24).

Robert David Redmile, The Apostolic Succession and the Catholic Episcopate in the Christian Episcopal Church of Canada (Maitland, FL: Xulon, 2006).

Neville Richardson, 'Apartheid, Heresy and the Church in South Africa', *The Journal of Religious Ethics* 14(1), 1986, pp. 1–21.

Royal Family, 'The consecration of the Coronation Oil', 3 March 2023, https://www.royal.uk/news-and-activity/2023-03-03/the-consecration-of-the-coronation-oil (accessed 10.1.24).

Ormond Rush, 'Reception Hermeneutics and the "Development" of Doctrine: An Alternative Model', *Pacifica* 6(2), 1993, pp. 125–40.

William L. Sachs, *Homosexuality and the Crisis of Anglicanism* (Cambridge: Cambridge University Press, 2009).

Peter Saunders, 'Sexual immorality is a first order salvation issue. It is time for The Church of England to go under the surgeon's knife', Anglican Mainstream, 15 February 2017, https://anglicanmainstream.org/sexual-immorality-is-a-first-order-salvation-issue-it-is-time-for-the-church-of-england-to-go-under-the-surgeons-knife/ (accessed 26.1.24).

Mary Frances Schjonberg, 'Same-sex spouses not invited to next year's Lambeth Conference of bishops', Episcopal News Service, 18 February 2019, https://www.episcopalnewsservice.org/2019/02/18/same-sex-spouses-not-invited-to-next-years-lambeth-conference-of-bishops/ (accessed 20.1.24).

Harriet Sherwood, 'Justin Welby criticises Ugandan church's backing for anti-gay law', *The Guardian*, 9 June 2023, https://www.theguardian.com/world/2023/jun/09/justin-welby-criticises-ugandan-church-backing-for-anti-gay-law (accessed 20.1.24).

Robert Slocum, 'The Chicago-Lambeth Quadrilateral: Development in an Anglican Approach to Christian Unity', *Journal of Ecumenical Studies* 33(4), 1996.

Oliver Slow and Andre Rhoden-Paul, 'Archbishop will not give new prayer blessing for gay couples', BBC News Online, 20 January 2023, https://www.bbc.co.uk/news/uk-64342940 (accessed 10.1.24).

Stephen Sykes, *Unashamed Anglicanism* (London: Darton, Longman and Todd, 1995).

Jonathan Tallon, *Affirmative: Why You Can Say Yes to the Bible and Yes to People Who are LGBTQI+* (Marlow: Richardson Jones, 2023).

William Taylor, 'St Helen's Bishopsgate breaks with the Bishop of London and will uphold the Bible's teaching on marriage and sex', Anglican Ink, 1 March 2023, https://anglican.ink/2023/03/01/st-helens-bishopsgate-breaks-with-the-bishop-of-london-and-will-uphold-the-bibles-teaching-on-marriage-and-sex/ (accessed 20.1.24).

Tertullian, 'Prescription Against Heretics', New Advent, https://www.newadvent.org/fathers/0311.htm (accessed 11.1.24).

The Anglican Church of Canada, 'The Lambeth Quadrilateral', https://www.anglican.ca/about/beliefs/lambeth-quadrilateral/ (accessed 10.1.24).

'The Church of England's Doctrine of Marriage', https://southwell.

anglican.org/wp-content/uploads/2023/01/The-Church-of-Englands-Doctrine-of-Marriage-paper.pdf (accessed 2.1.24).

The Episcopal Church, 'The Ordination of a Bishop', https://www.bcp-online.org/EpiscopalServices/ordination_of_a_bishop.html (accessed 20.1.24).

The Lambeth Commission on Communion, 'The Windsor Report', 2004, https://www.anglicancommunion.org/media/68225/windsor2004full.pdf (accessed 20.1.24).

The Lambeth Palace Library Blog, 'The first Lambeth Conference', https://monumentoffame.org/2020/07/03/the-first-lambeth-conference/ (accessed 10.1.24).

The Presbyterian Outlook, 'Church of England warns Swedish church on same-sex marriage', 24 July 2009, https://pres-outlook.org/2009/07/church-of-england-warns-swedish-church-on-same-sex-marriage/ (accessed 20.1.24).

The Society, 'A Catholic Life in the Church of England', https://www.sswsh.com/uploads/A_Catholic_Life_for_web.pdf (accessed 12.1.24).

Marcus Throup, *All Things Anglican: Who we are and what we believe* (London: Canterbury Press, 2018).

Vatican News, 'Doctrinal declaration opens possibility of blessing couples in irregular situations', 18 December 2023, https://www.vaticannews.va/en/vatican-city/news/2023-12/fiducia-supplicans-doctrine-faith-blessing-irregular-couples.html (accessed 20.1.24).

Vincent of Lerins, 'Commonitory', https://www.newadvent.org/fathers/3506.htm (accessed 11.1.24).

James Walters, 'Anglican Communion requires a rotating presidency', *Church Times*, 29 January 2022, https://www.churchtimes.co.uk/articles/2022/28-january/comment/opinion/anglican-communion-requires-a-rotating-presidency (accessed 22.1.24).

Jeff Walton, 'As bishops meet, Anglican future is already written', Anglican Ink, 2 August 2022, https://anglican.ink/2022/08/02/as-bishops-meet-anglican-future-is-already-written/ (accessed 20.1.24).

Devin Watkins, 'Pope at Ecumenical Vespers: "Christian journey to unity rooted in prayer"', Vatican News, 25 January 2024, https://www.vaticannews.va/en/pope/news/2024-01/pope-francis-ecumenical-vespers-week-prayer-christian-unity.html (accessed 27.1.24).

Samuel White, 'House of Lords: Lords Spiritual', *House of Lords Library Briefing*, 4 September 2017, https://researchbriefings.files.parliament.uk/documents/LLN-2017-0056/LLN-2017-0056.pdf (accessed 16.1.24).

Rowan Williams, 'Concluding Presidential Address to the Lambeth Conference', 3 August 2008, http://rowanwilliams.archbishopofcanterbury.org/articles.php/1350/concluding-presidential-address-to-the-lambeth-conference.html (accessed 20.1.24).

Women's Ordination Worldwide, 'Florence Li Tim-Oi', 25 January 2020, http://womensordinationcampaign.org/blog-working-for-womens-equality-and-ordination-in-the-catholic-church/2020/1/25/rev-florence-li-tim-oi-first-woman-ordained-in-anglican-communion (accessed 20.1.24).

Cindy Wooden, 'Love is the only path to Christian unity, pope says', United States Conference of Catholic Bishops, 25 January 2024, https://www.usccb.org/news/2024/love-only-path-christian-unity-pope-says (accessed 27.1.24).

World Council of Churches, 'Anglican churches', https://www.oikoumene.org/church-families/anglican-churches (accessed 20.1.24).

World Council of Churches, 'Baptism, Eucharist and Ministry: Faith and Order Paper No. 111', 1982, https://www.anglicancommunion.org/media/102580/lima_document.pdf (accessed 11.1.24).

World Council of Churches, 'What is the World Council of Churches?', https://www.oikoumene.org/about-the-wcc (accessed 20.1.24).

Tim Wyatt, 'Factsheet: The Church of England's General Synod', Religion Media Centre, 13 February 2020, https://religionmediacentre.org.uk/factsheets/synod-factsheet/ (accessed 10.1.24).

Index of Biblical References

Old Testament

1 Chronicles
30.12   81

Psalms
133   81-2

Malachi
2.10   81

New Testament

Matthew
12.25   103
15   85
16.18   84
18.14   85
18.15-17   85

Mark
7   84

Luke
1.47   17

John
13.35   84
13.36-38   84
14.17   82
15   83-4

15.1   84
15.4   83
15.5   84
15.9-11   84
15.12   84
15.17   84
16.8   82
16.12-15   82
17.3   82
17.11   82
17.17   93 n.4
17.20-21   83
17.21   79
17.22-23   82
17.23   83
17.24   83

Acts

2	86
2.43–47	87
2.38	86
2.39	86–7
2.41–42	86–7
4.32–35	85–6
15.1–2	87

Romans

2.1	90
2.2	90
2.5–11	90
13.10	90
14.19	90

1 Corinthians

1.10	88
5.6	89
5.11	79, 88
5.13	88
5.9–13	158
6.7	88
6.9–11	94 n. 13
6.11	88
11.22	89
11.26	158
12.3	94 n. 12
12.4	89
12.12–13	89
12.24–27	90
12.14–26	146
13.13	90
16.14	90

2 Corinthians

2.7–11	93 n.11
4.7–9	114

Galatians

3.27–29	91
5.22	4

Ephesians

2	91
2.13–16	91
2.20	91
2.22	91
4	8, 91
4.1–6	124
4.2–3	91
4.4–6	91
4.13	92
4.14–16	91–2
4.17	92
4.25	92
5.2	92

1 Peter

3	92
3.8	92

1 John

4.13–21	92
5.7	101

Index of Names and Subjects

Act of Uniformity (1662) 25
Acts of the Apostles, and
   unity 85–7
adiaphora 8, 66, 100, 105
Ambongo, Cardinal Fridolin
   42
American Anglican
   Council 120
Anglican Church of Canada,
   and sexuality 64, 66
Anglican Church in North
   America 47
Anglican Communion:
  and Anglican identity 40,
   47, 49–51, 53–4, 68–73,
   131, 134
  and ARCIC 117–18
  centralization 6–7, 65, 67,
   137, 153–4
  and Church of England 16,
   37–54, 113, 131–6, 151–3
  as communion of churches
   155–7
  and conservatism 42–3
  and culture and context
   41–9, 74 n.10, 134, 152
  and denominationalism
   38–40, 71–3, 137
  and doctrine 64–8, 70,
   121–2, 137, 156–7
  and ecclesiology 151–6,
   160–2
  and ecumenism 112, 113,
   121–2
  and excommunication 4,
   88, 157
  and focus of unity 30–2,
   46–7, 68, 153
  and imperialism 38, 40–2
  and Instruments of Unity
   40, 44–7, 67, 70, 72, 155,
   161
  and mutuality 63–6, 157
  and policymaking 41
  postcolonial views 39–41,
   43, 48, 134, 153–4, 159,
   161–2
  provinces 44, 51, 54, 63–4,
   67, 122
  resetting 52–4, 154, 158–9,
   165
  and See of Canterbury
   16–17, 30–1, 44–7, 51, 54,
   55 n.13, 68, 113, 133–5,
   152–3
  and sexuality 41–3, 49–53,
   64–7, 88, 132–5, 152, 159
  Standing Committee 67
  structure 44–7, 54, 65–6,
   134–7, 152, 158–9

and synodality 69, 111,
139, 151, 154–6
and unity 54, 63, 72–3,
120–1, 151, 163
weaponization 114, 131–2
Anglican Communion Office
45, 113, 155
Anglican Congress (1963)
66
Anglican Consultative
Council 30, 44, 47–8, 70,
132, 155–6, 165 n.1
Anglican Convocation
Europe 107 n.5
Anglican Covenant 64, 65–7,
72, 161
Anglican Mission in England
144
Anglican Mission in Europe
107 n.5
Anglican Network in Europe
107 n.5
Anglican–Roman Catholic
International Commission
see ARCIC
Anglicanism:
as contested term 6, 47, 79,
81, 136–7
and diversity 25, 39–40,
64, 81, 89–90, 120–1, 124,
145, 159–60
as gift to church
catholic 162
and mission and witness
162–3
and Scripture 39–40, 71–2,
144, 156
and worship 161

see also apostolicity;
catholicity; Church of
England; identity
anointing of the sick,
sacrament 112
Apostles' Creed 59, 98–100,
108 n.24
Apostolic Succession 68–9,
101
Apostolicae Curae 60, 110
apostolicity 104–5, 113, 120,
136, 138, 161–2
Archbishop of Canterbury:
and Anglican Communion
16–17, 30–1, 44–7, 51, 54,
55 n.13, 68, 113, 132–3,
postcolonial views 134,
153–4
as focus of unity 30–1,
44–6, 113, 134, 153
and General Synod 17,
30–1, 45–7, 152
leadership role 1–5, 16–17,
45–6, 52, 110, 143, 152–3
as Primate of All England
16, 45, 135, 153
Archbishops' Council 17
ARCIC 112, 113, 117–18
Ashey, Phil 120
Ashworth, Pat 14 n.1
Athanasian Creed 98, 99–100
Augustine of Hippo 102–4,
109 n.41
authority:
in Anglican Communion
44, 50, 67–8, 72, 116–17,
121
in early church 99

of Lambeth Conference 66
of Scripture 37, 59, 63, 73,
  121-2
in synodical church 29-30,
  143

baptism:
and Anglican identity
  59-61, 124-5
and Apostles' Creed 59, 99,
  101
availability 24
of infants 122, 125
and unity 86-91, 101-2,
  112, 122, 124-5
belief:
diversity 25, 64, 81,
  116-17, 140-1
and unity 97, 116-17
bishops:
and Anglican Communion
  153-4
appointment/election 45-6,
  69-70, 142
bishop-in-synod 30, 140-3,
  151, 156, 162
collegiality 19, 20, 70, 121,
  140-1, 153-6
diocesan 19-20
as focus of unity 30-2, 50,
  102-3, 134, 138-9, 140-1,
  143, 155, 159
geographical role 19, 20,
  22, 138, 142-3
in Global South 42-3, 64
and heresy 97
homosexual 49, 51, 64, 66,
  122-3

planting 28
role 17-19, 29-30, 32
suffragan 19-20, 69
teaching authority 29
Black Christians 132
blessing of same-sex
  relationships 30-1,
  36 n.40, 42, 117, 126 n.12
and Anglican Communion
  30-1, 152
call for 10, 62, 115, 146,
  150 n.26
moratorium on 66
opposition to 4, 21, 49-50,
  151
body of Christ, church as 18,
  65, 70, 89-92, 103-4, 124,
  146
Bonn Agreement 115
Book of Common Prayer
  (1662) 25-7, 99, 118, see
  also Ordinal
Book of Homilies 26
Bray, Gerald 26

Canon Law 26-7, 70,
  166 n.5
and Primates' Meetings
  75 n.31
and worship 25, 27, 144
catholicity:
and Anglican Communion
  49-51, 113-14, 138,
  161-2
and Church of England 8-9,
  27, 54, 69, 113-14, 120-2,
  136-9, 147
and creeds 101, 122

and doctrine 104–5
Central Services 17
centralization of Anglican
  Communion 6–7, 65, 67,
  137, 153–4
Chalcedon, Council 95
Chapman, Mark 72, 76 n.33
Chapman, Mark and Morris,
  Jeremy 55 n.1
Charles III, HM King 111
Chessun, Christopher, Bishop
  97
Chicago Quadrilateral
  59–60, 112–13, 136–7
Church:
  as body of Christ 18, 65,
    70, 89–92, 103–4, 124, 146
  four marks 104, 105
church catholic:
  Anglicanism as gift to 162
  apostolicity 104–5, 113,
    120, 136, 138, 161–2
  and denominational unity
    13, 59–61
  and excommunication 4, 88
  and sexuality 134
Church Commissioners 17
Church of England:
  and Anglican Communion
    16, 37–54, 113, 131–6,
    151–3
  and catholicity 8–9, 27, 54,
    69, 113–14, 120–2, 136–9,
    147, 151
  as comprehensive 71, 113,
    136–7
  and doctrine 70–2, 117–20,
    122, 144

as Established 16–17, 22–3,
  32, 38–9, 69–70, 72, 135,
  153
Evangelical Council 120,
  143
and exclusion from
  communion 3–11, 19, 80,
  158
first-order issues 98, 113,
  115, 119–20, 133
history 6, 37, 71–2,
  131–47, 151
as institution 11, 16–32
provinces 17
as Reformed 113
and Roman Catholicism 28,
  110–11, 148 n.14
structures 20, 21, 23–5,
  28, 32, 38, 54, 113–14,
  138–43, 152
Supreme Governor 15–19
see also bishops; College of
  Bishops; dioceses; General
  Synod; House of Bishops;
  leadership
church order 12–13, 22,
  60–1, 64, 72, 87, 102–3,
  122–3, 139
Church in Wales 38
churches, affirming 96
clergy:
  discipline 141
  gay and lesbian 146
  as limiting factors 22
Clement of Rome 106
Coakley, Sarah 127 n.21
Coggan, Donald, Archbishop
  50

College of Bishops 19, 30,
140, 141–2, 151
collegiality 19, 20, 70, 72,
121, 140–1, 153–6
colonialism 42–3, 45–6, 65,
67, 132, 135, 152, 155,
159, 162
Common Worship 25, 80,
144
Ordination 17–18, 31
Communion:
impaired 40, 47, 51, 54, 152
refusal of 3–11, 80
Communion of Saints 100,
108 n.24, 157
comprehensiveness 71, 113,
136–7
confirmation, sacrament 18,
61, 112
conservatism:
in Anglican Communion
42–3
evangelical 120–1, 139
and unity 8–10
Constantinople, First Council
104
Cranmer, Thomas 26
creeds 59, 61
and catholicity 101, 122
and first-order issues
98–101
and unity 98–101
see also Apostles' Creed;
Nicene Creed
Crown Nominations
Commission 45–6, 69, 142
culture, and theology 41–9,
74 n.10, 96, 106, 134

cure of souls 23, 33–4 n.14
Cyprian of Carthage 101–2,
106

Declaration of Assent 26
Denominations:
and Anglican Communion
38–40, 71–3, 137
and Church of England
113–14, 136–7
and church order 13
and identity 38, 40, 67,
70–3, 102, 162
and unity 10–11, 38, 40,
72–3
dioceses 17–19
and parishes 20–1, 32
strategies 21
discernment:
and church catholic 13
and development of doctrine
97–8, 141
disciples, and unity 82–4
discipline, and unity 80–1,
87–8
diversity:
and Anglicanism 25, 39–40,
64, 81, 89–90, 120–1, 124,
145, 159–60
and doctrine 39, 64–5, 92,
119, 122, 141, 145
in leadership 10
doctrine:
and Anglican Communion
64–8, 70–1, 121–2, 137,
156–7
and Church of England
70–2, 117–20, 122, 145

development 24, 96–8,
  104–6, 114–17, 122
and diversity 39, 64–5, 92,
  119, 141, 145
and ecclesiology 23–4,
  37–8, 64–6, 73, 156–8, 160
and ecumenism 111
and love 85, 91–2
reception 97, 100, 114–16,
  122
and Scripture 51–2, 133–4
and sexuality 34 n.23,
  64–8, 88, 98–100, 133–4,
  166 n.14
and theology 104–5,
  118–19
and unity 34 n.23, 53–4,
  61–2, 85–6, 91–2
Donatism 102
Dunnett, John 120

Eames, Robin, Primate of All
  Ireland 65
early church:
  and doctrine 101
  and unity 85–6, 98–106
ecclesiology:
  and Anglican Communion
    151–6, 160–2
  crisis of confidence in 159
  and doctrine 23–4, 37–8,
    64–6, 73, 156–8, 160
  and finance 21
  neglect of 22, 144–5
  and parishes 23–4, 54
  place-based 23–5
  and Scripture 87–8
  secularization 6–7

ecumenism 15 n.8, 110–25
  and Anglican identity
    119–23
  and institutional unity
    11–12, 102
  and Lambeth Quadrilateral
    59–60, 112–13, 121–3
  and walking together 164
Elizabeth II, HM Queen 111
Episcopal Church (USA):
  and Anglican Communion
    44, 50, 66, 123, 138
  election of bishops 69–70
  and unity 31, 59, 64, 88
episcopate:
  catholicity 138
  historic 60–1, 68–9,
    143, see also Apostolic
    Succession
  local 142–3
  and theology of taint 12
  women in 6, 12, 33 n.9,
    122–3, 126 n.8
  see also bishops
Establishment 16–17, 22–3,
  32, 39, 69–70, 136, 152
  and Anglican Communion
    38
Eucharist:
  and Anglican identity 59–61
  centrality 112
  and church order 12, 102–3
  diversity of beliefs 25, 64,
    81, 122, 157–8
  and union with Christ 4,
    89, 103, 159–60
excommunication 3–11, 88,
  89, 95

faith:
  and holy living 97–9
  and unity 95, 141–2
  and works 79, 99–100
Farewell Discourse 82–4
Fathers, early church 7, 101–6
fellowship, sacramental 47,
  65–6
Fiducia Supplicans 42, 112,
  117
First-order issues:
  and creeds 98–101
  and ecumenism 119–20
  and sexuality 98–100, 105–
  6, 113, 115, 133, 158, 160
formularies, historic 26–8,
  37, 39, 61, 72, 134
Francis II, Pope 110–11
funerals, availability 24

GAFCON 51–4, 135, 143,
  154
gender *see* sexuality
General Synod 13, 17, 111,
  139, 142
  and Archbishop of
  Canterbury 17, 30–1,
  45–7, 152
  and decision-making 29–31
  sexuality debates 98, 132,
  140, 159
  Standing Orders 35 n.36
Global Anglican Future
  Conference *see* GAFCON
Global North 43, 131, 160,
  161
Global South 41–3, 64,
  131–2, 154

Global South Fellowship of
  Anglicans (GSFA) 50–1,
  53, 134
Gospels, and unity 82–5, 101
Great Schism 95
growth:
  focus on 21–2
  and uniformity 9

Hahn, Scott 99
Heckel, Ulrich 124
heresy 96–106
  definition 96
  disunity 97
  and schism 103–6
holiness 97–9, 136
  and unity 92, 105, 163
Holy Communion *see*
  Eucharist
Holy Spirit, and unity 8–9,
  37, 63, 82–3, 86–7, 91,
  101, 131, 163–4
homophobia 64, 132–3
homosexuality *see* sexuality
Hooker, Richard 37, 71
House of Bishops 17, 19,
  30–1, 140–1
House of Clergy 29
House of Lords, bishops in
  20, 39
Huntington, William Reed
  59

IARCCUM 111–12, 113
identity, Anglican:
  and Anglican Communion
  40, 47, 49–51, 53–4,
  68–73, 131, 134, 154

and Chicago–Lambeth
Quadrilateral 59–60,
61–2, 65, 66, 73, 112–13,
121–3
and Church of England 22,
26–7, 32, 37–40, 54, 67,
70–3, 118, 136
as distinctive 162
and ecumenism 119–23
and unity 59–73, 113,
119–23, 160, 164
see also episcopate
Ignatius of Antioch 102–3
imperialism, and Anglican
Communion 38, 40–2, 45
Instruments of Communion
see Instruments of Unity
Instruments of Unity 11–14,
16, 39–40, 44–7, 52, 66,
72, 161
and Anglican Communion
40, 44–7, 67, 70, 72, 155
as foci of unity 46, 47, 50,
67
Lambeth Conference 44,
47, 50, 143, 154, 156–9
Primates' Meetings 44, 47,
50, 52, 63, 83, 165 n.1
see of Canterbury 30–1,
44–6, 113, 133–5
intercommunion:
and Bonn Agreement 115
and Methodist Church 28
International Anglican-
Roman Catholic
Commission for Mission
and Unity
see IARCCUM

Issues in Human Sexuality
149 nn.19,22

Jerome 103
Jesus Christ:
and Eucharist 4, 89, 103,
159–60
unity with 82–5, 87–92,
131, 157, 163
justification 55 n.3, 60, 64,
133

Kasper, Walter, Cardinal
126 n.8
kenosis 90, 131
Kigali Commitment 52, 53
koinonia, and unity 29–30,
51, 112, 157
Kwok Pui-lan 159–60

Lambelet, Kyle 159
Lambeth Conference:
1867 48, 59
1888 59–60
1958 167 n.21
1988 117–18, 147 n.1
1998 48–9, 75 n.13, 133
2022 43, 49, 51, 94 n.17,
134, 154
authority 66
Calls 49, 134, 154
future 49–50
as Instrument of Unity 44,
47, 50, 143, 154, 156–9
Resolution I:10 49, 63–4,
133–4, 137
Resolution II 59–60
Lambeth Quadrilateral 61–2,

65, 66, 73, 99, 112–13,
120–3, 136–7
leadership:
in Anglican Communion
43, 45, 51–2, 134–5,
152–5
in Church of England 1–5,
16–17, 28–9, 110
diversity of views 10,
141–2
secularization 6–7
Leo XIII, Pope 60, 110
LGBTQIA Christians:
and discernment 97–8
discrimination 167 n.23
in episcopate 49, 123
and Global South 41–3, 64,
132, 135, 152–3
rejection of 96, 132–3, 159
and Roman Catholic
Church 117
liberals/liberalization 24, 48,
51, 132
liturgy see worship
living, holy see holiness
Living in Love and Faith 7,
149 n.22
love, and unity 84–5, 87,
89–92, 110

Magisterium, Roman
Catholic 9, 117, 118
marriage:
and orthodoxy 133–4
as sacrament 112
same-sex 10, 23, 115–16,
132
McGrath, Alister 96

Methodist Church:
and intercommunion 28
and threefold order 60
Metropolitan Community
Churches 96
Milbank, Alison 20, 33 n.14
ministry:
ordained 22
priestly 28–9, 60–1
sacramental 29–30, 32,
60–1
threefold 23, 28–30, 32,
60–1, 68
mission and witness:
and Anglican Communion
44, 64–5, 154, 160
and Anglicanism 162–3
and ecumenism 112
and unity 80, 83, 163
Mission-Shaped Church 21
Monophysites 95
Morris, Jeremy 72
mutuality 63–6, 141, 157

National Church Governance
Report 29–30
National Church
Institutions 17
National Society 17
Naziism, church responses
to 95
Nederduitsch Hervormde
Kerk 95
Nederduitse Gereformeerde
Kerk 95
New Testament see Acts;
Gospels; Paul, St
Nicaea, Council (325) 99

Nicene Creed 59, 98–9, 101

occasional offices 71
Old Catholic Church 115, 119
Old Testament, and unity 81–2
orders, Anglican:
  and ecumenism 60, 110–11
  threefold 23, 28–30, 32, 60–1, 68
Ordinal 26–7, 31, 118
ordination:
  as sacrament 112
  and sexuality 49
  of women 138–40, 146, in Anglican Communion 43, 64, 75 n.13, as necessity 61, opposition to 12–13, 21, 138–40, 146
orthodoxy, and Anglican Communion 3, 40, 51–3, 96, 127 n.21, 133
Ozanne, Jayne 98

parishes:
  and dioceses 20–1, 32, 138
  and ecclesiology 23–4, 54
  and mission and evangelism 22
  and worship 26
Partnership, Ten Principles 66, 161
Paul, Ian 107 n.3
Paul, St 80–1, 87–92, 99, 124, 146, 158
Pensions Board 17
Pentecostalism 152

planting:
  of bishops 28
  of churches 51–2, 143
policy-making 2–5, 20–1, 29–30
  and Anglican Communion 41
politics:
  and Anglican Communion 131–3
  in early church 99, 106
  and General Synod 140, 142
  and Primates' Meetings 50, 64
  and theology 1, 7–10, 13, 24, 37, 41, 72, 137, 156, 165 n.6
Porvoo Communion 115
practice, and unity 23–4, 37, 72, 95, 97
Primates' Meetings:
  and canon law 75 n.31
  and communion 52, 154
  as Instrument of Unity 44, 47, 50, 52, 63, 83, 143, 165 n.1
  and sexuality 64–6, 122–3, 133, 137
Protestantism see Reformation
provinces:
  Anglican Communion 44, 51, 54, 63–4, 67, 122, 152
  autonomy 44, 64, 123
  and episcopate 69, 142
  and mutuality 63–6

possibility of third 153
provincial episcopal visitors
    19, 32, 138–9

racism 42–3, 132
Ramsey, Michael, Archbishop
    69
reason, and Scripture and
    tradition 71, 72, 113
reception of development 97,
    100, 114–16, 122
reconciliation, sacrament
    112
Reformation:
  and Anglican Communion
    40
  and current debates 5–6,
    28, 37, 139
  and Roman Catholicism 28
Reformed churches, and
    ecumenism 112, 113
relationships, same-sex:
  criminalization 42
  opposition to 96, 120–1,
    131, 133, 139–40, 143,
    153, 158, 160
  support for 100, 140–1
  see also blessing; marriage
Robinson, Gene, Bishop 51,
    64, 122–3
Roman Catholicism:
  and Church of England 28,
    110–12, 148 n.14
  and sexuality 42, 117–18,
    134

sacraments 29–30, 32,
    59–60, 101–2, 162

number 61
  see also baptism; Holy
    Communion
salvation: by faith 79
  see also first-order issues
Save the Parish campaign 20
schism:
  and heresy 103–6
  and refusal of communion
    11, 95, 97, 126 n.8
Scripture:
  and Anglicanism 39–40, 73,
    144
  authority 37, 59, 63, 73,
    121–2
  canon 99
  and doctrine 51–2, 133–4
  interpretation 39–40, 63,
    79, 120–2, 133–4, 141–2,
    144
  and tradition and reason
    71, 73, 79, 113
  and unity 79–81, 101–2,
    144
Second Vatican Council 111
sexuality:
  and Anglican Communion
    41–3, 49–53, 64–7, 88,
    114, 132–3
  differences over 3–7, 23,
    49–53, 152, 161, 164
  and doctrine 39, 64–8, 88,
    133–5, 166 n.14
  and first-order issues
    98–100, 105–6, 113, 115,
    133, 158, 160
slavery 45
Society, The 122

stasis, risk of 8, 10–12, 45,
    146, 152–3, 162
subsidiarity 66
suffragan bishops 19–20, 69
Sykes, Stephen 7
synodality 10, 29, 69, 111,
    139, 143, 151, 154–6, 167
    n.24

taint, theology of 12
Ten Principles of Partnership
    66, 161
Tertullian 104
theology:
  Anglican 72, 118
  and culture 41–9, 74 n.10,
    96, 106, 134
  and doctrine 104–5,
    118–19
  and policy–making 2–5,
    20–1, 29–30
  and politics 1, 7–10, 13, 24,
    37, 41, 72, 137, 156, 165
    n.6
  and unity 6–11, 13–14, 73,
    81, 161–2
Theophilos III, Patriarch 111
Thirty-Nine Articles 26, 61
Tim-Oi, Florence Li 61
tradition, and Scripture and
    reason 71, 73, 79, 113
traditionalists 13, 139, 148
    n.14
Trinity, and unity 82–5, 92,
    112, 124, 131, 163
truth, and unity 82–5, 92,
    106, 163

uniformity:
  and growth 9
  and unity 6–10, 16, 39, 81,
    97, 100, 121, 147
  of worship 25–6, 144
United Nations, and Anglican
    Communion 44
unity:
  in Acts 85–7
  at all costs 43, 138, 144,
    146
  and Anglican identity
    59–73, 113, 119–23, 160,
    164
  in Anglicanism 134–5
  in baptism 86–91, 101–2,
    112, 122, 124–5
  and belief 97, 116–17
  bishops as focus of 30–2,
    50, 102–3, 134, 138–9,
    140–1, 143, 155
  challenges to 12
  with Christ 82–5, 87–92,
    131, 157, 163
  as contested notion 4–5,
    8–10, 81
  and creeds 98–101
  and discipline 80–1, 87–8
  and diversity 145–6,
    159–60
  and doctrine 34 n.23, 53–4,
    61–2, 64–6, 91–2
  in early church 85–6,
    98–102
  enforced 9–10
  as gift of Holy Spirit 8–9,
    37, 63, 82–3, 86–7, 91,
    101, 131, 157, 163–4

in God 81
in Gospels 82–5, 101
and historical continuity 21
institutional 11–14, 16,
    102, 158–62
internal 61, 105, 120
as kenotic 90, 131
and *koinonia* 29–30, 51,
    112, 157
and liturgy 34 n.23
local 13
and love 84–5, 87, 89–92,
    110
metaphysical 63, 80,
    108 n.24, 134, 145, 163
and mission and witness 80,
    83, 163
in Old Testament 81–2
and Reformation 5–6, 28
risks 145–7
and Scripture 79–81, 101–2
and theology 6–11, 13–14,
    73, 81, 161–2
and Trinity 82–5, 92, 112,
    124, 131, 163
and truth 82–5, 92, 106,
    163
and uniformity 6–10, 16,
    39, 81, 97, 100, 121, 147

visible 12, 31, 60–3, 80,
    85–6, 92, 102–3, 111,
    134–5, 144, 146, 156, 158

via media 5–6, 28, 37, 39,
    71, 113
Vincent of Léris 104
Virginia Report 147 n.1

Welby, Justin, Archbishop 58
    n.43, 68, 110–11, 126
    n.12, 132, 165 n.1
Welsh Church Act (1914) 38
Williams, Rowan,
    Archbishop 70, 162–3
Windsor Report 64–6, 97
women:
    in episcopate 6, 12, 33 n.9,
        122–3, 126 n.8
    ordination *see* ordination
works, and faith 79, 99–100
World Council of Churches
    110, 112
worship:
    and common liturgy 25–6
    uniformity 25–6, 144
    and unity 34 n.23, 161